ISRAEL HOROVITZ

ISRAEL HOROVITZ

A Collection of Critical Essays

Edited by
LESLIE KANE

Contributions in Drama and Theatre Studies, Number 55

GREENWOOD PRESS
Westport, Connecticut • London

PS'
3558
069
Z7
1994

Library of Congress Cataloging-in-Publication Data

Israel Horovitz : a collection of critical essays / edited by Leslie
   Kane.
          p.   cm.—(Contributions in drama and theatre studies, ISSN
   0163–3821 ; no. 55)
       ISBN 0–313–29147–0
       1. Horovitz, Israel—Criticism and interpretation.   I. Kane,
   Leslie, 1945– . II. Series.
   PS3558.069Z7   1994
   812′.54—dc20   93–43794

British Library Cataloguing in Publication Data is available.

Library of Congress Catalog Card Number: 93–43794
ISBN: 0–313–29147–0
ISSN: 0163–3821

First published in 1994

Greenwood Press, 88 Post Road West, Westport, CT 06881
An imprint of Greenwood Publishing Group, Inc.

Printed in the United States of America

∞™

The paper used in this book complies with the
Permanent Paper Standard issued by the National
Information Standards Organization (Z39.48–1984).

10 9 8 7 6 5 4 3 2 1

Copyright Acknowledgments

The editor and publisher gratefully acknowledge permission for use of the following material:

Excerpts from the following plays by Israel Horovitz: *Henry Lumper* (1990), *Stage Directions*
(1977), *Mackerel* (1979), and *The Widow's Blind Date* (1989).

Emily Dickinson's poem #1206 "The Show Is Not the Show," from *The Complete Poems of Emily
Dickinson*, edited by Thomas H. Johnson. Copyright 1957, Little, Brown and Company, Boston,
Massachusetts.

Excerpts from *The Orestes Plays of Aeschylus*, translated by Paul Roche. Translation Copyright ©
1963, renewed 1990 by Paul Roche. Used by permission of Dutton Signet, a division of Penguin
Books USA Inc., New York.

Excerpts from "The Widow's Blind Date: 'A Shitload of Getting Together'," by Leslie Kane in
Public Issues, Private Tensions: Collection of Critical Essays on Contemporary American Drama,
edited by Matthew Roudané. Copyright 1993, AMS Press Inc., New York, New York.

For Stu

Contents

Preface

Israel Horovitz: A Collection of Critical Essays is the first collection of scholarly essays to assess Israel Horovitz's long career in the theatre. The twelve essays, with the exception of my own (reprised and expanded), which was recently published in *Public Issues/Private Tensions*, have been commissioned for this book from scholars identified with critical appraisals of the author's work or theatre and film studies. Others have been chosen for their professional expertise. Cumulatively, these essays present the most current and provocative thinking on Horovitz's canon, commence a dialectic on performance and structure, and substantially advance our knowledge of the playwright and his plays. This book includes an interview with the playwright conducted specifically for this collection.

Reflecting the breadth, theatricality, imagination, and diversity of Horovitz's work, the chapters provide a range of critical approaches that offer retrospectives and perspectives on Horovitz's drama, including two recent screenplays, and encompassing his work from the early absurdist parable, *Line*, to *Strong-Man's Weak Child*. Employing diverse approaches, and subjects, chapters cover the entirety of Horovitz's career, thematic explications to examinations of individual plays. The dominant focus is on several principal works, such as *The Indian Wants the Bronx, The Widow's Blind Date, The Wakefield Plays,* and *The Gloucester Plays*, but chapters on lesser-known plays, such as *Mackerel* and *The Sault Ste. Marie Trilogy*, will familiarize readers with the continuity of theme, the variety of rhetorical mode, the technical virtuosity, and the social consciousness that characterizes Horovitz's substantive body of work. Whether contradicting or complementing one another, these scholarly essays initiate a much-needed dialogue on Horovitz's contribution to the American theatre during the past twenty-five years.

I thank all of the contributors for generously tailoring their research to my proposals, sending their manuscripts in a timely fashion, and responding to my remarks receptively and immediately. And for their kind suggestions of scholars who were interested in Horovitz's work, I thank Michael Hinden, Matthew Roudané, Karelisa Hartigan, and Susan Haedicke.

For his advice and patience, I thank Peter Coveney, my editor at Greenwood Press. I also acknowledge a debt to my graduate research assistant, Robert Schaaf, for his meticulous preparation of the bibliography and for his assistance at every stage of production, and to the research librarians at the Billy Rose Theatre Collection, New York Public Library for the Performing Arts at Lincoln Center, where the Horovitz papers are retained.   Special mention should also be made of David Kane and Robyn Miliano for the preparation of the manuscript.   And I am indebted to Israel Horovitz for the inspiration of his work, for his generous gift of innumerable manuscripts, and for his warmth, accessibility, and candor.

Finally, I especially thank my husband, Stu, for his unqualified support, his continuing patience, and his suggestion that I undertake this project.

Chronology

1939   Arthur Israel Horovitz is born on March 31 to Julius Charles and Hazel Solberg Horovitz in Wakefield, Massachusetts.

1939–56 Horovitz grows up and attends high school in Wakefield, a community on the North Shore of Massachusetts, whose distinctive linguistic patterns and accents will characterize numerous Horovitz plays set in either Wakefield or Gloucester. While he is a teenager, Horovitz begins a life-long commitment to running and a prolific career as a writer, submitting his first novel, *Steinberg, Sex, and the Saint,* at the age of thirteen.

1958   *The Comeback*, Horovitz's first play, written at the age of nineteen, premieres at Suffolk University with Israel Horovitz in the role of the son and Suffolk University theatre instructor Peter MacLean as the father. The production tours to Emerson College, Boston, where *The Comeback* is a curtain-raiser to Arthur Miller's *A Memory of Two Mondays*.

Horovitz marries Elaine Abber.

1959   Horovitz's marriage to Elaine Abber is annulled. On December 25, Horovitz marries Doris Keefe. They have three children; Rachel, Matthew, and Adam.

1960   Il Cafe Cabaret, South Orange, New Jersey, stages *The Death of Bernard the Believer.*

1961   Horovitz becomes a fellow at the Royal Academy of Dramatic Art in London.

This Play Is about Me is produced at Il Cafe Cabaret.

1962   Il Cafe Cabaret Theatre presents *The Hanging of Emmanuel.*

1963   *The Killer Dove* is produced by Theatre-on-the-Green, West Orange, New Jersey.

Hop, Skip and Jump is staged at Il Cafe Cabaret Theatre.

1964   Il Cafe Cabaret Theatre presents *The Simon Street Harvest.*

1965   Horovitz is the first American playwright selected playwright in residence at the Royal Shakespeare Theatre, Stratford-upon-Avon, and he holds an appointment concurrently with that of playwright in residence at the Aldwych Theatre, London.

Horovitz is a charter member of the Eugene O'Neill Memorial Theatre Foundation Waterford, Connecticut.

1966   *The Indian Wants the Bronx* receives a staged reading at the Eugene O'Neill Memorial Theatre Foundation.

1967   *Line* opens on November 29 in New York's La Mama Experimental Theatre Club, starring Richard Dreyfuss, and featuring Horovitz, who had never acted before, in the role of the line-eater.

Horovitz conducts a playwrighting workshop at New York University.

It's Called the Sugar Plum receives a staged reading at the Eugene O'Neill Memorial Theatre Foundation on July 18.

The Indian Wants the Bronx is staged in Provincetown, Massachusetts, featuring Al Pacino and John Cazale.

1968   *The Indian Wants the Bronx*, starring Al Pacino, Matthew Cowles, and John Cazale, and *It's Called the Sugar Plum*, featuring John Pleshette and introducing Marsha Mason, open on January 17, at the Astor Place Theatre, New York, as a double bill directed by James Hammerstein.

Horovitz is appointed professor of English and playwright in residence at City College, New York.

The Indian Wants the Bronx and *It's Called the Sugar Plum* are presented in Watford, Hertfordshire, England.

The Honest-to-God Schnozzola is produced in Provincetown, Massachusetts.

Acrobats is produced in New York.

Chiaroscuro is presented in July at the Festival of Two Worlds in Spoleto, Italy.

Chiaroscuro, produced as *Morning* in the triptych *Morning, Noon, and Night*, by Horovitz, Terrence McNally, and Leonard Melfi, music by John Hall, lyrics by Horovitz, opens on November 28 at Henry Miller's Theater in New York. The show features Charlotte Rae, Robert Klein, Sorrel Beeke, Jane Marla Robbins, and John Heffernan.

The Indian Wants the Bronx wins Horovitz the Obie Award for Best American Play, the Vernon-Rice Drama Desk Award, and the *Jersey Journal* Best Play Award.

Rats, starring Scott Glenn and Tom Rosqui, is presented at the Cafe Au Go Go on May 8, one of eleven short plays in the collection *Collision Course*, which includes pieces by Leonard Melfi, Terrence McNally, Jules Feiffer, and Sam Shepard.

1969   Horovitz is a recipient of a Rockefeller Fellowship. *A Play for Trees* is produced on WNET television in New York.

Rats and *The Indian Wants the Bronx* open in London, England.

L'Indien Cherche le Bronx with Laurent Terzief is performed at Théâtre de la Gaité–Montparnasse, Paris.

Horovitz wins his second Obie for *The Honest-to-God Schnozzola* and *Leader*, which open at the Gramercy Arts Theater in New York on April 21. This double bill, directed by Rip Torn, features Lane Smith and Ann Wedgeworth.

It's Called the Sugar Plum wins the Play and Players Best Foreign Play Award in England. *Sucre d'Orge*, with Laurent Terzief, opens at Théâtre de la Gaite–Montparnasse.

1970   Four movie screenplays are completed for MGM: *Machine Gun McCain, The Strawberry Statement, Believe in Me (Speed Is Everything)*, and *Alfredo*.

Horovitz wins the French Société des Auteurs' Best Foreign Play Award for *The Indian Wants the Bronx*.

Chiaroscuro, produced as *Clair-Obscur*, opens on April 10 at the Théâtre Lucernaire in Paris, and at Théâtre de la Gaité–Montparnasse with Gerard Depardieu.

Line is produced in London.

Acrobats opens on October 20 at the Miskery Theatre, Amsterdam.

The Strawberry Statement, with Horovitz's screenplay adapted from James Simon Kunen's novel, is awarded the Cannes Film Festival Prix du Jury.

1971   Horovitz is a columnist until 1977 for *Magazine Literaire* in Paris.

Line (revised) with *Acrobats* opens as a double bill at the Theatre de Lys, New York, February 15, with Richard Dreyfuss, Ann Wedgeworth, Barnard Hughes, John Randolf, and John Cazale.

Hero is produced at the New York Shakespeare Public Theatre in New York on May 7.

Shooting Gallery is presented at the Workshop of the Players Art Theatre in New York on June 22.

Horovitz completes two screenplays, *The Sad-Eyed Girls in the Park* for Columbia and *Camerian Climbing* for MGM.

Horovitz is the recipient of a New York State Council of the Arts Fellowship.

It's Called the Sugar Plum is staged in London.

1972   At the National Playwrights Conference (director, Lloyd Richards), Horovitz reads from his *Spider Poems*.

Alfred the Great is produced at the Théâtre du Centre Cultural Americain, Paris, on January 28. Horovitz directs this production.

Alfred the Great is produced in Great Neck, New York.

Acrobats is adapted for the screen by Horovitz from his play and is directed by the author for Walker Stuart Productions.

Horovitz directs the television production of his *Play for Germs*, the longest segment of the Emmy-winning *V.D. Blues*, for Public Television.

Dr. Hero, a revised version of *Hero*, is produced in Great Neck, New York.

Line (Le ler) premieres, with Loleh Bellon, Max Vialle, Georges Staquet, Jean-Claude Dauphine, and Ives Bureau at Théâtre de Poche-Montparnasse (runs 1972-1983). This production is directed by Horovitz and Michel Fagadau.

1973   Horovitz is Fanny Hurst Professor of Theatre at Brandeis University, Waltham, Massachusetts until 1975.

Alfred the Great is produced at the Pittsburgh Playhouse, Pittsburgh, Pennsylvania, on March 16.

Dr. Hero, directed by Edward Berkeley, is produced at the Shade Company Theatre, New York, on March 19, and opens in Paris at Théâtre La Bruyère.

Our Father's Failing, the second play in *The Alfred Trilogy*, is produced at the Eugene O'Neill Memorial Theatre Foundation on July 21.

Alfred the Great is staged at the Actors Studio, New York, as an open rehearsal for a work in progress. It premieres on November 23 at the Trinity Square Repertory Company, Providence, Rhode Island, directed by Jack O'Brien.

Horovitz wins the French Critics Prize for *Line*.

1974   Horovitz receives a National Endowment for the Arts Fellowship.

Hopscotch, starring Lenny Baker and Swoosie Kurtz, is produced at the Manhattan Theatre Club, New York, on March 21, under the direction of Horovitz.

Alfred the Great, directed by Michael Redgrave, opens in April at the Hampstead Theatre Club.

Turnstile is produced at Dartmouth College, Hanover, New Hampshire, on August 18.

Horovitz wins the Prix du Plaisir de Théâtre for *Line*.

The First, The Last, The Middle: A Comedy Triptych written by Horovitz, Terrence McNally, and Leonard Melfi, is produced at the Cubiculo Theatre, New York, in December.

Our Father's Failing is produced in New York.

1975   Horovitz is recipient of a New York State Council of the Arts Fellowship.

Horovitz founds the New York Playwrights Lab (NYPL), a weekly workshop for full-time, professionally produced playwrights at the Actors Studio. Still active, the NYPL is now a project of the Joseph Papp Public Theatre; Horovitz continues to serve as its artistic director.

In April at the Centre Cultural Americain in Paris, *Hopscotch* and *Spared*, with Lenny Baker, are staged in English. Horovitz directs.

Uncle Snake: An Independence Day Pageant is produced at Federal Hall, New York.

Start to Finish, a Horovitz teleplay, is aired on CBS's "Playhouse 90."

Horovitz receives a Fulbright Fellowship and an American Academy of Arts and Literature Award.

Horovitz wins an Emmy for *Play for Germs* of the "V. D. Blues" series.

Hopscotch is produced in November in New York.

The Primary English Class, with Horovitz as director, is staged at the Eugene O'Neill Memorial Theatre Foundation.

1976   *The Primary English Class*, directed by Edward Berkeley, is produced at the Circle in the Square Theatre in New York on February 16, featuring Diane Keaton, and runs for 104 performances.

Horovitz receives the Christopher Award for *Play for Germs*.

Our Father's Failing, directed by John Dillon, opens on April 1 at the Goodman Theatre, Chicago.

Stage Directions premieres at the Actors Studio in New York on May 31, featuring Lenny Baker, Laura Esterman, and Nancy Mette.

The 75th is first presented by the Aleph Company, University of Wisconsin, Milwaukee, in November.

The Reason We Eat is produced at the Hartman Theatre, Stamford, Connecticut, on November 3.

The Quannapowitt Quartet (*Hopscotch, The 75th, Spared,* and *Stage Directions*) is produced at Davenport College Theatre at Yale University, New Haven, Connecticut.

A television play, *The Making and Breaking of Splinters Braun,* is aired on CBS.

Line opens at the 13th Street Theater and runs for fifteen years, off-Broadway's longest-running play.

1977   Horovitz receives a National Endowment for the Arts Fellowship and a Guggenheim Fellowship.

The world premiere of *Alfred Dies,* directed by John Lion, is staged at the Magic Theatre, San Francisco, on March 26.

Man with Bags, a play adapted from Eugene Ionesco's *L'Homme aux valises,* translated by Marie-France Ionesco, is produced at the Towson State University Theatre, Baltimore, Maryland, on September 13. Carly Simon's incidental music beautifully complements the brilliantly orchestrated production, which features Dwight Schultz in the role of First Man.

Alfred the Great, produced in December at the Actors Studio with Michael Moriarty in the role of Alfred, also features Jill O'Hara, Paul Gleason, and Lois Markle.

The Former One-on-One Basketball Champion and *The Lounge Player* are staged at the Actors Studio.

1978   *Cappella,* a Horovitz novel, adapted for the theater by Horovitz and David Boorstin, opens in January at the Off-Center Theatre in New York.

Two plays of *The Alfred Trilogy, Alfred the Great* and *Our Father's Failing,* are workshopped in New York at the Actors Studio.

Mackerel is produced at the Old Place by the Hartford Stage Company, Hartford, Connecticut, on March 23. A revised version is staged by the Folger Theatre Group, Washington, D.C., on April 12, with Brian Hartigan, Pat Karpen, Jo Henderson, and Elizabeth Kemp.

Stage Directions is performed in Richmond, Surrey, England.

A Christmas Carol: Scrooge and Marley, an adaptation of Dickens's novel, using song, dance, color, and sounds to recreate the period, is produced at Center Stage in Baltimore in December.

Three Horovitz television plays are aired: *A Day with Conrad Green,* from a Ring Lardner story, and *Bartleby the Scrivener,* from the story by Melville, both for Maryland Public TV; and *Growing Up Jewish in Sault Ste. Marie,* a five-part mini-series adapted from Morley Torgov's *A Nice Place to Come From*, for Canadian Broadcasting.

1979   Horovitz founds the Gloucester Stage Company in Massachusetts and serves as both its producer and artistic director.

The Great Labor Day Classic is staged on January 26 by the Actors Theatre of Louisville as part of the 3rd Annual Festival of American Plays. Works by Tom Eyen, John Guare, Preston Jones, Marsha Norman, Megan Terry, Douglas Turner, and Lanford Wilson are also performed under the collective title *Holidays*.

The Good Parts is staged by the Actors Studio in New York.

The Widow's Blind Date is produced as a staged reading in May by the New York Playwrights Lab under the auspices of the Actors Studio. The cast includes then-unknown Jill Eikenberry, Robert Fields, and Ebbe Roe Smith.

A Special Tribute to Israel Horovitz is held in April for his fortieth birthday to celebrate the completion and publication of *The Wakefield Plays*. Elizabeth Wilson, Jill Eikenberry, Paul Simon, and Christopher Walken appear in this Poets at the Public Series event at Joseph Papp's Anspacher Public Theater, New York.

Horovitz writes a television play adaptation of Norman Mailer's novel, *The Deer Park*, for Lorimar Productions.

The Primary English Class, adapted and directed by Nicole Anouilh (wife of dramatist Jean Anouilh), premieres at Lucernaire-Forum, Paris.

1980   *The Primary English Class* and *Hopscotch* are staged in London.

Sunday Runners in the Rain, directed by Sheldon Larry, is workshopped at the Public Theatre, with Maureen Alderman, William Hickey, Judith Ivey, and Peter Riegert.

Horovitz writes *Fast Eddie*, his first screenplay since the early 1970s.

Horovitz's adaptation of a Ring Lardner story, *A Day with Conrad Green*, is produced by WNET.

The Widow's Blind Date enjoys a successful production at the Los Angeles Theatre Center.

Horovitz wins the Los Angeles Drama Critics Circle Award.

1981   Actors Studio in New York stages a revival of *Alfred the Great* and *Our Father's Failing*, starring Michael Moriarty.

Horovitz marries Gillian Adams, former British (Women's) Marathon Champion.

1982   *The Good Parts*, staged at the Astor Place Theater in January, is directed by
Barnet Kellman and stars Tony Roberts and Stephen Strimpell.

Horovitz writes two screenplays, *Fell* and *Berta*.

1983   *Author! Author!* a screenplay, is completed by Horovitz, with Al Pacino in the
starring role.

Horovitz wins the Los Angeles (Weekly) Critics Prize.

Bill Bushnell directs a revised *The Widow's Blind Date* at the Gloucester
Stage.

1984   *Park Your Car in Harvard Yard* is produced in Gloucester at the Gloucester
Stage Company. The production is directed by Richard Hughes and stars
Dossy Peabody and Thomas Celli.

1985   *Henry Lumper* is premiered by the Gloucester Stage Company. A cast of
twenty-two, many of them doubling roles, is led by Ted Kazanoff and Paul
O'Brien.

Twins, Hannah and Oliver, are born to Gillian Adams and Israel Horovitz at
Addison-Gilbert Hospital, Gloucester.

The Former One-on-One Basketball Champion is staged in San Francisco,
starring Boston Celtics great Bill Russell.

Light Years, a screenplay, is written.

Screenplay *Author! Author!* is translated into French as *Avec des compliments
de l'auteur*.

1986   The world premiere of *Today, I Am a Fountain Pen* is staged at the American
Jewish Theater of Ninety-second Street in New York on January 2 and stars
Josh Blake, Sol Frieder, and Marcia Jean Kurtz.

A Rosen by Any Other Name is given its world premiere on March 4 at the
American Jewish Theatre and features Maddie Corman, Barbara eda-Young,
Sol Frieder, Michael Ornstein, and Peter Riegert.

The world premiere of *The Chopin Playoffs* is staged at the American Jewish
Theatre on May 15. With *Today, I Am a Fountain Pen* and *A Rosen by Any
Other Name*, the play forms the *Sault Ste. Marie Trilogy*, which is adapted
from a novel and short stories by Morley Torgov. All three productions are
under the direction of Stephen Zuckerman and were originally commissioned
by the Community Theatre Project of the National Foundation for Jewish
Culture.

In May, Horovitz is awarded the Eliot Norton Prize for outstanding
contributions to the theater of Boston, primarily for his creative work as
founding artistic director of the Gloucester Stage Company.

North Shore Fish is given its world premiere on August 24, at the Gloucester Stage. The production is directed by Grey Cattell Johnson and features Mary Klug, Marina Re, and John Fiore.

Year of the Duck is staged in Portland, Maine.

Firebird at Dogtown is workshopped at the New York Shakespeare Festival.

1987   *North Shore Fish*, directed by Steve Zuckerman, opens in January at WPA Theatre in New York, starring John Pankow, Christine Estabrook, and Mary Klug. Set design by Edward T. Gianfrancesco.

Horovitz and Diane Kurys co-author *A Man in Love*, a screenplay.

Year of the Duck opens in August at the Gloucester Stage and in October at the Hudson Guild Theater. Directed by Geoffrey Sherman, the latter production features Paul O'Brien, Kathryn Rossetter, and Ann-Sara Matthews.

North Shore Fish is nominated for a Pulitzer Prize.

1988   *Year of the Duck* is the Hudson Guild Theater entry.

Un Homme amoreux is translated from the screenplay *A Man in Love*, co-authored by Horovitz and Diane Kurys.

Payofski's Discovery, a screenplay, is written.

Faith, Hope and Charity marks the twentieth reunion of the collaboration of Israel Horovitz, Terrence McNally, and Leonard Melfi. Directed by Edward Berkeley, the triptych is staged at South Street Theater, New York, in December.

1989   *Henry Lumper* opens January 31 at the Actors Outlet Theatre, off-Broadway, a co-production of the Working Theatre and the Gloucester Stage Company. Directed by Grey Cattell Johnson, *Lumper* features a cast of twenty-two actors performing forty-six roles.

Horovitz completes two screenplays, *The Pan* and *Letters to Iris*.

The Widow's Blind Date enjoys an extended run of several months at the Gloucester Stage before reopening in New York at Circle in the Square Downtown on November 7. This production, directed by Horovitz, features Paul O'Brien, Tom Bloom, and Christine Estabrook.

1990   *Park Your Car in Harvard Yard* is workshopped at the Manhattan Theatre Club with Burgess Meredith and Ellen Burstyn.

The French version of *Park Your Car in Harvard Yard*, *Quelque part dans cette vie* (Somewhere in This Life), with Jane Birkin and Pierre Dux opens in Théâtre des Bouffes Parisiens, Paris.

Screenplay for *The Deuce* is completed.

1991   Horovitz is awarded an honorary doctor of arts degree by Salem State College, Salem, Massachusetts.

It's Called the Sugar Plum is featured on A&E Cable Network, starring Ione Skye and Fisher Stevens.

Faith is staged off-Broadway in the Horovitz-McNally-Melfi revival of their triptych, *Faith, Hope, and Charity.*

Strong-Man's Weak Child has a joint world premiere at Los Angeles Theatre Center and, subsequently, at Gloucester Stage. Horovitz directs the LATC and   Gloucester productions, which star Don Yesso and John Fiore.

Park Your Car in Harvard Yard, starring Jason Robards and Judith Ivey, opens on Broadway at the Music Box Theater on November 7.

1992   Horovitz directs a New York revival of *Spared*, which stars William Hickey as an aging and helpless Alfred in the finale of *The Wakefield Plays.*

Judith Ivey wins a Tony Award for her performance in *Park Your Car in Harvard Yard.*

Fighting over Beverley, the eighth play of the Gloucester cycle, receives a staged reading at the Public Theatre in October.

The Widow's Blind Date is performed in France, Germany, Spain, and Israel.

Feature film rights to *Strong-Man's Weak Child* are purchased by Tri-Star Pictures. Horovitz has recently completed the screenplay, *Strong-Men.*

Horovitz is writing two screenplays for Warner Brothers. The first, *Damon*, is scheduled to shoot in Cambridge, Massachusetts; the second will be based on the life of James Dean.

1993   *Hopscotch* and *Stage Directions* in French, directed by Horovitz, open in Paris at the Théâtre Lucernaire with Olivier Granier, Rafaèle Montier, Jean-Pierre Stewart, and Laura Zichy. A huge success, the production is extended until July.

North Shore Fish, with Grey Cattell Johnson directing the original cast, airs on WGBH Public Radio on May 8. The play, selected to be a representative work of New England playwrights, is part of the New England Theatres on the Air.

Adapted and directed by Horovitz, *Hopscotch*, is taped for future airing on French television.

Fighting over Beverley receives a staged reading at the American Repertory Theatre on May 24 with Jeremy Geidt, Ted Kazanoff, Julie Harris, and Marina Re.

Fighting over Beverley, directed by Patrick Swanson, premieres on August 25 at the Gloucester Stage Company, starring Judy Holmes, David Jones, Ted Kazanoff, and Marina Re.

Park Your Car in Harvard Yard opens October 12 at Hasty Pudding Theatre in Cambridge, Massachusetts, starring E. G. Marshall and Mary Plunkett.

ISRAEL HOROVITZ

1

Introduction

Leslie Kane

Addressing a conference of Eugene O'Neill scholars in 1987 with idiosyncratic wit, Israel Horovitz recalled,

When I was born, in 1939, O'Neill had already established himself as the American Master. By June of my birth-year, O'Neill had already written down his plans for *Iceman*, and *Long Day's Journey*. I am not yet on solid food, and O'Neill is three years past his Nobel Prize, a quarter dozen Pulitzers, and outlines for two of the three best plays in American English. I look out of my crib . . . and write in my notebook, "O'Neill will be tough competition." [1]

A precocious teenager from Wakefield, Massachusetts, whose introduction to literature came in the form of books he was paid to destroy in his uncle's junk shop and baling room, Horovitz's writing career began when he submitted a novel, *Steinberg, Sex and the Saint*, at the age of thirteen. Horovitz, whose dazzling productivity, high energy, and tenacious competitive spirit characterize his life and his art, credits its rejection and praise for launching his career as a playwright.

Horovitz's first dramatic work, *The Comeback*, a reworking of *Richard II* in which he dramatizes the experiences of a father-son acting team, written when he was seventeen, had its premiere at Emerson College, Boston, as a curtain-raiser for Arthur Miller's *A Memory of Two Mondays*. After honing his craft at the Old Poets Theatre in Cambridge, Massachusetts, and attending Salem State College for one year, the young playwright from Wakefield, a small working-class town north of Boston, became a Fellow at the Royal Academy of Dramatic Art in London, where in 1965 he earned the distinction of being the first American playwright to be appointed playwright-in residence at the Royal Shakespeare Company and the Aldwych Theatre in London.

At twenty-eight Horovitz burst upon the New York theatre scene in 1967–68 when successful productions of four one-act plays, *Line*, *The Indian Wants the Bronx*, *Rats*, and *It's Called the Sugar Plum,* heralded him as a brilliant, new, socially committed playwright. *Line*, a grotesque allegory of the American success myth, which opened at La Mama in New York in 1967, also occasioned Horovitz's acting debut when the playwright took the part of the line-eater who left New York for Hollywood on the eve of the play's opening night. Since that time, Horovitz has won acclaim for *Line*, the longest running off-Broadway play in New York history; The *Indian Wants the Bronx*, now considered a genre classic of violence; *The Wakefield Plays; North Shore Fish; The Primary English Class*; and *An Israel Horovitz Trilogy*. More recently, *The Widow's Blind Date*, which played to standing-room-only audiences in Gloucester, Paris and Darmstadt, Germany, for the run of production, reopened off-Broadway in 1989 and enjoyed successful productions in Spain and Israel. *Park Your Car in Harvard Yard,* which workshopped at the Manhattan Theatre Club with Burgess Meredith and Ellen Burstyn, earned critical acclaim in Paris and on Broadway. And, most recently, Horovitz's *Fighting over Beverley*, the ninth play of his Gloucester cycle, whose world premiere production in August 1993 at the Gloucester Stage Company garnered strong reviews. Scheduled for a Paris production, *Beverley* is the poignant and moving portrayal of a woman worth fighting over that dramatizes her growing independence from and rejection of the male combatants who view her as a prize rather than their equal.

Winner of two Obies, the French Critics Prize, the Prix du Plaiser de Théâtre, the Vernon–Rice Drama Desk Award, the Emmy, the Los Angeles Critics Prize, and the Eliot Norton Award for outstanding contribution to the theater of Boston, as well as a Fulbright Foundation Award, Guggenheim Fellowship, and a National Endowment for the Arts Award, Israel Horovitz, who has written more than fifty plays, been translated into twenty languages, and produced in cities from Tokyo to Rome, continues to be one of the most prolific and theatrically innovative playwrights in America. No other American playwright, with the exception of O'Neill, has had more plays produced in the French language. Founder of the New York Playwrights Lab and founder and artistic director of the Gloucester Stage Company, Horovitz has also directed the world premiere productions of many of his plays in English and French, including *Spared, Hopscotch, Strong-Man's Weak Child, The Widow's Blind Date, and Line* (with Michel Fagadau).

A number of actors have made their debuts as Horovitz characters, among them Al Pacino, Richard Dreyfuss, Jill Clayburgh, John Cazale, Marsha Norman, and Diane Keaton. In addition to his substantial literary output, the playwright has been a producer, director, stage manager, actor, and screenwriter. Author of the screenplays *The Strawberry Statement* (Cannes Film Festival Prix du Jury), *Author! Author!* and the recently completed

Strong-Men, *The Deuce*, *Letters to Iris*, and *Payofski's Discovery*, Horovitz has also written a novel, a novella, and a collection of poetry.

Horovitz's fascination with self-sustaining fictions, characters as an expression of social dislocation, intimations of menace, seemingly aimless, colloquial speech laced with innuendo, realistic props metamorphosed into instruments of torture, and intrusion of memory and betrayal suggest obvious comparisons with Samuel Beckett, with whom Horovitz enjoyed a close personal relationship and whose influence he readily acknowledges, and Harold Pinter, whose *Homecoming* was in rehearsal when the young playwright was in residence at the Royal Academy of Dramatic Art. "There had never been anything   like that before," recalls Horovitz, who found it a "stunning revelation that you could write that way." [2] His criticism of wanton violence and moral void, his consideration of the delicate balance between illusion and reality, and the use of trilogies place him firmly in the tradition of American drama and invite comparison to both O'Neill and Edward Albee. But it is his refusal to repeat himself, reflected in a body of work composed of realistic plays, absurdist fantasies and parables, and dark chamber plays, that are characterized by "a rich and gorgeous theatrical sense and real breathing, living people" that clearly account for his worldwide appeal. [3]

Although Horovitz's recent work is largely realistic, psychological, darker, and more personal than earlier plays, his technical virtuosity, superb ear for dialogue, images of alienation, powerful central metaphor, taut balance between the comic and the terrifying, and social consciousness account in large part for his staying power and critical respect.[4] Indeed, dramatizing how violence can and does spring from futility and frustration, Horovitz's theatre is an extraordinary study of the psychology of terrorism. Turning back to the issues of power and fear that occupied him in the 1960s, Horovitz seems to be fulfilling earlier promise by addressing issues of social terror, personal responsibility, and essential vulnerability with a verbal dexterity and control of character and plot that attests to his maturity and has never been more relevant. "If Horovitz previously resorted to violence and bloodshed in early works to blow them [audiences] out of their conformist armchairs," observes Peter Sagal, more recently he "is dedicated to an increasingly gentle portrayal of human frailty."[5]

Horovitz's monumental *The Wakefield Plays*, composed of the *Alfred Trilogy* and its companion quartet, *The Quannapowitt Quartet* (named for Lake Quannapowitt, where the young Horovitz, a marathoner, regularly ran), combining allegory and dark comedy to depict sexual greed, guilt, and impotence, portrays the adventures of Alfred, a celebrated citizen of Wakefield who returns to unravel a confusing narrative of his past. The trilogy and the quartet depict, with great humor and almost perfect dramatic unfolding, human loss, the power of mythology of the past, the poignancy of human failure, and the universality of the quest to dig up old truths in search of present understanding.

Whereas *The Wakefield Plays* are weighty with buried betrayals and mythic importance, Horovitz's most recent cycle of plays (nine at last count) are set in his adopted home town, Gloucester, Massachusetts, a declining fishing community of great beauty where Horovitz maintains a home on Cape Ann, runs with the Wingeraesheek Runners, and in the playwright's view, "the stars are the people who built their houses with their own hands."[6] Its self-appointed local bard dramatizing the staunch pride and vicissitudes of "livin' local," dedicated to capturing and preserving the speech patterns and idioms of the community, Horovitz has "fashioned himself as the voice and the heart and the conscience" of the picturesque community that has inspired such artists as T. S. Eliot, Winslow Homer, and Edward Hopper. In stark contrast to spare, early plays, whose tension derives from the complicity between surrealism and logic, his recent work, which may be his best, is largely realistic. Reflecting the playwright's maturity, sensibility, and social consciousness, the Gloucester plays vitally portray a working-class people confronting an insidious drug problem, a dying trade, and a community falling prey to mechanization and gentrification. [7]

In the early 1970s, Horovitz began presenting his plays in Gloucester in any available space, including movie theatres, chapels—even a pizza parlor—but in 1979 he founded the Gloucester Stage Company as a venue for new and mostly American plays, including his own. The back room of the Blackburn Tavern, a local watering hole, served as its official home until the tavern was sold in 1986, at which time the Gloucester Stage moved to the cavernous fish warehouse owned by Gorton's of Gloucester, a local fish-packing company, that served as a fitting setting for its first production, *North Shore Fish,* and subsequent Gloucester cycle plays. Despite the financial struggle to maintain the solvency of the Gloucester Stage, Horovitz is apparently inspired by the sea and the setting. *Fighting over Beverley*, which Horovitz discusses in an interview in Chapter 15, demonstrates yet again his refusal to repeat himself and his new commitment to strong women's roles. "With these plays," Horovitz recently remarked, "I have taken the position that changing times in Gloucester is an essential metaphor for changing times in our country and our world."[8]

The time is propitious for a collection of essays devoted solely to Horovitz's work in the theatre. The rationale for such a collection is provided by Israel Horovitz himself. Few others in the American theatre continue to demonstrate sensitivity to language and examine violence with such breadth, imagination, theatrical audacity, social consciousness, and continuing productivity, tempering gravity and seriousness with humor and economy. Currently, no scholarly book or collection of essays has been published on Horovitz's more than fifty plays, and few scholarly essays have been published within the past ten years, with the exception of my own on *The Widow's Blind Date* (revised and reprised here). Yet Horovitz's powerful dramas, worldwide productions, and enormous success in France and Germany (as yet unmatched in the United States) suggest that he may soon gain his rightful place among important American playwrights.

Reflecting the breadth, theatricality, imagination and diversity of Horovitz's canon, I have provided a range of critical approaches that offer retrospectives and perspectives on Horovitz's drama, including two recent screenplays, and encompassing his work from the early absurdist parable, *Line,* to *Strong-Man's Weak Child.* Moreover, specific plays and Horovitz's prolific body of work invite thematic, rhetoric, and comparative consideration, as well as an exploration of recurring paradigms such as the bonding among characters behind which lurks a confrontational friendship, disillusionment of male relationships, the use of talent, tricks, sex, or guilt to achieve advantage, and analogues to Chekhov, Beckett, O'Neill, and Albee.

In order to provide a comprehensive and cohesive context, I have chosen essays that are broadly sketched and specifically focused on major plays. The dominant focus will, of course, be accorded to several principal works, such as *The Indian Wants the Bronx, North Shore Fish,* and *The Widow's Blind Date.* In addition to essays that offer differing perspectives on well-known plays, essays on lesser-known works, such as *Mackerel, Morning, The 75th,* and *Henry Lumper,* will familiarize readers with the variety in theme, rhetorical mode, and technical scope that characterizes Horovitz's substantial canon.

This collection presents thirteen essays—twelve original essays and one reprised and expanded—that cohesively establish a context for thinking about the drama of Israel Horovitz and initiate a dialectic on performance and structure. Each makes a sound argument independent of the other essays. Together, the essays provide a cohesive overview of Horovitz's plays and recent screenplays and provide a context for furthering our understanding of them. Although I do not concur with some interpretations presented in this book, the arguments have been carefully delineated and articulated. That critics hold opposing viewpoints is a reflection of both the critic's philosophy and the richness of Horovitz's writing. Additionally, this book includes a substantive interview with the playwright that immeasurably furthers our understanding of the artist and his art. The chapters have been arranged mostly on the basis of chronological order, but this has proved impossible in several that consider both early and late work. The chronology of Horovitz's prodigious career, at the beginning of this book, aquaints readers with the sequence of productions (and clearly reflects Horovitz's popularity in France); comprehensive primary and selected secondary bibliographies, at the end of the book, will assist scholars and students.

William Demastes's provocative essay, "'We Gotta' Hang Together': Horovitz and the National Cycles of Violence," initiating a dialogue on the subject that would seem to defy reasonable discussion, opens this collection with a study of Horovitz's work. With a breadth and depth that reveals a stunning grasp of the playwright's philosophy, dramaturgy, influences, and intent, Demastes presents a perceptive explication of personal impotence and the correlation between competition and capitalism and the dissolution of culture and community and cogently persuades us that the physical, verbal, and psychic violence that typify Horovitz's drama are "the result of a marked breakdown of social structures" and contracts that have proved themselves ineffective in preventing what he terms "primitive and violent response." Drawing upon a plethora of evidence from works both familiar and less so, both early and late, such as *Rats, Indian, The Alfred Trilogy, Henry Lumper, and The Former One-on-One Basketball Champion,* Demastes's thematic approach presents a strong case that even at this stage of Horovitz's career, the playwright continues "to personally howl at the injustices" individuals inflict upon one another. Even if his plays do not always succeed, argues Demastes, Horovitz, who originally attracted attention in 1967 as a socially committed playwright, has never desisted in addressing America's need to confront itself. Unlike his characters, for whom violence serves as impotent rage or self-empowering revenge, the playwright, neither visionary nor apocalyptic, is firmly grounded in reality, aware that America as a culture "can and must" find the spiritual and political resolutions to disrupt the "cycle of violence that epitomizes so much of what is wrong with this country."

Approaching the broad issue of community and culture in Horovitz's drama from a slightly different perspective, Robert Skloot's "Ins and Outs: The Ethnic World of Israel Horovitz" narrows the focus to Horovitz's pervasive concern with the "newcomer/outsider," a theme, Skloot maintains, that is particularly consistent in the playwright's canon. Arguing convincingly that Horovitz's drama, however comic, is typified by its social commentary on the ethnic condition in America, Skloot marries his own seriousness of purpose with humorous and piercing insight. Amply illustrating his thesis, Skloot scrutinizes plays from "three different culturally and otherwise decades": *The Indian Wants the Bronx, Morning, The Primary English Class,* and *The Saute Ste. Marie Trilogy,* representing the 1960s, 1970s, and 1980s, respectively.

Although clearly there is nothing comic about racial prejudice, Skloot astutely recognizes that the comic violence that erupts in *The Primary English Class* and the ferocious satire that typifies *Morning,* a one-joke play that harshly employs "ethnic language" to expose "the evils of racism," are of a piece, that is, they, like *Indian,* expose "intolerance at the heart of humanity." Skloot, however, is especially insightful on what he terms Horovitz's "ethnic masterpiece," his personal and deeply felt "Growing-up Jewish plays" chronicling the struggle of Jews "to assimilate into the larger, ethnically diverse cultures of America," and dramatizing universal, generational, and ethnic conflicts. Throughout the chapter, Professor Skloot brings the keen eye of a director to bear upon the stage instructions that, in the case of *The Chopin*

Playoffs, for example, forbid a director and designer to employ "stereotypes" and "stereotypically Jewish intonation." And, citing *Rosen* as the strongest expression of "social and familial tension" in the trilogy (and the one on which the playwright has apparently "lavished great love") engendered by ethnic struggle, Skloot unswervingly maintains that the playwright's comic world is continually disrupted by violence born of ethnic tension in this play and others under discussion. We are all profoundly diminished, concludes Skloot, if we fail to value both the range and skill of these plays that illustrate that for Horovitz "being in and being out is a comic and serious thematic preoccupation."

Although Ionesco and Beckett are traditionally cited as the principal influences on Israel Horovitz's dramaturgical and philosophical development, Robert Combs's compelling comparative essay, "O'Neill and Horovitz: Toward Home," encourages us to (re)consider the extent, persistence, and prevalence of O'Neill's influence on Horovitz's work. He draws upon his vast knowledge of O'Neill's drama to formulate and lay the foundation for his argument that the earlier playwright's drama prefigures, anticipates, and sets the stage for Horovitz's development of theme, character, and subject. Fresh readings of O'Neill's major dramas and Horovitz's *Line, Indian, and Widow* lead Combs to conclude that Horovitz, like O'Neill, perceiving the betrayal of the American soul, has looked inward to "the family of all humankind . . . to mitigate sins of greed." Whereas Combs wonderfully captures the essence of Horovitz's comedic philosophy and structure as an "engaging celebration of humanity in an age that has tended to glamorize business," he nevertheless is acutely aware that Horovitz's humor—"often quite dark"—is staged against a backdrop of a "wasteland of unfulfilled dreams first charted by O'Neill." The strength of this perceptive essay lies in Combs's ability to elucidate the rarely discussed *The 75th*, a charming (and ostensibly slight) one-act play informed by the rhythm of reunion, reassessment of the past, the dynamics of family (however extended), and self-deception with the same acuity that he brings to the massive *Henry Lumper,* a play that dramatizes "a family-centered world breaking apart into factions," modeled on Shakespeare's *Henriad.* The conclusion that Horovitz—and formerly O'Neill—arrive at is that home can yet be a refuge for individuals struggling with the "large forces of their inner and outer worlds."

A critic-in-residence at the Eugene O'Neill Playwrights Conference (of which Horovitz was a charter member) when the playwright's *Alfred Trilogy* was staged as a work-in-progress, Martin Esslin, who called the Wakefield plays an "American Oresteia," believed them to be a brilliant response to the sterility and impotence of the Vietnam War. Thus, Dennis Klein's essay, "The Influence of Aeschylus' *Oresteia* on Israel Horovitz's *Alfred Trilogy*," taking his cue from Esslin's well-known observation, is justifiably a massive one that not only thoroughly acquaints the reader with the elements of plot, theme, characterization, imagery, and technique that typify Aeschylus' *Oresteia* but persuasively argues that Horovitz's "masterfully paced trilogy of revelation of past events," a treatment of such subjects as matricide, adultery, revenge, and retribution, thematically and structurally parallels Aeschylus' masterpiece. Indeed, Klein's formidable breadth of knowledge of the classical trilogy informs his pointed comparative examination of Aeschylus' and Horovitz's *Oresteia*, as well as a variety of strategies, including conforming to the classical unities, the paradigm of reunion, gradual revelation and discovery, the promotion and prevalence of death, and themes of infertility and impotence. Although both trilogies are, in Klein's view, "parallel to the extent that both begin with triumphant returns, and end with protagonists on trial," Klein's impressive argument captures the intent, irony, and artistry of Horovitz's trilogy, as well as its companion, *The Quannapowitt Quartet*. Klein's contribution is a tour de force that finally affords Horovitz's *The Wakefield Plays* the attention long denied them.

"The tricks played on our mind by our memory," observes Liliane Kerjan, "provide the starting impulse" of *The Quannapowitt Quartet*, composed of *Hopscotch, The 75th, Stage Directions,* and *Spared*, whose perspective is "private, narcissistic, and confessional, to a point." Analyzing its "mixed moods," a tripod of "resilience and reticence and absence," and Horovitz's art of economy with enormous sensitivity to sound and space, Kerjan expands our understanding of these minimalist gems. Kerjan, a French critic and scholar, was, like Esslin, in residence at the O'Neill Playwrighting Conference when these plays were first staged; her familiarity with these works spans nearly twenty years, affording readers not only a unique perspective on the quartets but ample rationale for the enormous appeal and success of Horovitz's plays in France. Resonating with references to Bach, Beckett, Flaubert, Balzac, and Albee, Kerjan's essay, "Double Mixed Memories," elucidates the elusive quartets—double duets oscillating "between rage and frustration"—and explicates each play's dramatization of fantasy and emotion. Whereas in *Stage Directions* "the confrontation of memories and the memory of past confrontations generate a regression toward self-destruction," memories in *Spared*, observes Kerjan, "inspire construction and urgent life." Similarly, "the September stance of *Hopscotch*," with its "keynotes of regrets," is succeeded by its twin duet, *The 75th*, thereby achieving a perfect confessional symmetry. Although this chapter is consistently illuminating, Kerjan's analysis of both *Stage Directions* and *Hopscotch* is especially luminous, guiding readers through the paces and places of loss.

My own essay on *The Widow's Blind Date* extends Kerjan's discussion on mixed memory, buried history and betrayals, and the delicate balance of rage and frustration. Paralleling dramas of great poignancy and power such as *Indian, Sugar Plum,* and *North Shore Fish, Widow* derives its power from wanton destructiveness, where violence takes the form of a gang rape—at once realistic and symbolic. A brilliantly imagined and chillingly executed drama that might have been a revenge drama on the order of Durrenmatt's *The Visit* (and has been viewed as such by other contributors to this book), *Widow* is approached as a fascinating exploration of victimization of victim and victimizer. Benefiting from attendance at the world premiere, access to performance scripts, revisions, and author's notes, as well as extended discussions with the playwright on the entrapment of young men in small towns (like the one in which Horovitz grew up and now resides) that gives rise to fierce competition, failure, and frustration, I have traced the history of *Widow* from its first reading to its final stage version.

Widow shares a number of paradigms with other Horovitz plays—territorial, intellectual, and sexual dominance, a secret history that is progressively revealed, moral and ethical blindness, and a central metaphor—as well as compatibility with Pinter's drama, specifically in the untrustworthiness of narrative, the intimations of menace, and the experience of entrapment. However, I refute critics who view Margy as the villain of the piece. Rather, in my fresh reading of this work, I maintain that Horovitz has effectively broken new ground in *Widow* by amply illustrating that his sympathies lie with his empowered protagonist, as evidenced by his arming her with the linguistic weapons and emotional strength to even the playing (and killing) field. My analysis of this play encourages reevaluation of *Widow* and of Horovitz as a socially committed humanist outraged by the emotional and psychic rape of women too long foxed out of first place.

John Watkins and Andrew Elfenbein in "The Unkindness of Strangers" have coauthored a disturbing chapter on the prevalence and persistence of violence and homosexual subtexts in Israel Horovitz's plays. Rereading *The Indian Wants the Bronx* and *The Widow's Blind Date* in the light of the Jeffrey Dahmer case, Watkins and Elfenbein approach linguistic and physical violence from the vantage point of the contemporary minefield of social politics. Convincingly, they analyze "the uncomfortable tensions in sexual definition" that characterize "relations between men who think of themselves as being just 'friends,'" arguing that although Horovitz's plays are typically sympathetic, "that sympathy is never innocent." Rather, linking violence to class and social awareness, Watkins and Elfenbein unmask Horovitz's plays as "pretexts for more disturbing inquisitions" of ostensibly liberal American values regarding marginalized social groups.

Taking up the question of friendship between men, namely Samuel Beckett and Israel Horovitz, Robert Scanlan observes that it is difficult to imagine two more widely disparate personalities and creative talents; however, between 1972 and 1976, when their friendship was new and the playwright young, Horovitz was drawn into "the metaphysical whirlpool that was Beckett's influence." Scanlan initiates a lively debate on the nature of this influence, the extent of "ingenuous imitation," and "the considerable sympathy and indulgence" that Beckett, then sixty, extended to his young American friend.

Subjecting several dramatic and prose pieces written during the early 1970s—what he terms Horovitz's "Beckett phase"—to a close reading, Scanlan concludes that Horovitz openly imitated Beckett's subject and structure in *Capella,* with its hospital room setting and first-person narrator identified as "the copyist," and two Beckett-like one-act plays, *Stage Directions* and *Spared.* But, while one may consider such deliberate mimicry "as presumptuous or invasive" of a fellow artist, Horovitz, Scanlan maintains, was motivated by open admiration. Clearly, Beckett's influence "altered and shaped Horovitz's life," but if he was "drawn to the *tone* in Beckett," observes Scanlan, Horovitz abandoned and replaced it with a new style and tones unrelated to any in Beckett.

A native of the North Shore of Massachusetts, where both Wakefield and Gloucester are located, Thomas F. Connolly contributes a unique and most welcome perspective on the history, language, and community of Gloucester that has served as Israel Horovitz's adopted home and, since the 1980s, the inspiration for his cycle of Gloucester plays. A finely tuned piece of scholarship, "The Place, the Thing: Israel Horovitz's Gloucester Milieu" views (or hears) a number of plays in the Gloucester cycle from the panorama of "theatrical local color, theatricalized location, and local locution" with the depth of understanding that both (re)focuses the spectator's and reader's vision and heightens awareness to resonance among the plays. As Connolly wisely observes and Horovitz's plays portray, Gloucester is a community whose traditions, trade, and very property are threatened by obsolescence and gentrification but whose "proletarian code of honor" and work ethic are absolutely integral to survival. Thus, maintains Connolly, "the more 'precisely Gloucestrian' Horovitz's plays . . . the more universal they are as dramas." Drawing sharp distinctions between those plays for which Gloucester serves as local color and those for which Gloucester is "site specific," Connolly concludes that plays such as *Henry Lumper* and *North Shore Fish* that are site specific have "a greater resonance as plays about Gloucester life" than do *Mackerel* or *Year of the Duck.* Connolly persuasively argues that possessed of "a historical continuity and dramaturgical unity," Horovitz's Gloucester plays not only "constitute the portion of his work that is most successful" but the cycle "where he has managed to find his own sound."

Susan C. Haedicke's "Portraits of (Wo)Men" offers a provocative feminist perspective on the women in *North Shore Fish* and *Park Your Car in Harvard Yard* who, for this critic, "exemplify metaphoric cross-dressed characters following a script defined by the dominant patriarchal culture." Haedicke addresses the issues of enforced aphasia of the female voice, female characterization as sex objects, and otherness with depth, sensitivity, and expert knowledge of both theory and theatrical practice. A director, Haedicke draws upon a wealth of theatrical experience and expertise to guide our attention to costume, lighting, blocking, and dialogue in order to illustrate how these dramatic elements direct and focus the spectator's vision. Haedicke's central thesis is that a male playwright "writing about a woman and foregrounding her life does not give her a voice if she is living out a male-derived narrative."

While conceding that Horovitz is not alone in silencing the female voice, Haedicke maintains that he "follows a long and dramatic tradition" that "marginalizes" women. Haedicke is especially convincing when she strengthens her critical posture by referring to Simone de Beauvoir on otherness and Mikhail Bakhtin's distinction between heteroglossia and monoglossia (or unitary language) upon which Haedicke argues that Horovitz relies. Illustrating her premise that the portrayal of Horovitz's Gloucester women—however sympathetic—is monoglossic (single-voiced) and that their representation as female characters is either erotic or generated by "a male fantasy of the loyal and loving woman," Haedicke's trenchant study of *North Shore Fish* and *Park Your Car* unmasks ostensibly empowered women by exposing them as women living stories delineated and "defined by the male perspective." "Foregrounding female characters," Haedicke maintains, as Horovitz does in these two Gloucester plays, does not necessarily "valorize gender difference"; on the contrary, it "can, in fact, reinforce the dominant culture."

Ann C. Hall's "Machismo in Massachusetts: Israel Horovitz's Unpublished Screenplays *The Deuce* and *Strong-Men*" is a superb study of both machismo as it functions in Horovitz's world—not only in these screenplays but in numerous plays—and the feminine spectator's response to screenplays in which macho men wrestle with issues that threaten their manhood. From a feminist and female perspective, Hall finds much that is refreshing in *The Deuce* and *Strong-Men*: Patriarchal biases are treated as a character's "tragic flaw"; macho behavior results in consequences; and men, redressing biases by compromising and/or sacrificing, undergo significant transformation. Hall concludes that although macho sexist behavior is condemned by Horovitz, a theme repeatedly emphasized by his envisioning collaboration in lieu of competition, female characters are, nonetheless, objectified and marginalized in these screenplays. Interestingly, Hall does not perceive some hidden misogenistic agenda on the part of the screenwriter. Rather, the fault appears to lie with the Hollywood screenplay, a form that continues to be reluctant to forgo a winning formula.

Notably, Hall strengthens her argument by detailed exegesis of *The Deuce* and *Strong-Men*, citing examples in which men, having exhibited patronizing or misogynist behavior, do not experience epiphanies and improve their treatment of their wife/women.   Rather, the screenplays depict "the men brutally beating other men" who have yet to reform macho behavior, as well as disappointing stereotyping of female characters "left in the shadows or the grave." But Hall's intelligent and incisive study concludes that on balance Horovitz's new screenplays tip the scales toward a more "complicated" and welcome "representation of masculine behavior" that celebrates "masculine flexibility rather than macho rigidity or patriarchal paralysis."

Steven H. Gale's insightful and instructive essay, "Israel Horovitz's *Strong-Man's Weak Child/Strong-Men*: From Stage Play to Screenplay," is a wonderful piece of scholarship that simultaneously enhances our understanding of the creative process in each medium and the evolution of Horovitz's perspective, which, like a camera lens, widens to encompass more in his screenplay than initially conceived by the playwright in his stage play. Gale carefully analyzes several unpublished versions of *Strong-Man's Weak Child*, a two-act, five-character play about "a trio of thirty-something weight lifters" (Franny, Fast Eddie Ryan, and Auggie) who attended high school together in Gloucester, the setting of several Gloucester cycle plays. Benefiting from Horovitz's script annotations and director's notes, he delineates cosmetic and integral revisions in the stage play, perceptively elucidating the theatrical and thematic rationale for these revisions while simultaneously establishing a vantage point for his comparative study of the stage play and screenplay.

Markedly different from any of the stage revisions, notes Gale, *Strong-Men* contains eight scenes (including sites only alluded to in the stage version and the "concurrent addition of characters to fill these scenes") that facilitate a film director to cut from scene to scene, crossediting and strengthening the film's parallel plots and subplots. "Among the technical advantages of film that Horovitz utilizes," observes Gale, are "the camera as a means of focusing on an object or person in a way not possible on the live stage," the ability to focus the audience's attention on the present connections" and the concomitant "ironic tone" that these contrasts elicit, the immediate and direct introduction of Eddie, and the scenic depiction of fall foliage now extended to December to "evoke the family feelings that surround the holidays of the season."

Gale's perspective and detailed examination of versions of *Strong-Man/Men* offers impressive evidence that these variations "illustrate the author's movement from the exploration of the character of a few individuals to the exploration of the character of a community" and confirms that Horovitz continues to manifest a receptivity to revision that has previously characterized his dramatic work.

Whereas many scholars decline to take on the challenge of Horovitz's *Mackerel* because they view it as an anomaly in his canon, or because they dismiss it as unimportant, or because they can make absolutely no sense out of its absurdist parable, Martin J. Jacobi's "Ed Lemon: Prophet of Profit" is a brilliant essay that cohesively corroborates Horovitz's ability to employ absurdism to depict social bankruptcy chillingly and persuasively. Expanding upon Kenneth Burke's view that a work of art can become "equipment for living," Jacobi's wickedly funny and searingly accurate treatment of *Mackerel* as "an absurdist play that does more than entertain" is an incisive critique of the play that preserves Horovitz's wit while exposing the half-wits that expound its truism as truths. With a clarity that has long eluded other critics of this play, or for that matter Horovitz's drama, Jacobi astutely argues that *Mackerel* is not another fish story. Rather, it does nothing less than depict the corruption in modern American family, religion, and business" while exposing "business as a heartless, corrupt and corrupting, sometimes evil system, and religion as either the refuge of the mad or the cynical resort of scoundrels." Cogent, cohesive, and compelling, Jacobi's stunning essay is not only illuminating; it convinces us, as does Horovitz's play, to reexamine "a truly ugly American" and to respond by reevaluating our own familial and social attitudes.

NOTES

1. Israel Horovitz, "The Legacy of O'Neill," *Eugene O'Neill Newsletter* 11, no. 1 (Spring 1987):3.

2. Israel Horovitz interview, 22 March 1993.

3. Clive Barnes, Review of *Line* and *Shooting Gallery*, *New York Times*, 22 March 1976, 20.

4. Kim Peter Kovac, "Israel Horovitz," in *Dictionary of Literary Biography: Twentieth Century American Dramatists*, ed. Frank N. Magill (Detroit: Gale Research, 1981), 303.

5. Peter Sagal, "The Mellowing of Israel Horovitz," *Boston Magazine* (October 1986): 247.

6. Peter Berkrot, "Israel Horovitz," *American Theatre* (October 1992): 39.

7. Patti Hartigan, "Horovitz's Life as a Town Bard," *American Theatre* (December 1989): 58.

8. Horovitz quoted in Peter Sagal, "Strong Men in Tough Times," *Playbill for Strong-Man's Weak Child*, Gloucester Stage Company, 1990.

2

"We Gotta' Hang Together": Horovitz and the National Cycles of Violence

William Demastes

Israel Horovitz's drama is fraught with acts of physical and verbal violence, generally stemming from either an impotent sense of rage or a final self-empowering attempt at revenge. In both cases, the violence is the result of a marked breakdown of social structures that would or should otherwise prevail in resolving conflict. Horovitz's central interest in such a breakdown has led him to a brand of drama that critics such as Scott Giantvalley claim places Horovitz "in the Beckett-Ionesco tradition of modern absurdity."[1] The world has lost its center, civilization's glue ceases to bond, and humanity is reduced to searching for alternative social contracts that are either themselves basic and primitive or are inevitably too weak to prevent the primitive and violent responses that Horovitz presents on stage.

This summary generally applies to all of Horovitz's vast dramatic output. He does present brutal acts with often brutal honesty, but there are crucial, mollifying exceptions. For example, in the one-act 1978 play, *The Former One-on-One Basketball Champion*, a former National Basketball Association great returns to an inner-city neighborhood to confront a youth whose father was murdered by the star's son. Giving himself up to revenge, the former star meets this youth and sets himself up for sacrifice, but after an emotion-draining confrontation, the two begin to understand each other and depart, promising to meet again next year. The result is a bond born out of grief and suffering, but a bond is established nonetheless, rather than a continuation of violence. Less consequential, but no less telling, is the 1979 one-act play, *The Great Labor Day Classic*, depicting a long-distance race between three pairs of runners whose struggles against exhaustion, the elements, and themselves produce winners and losers at the finish line but also genuine mutual admiration and respect rather than the perhaps expected competitive hostility.

What do such plays suggest about placing Horovitz in a Beckett-Ionesco tradition? Perhaps as Martin Esslin suggested in the 1960s in *The Theatre of the Absurd*, American thought never fully captures the full sense of despair felt about humanity by European contemporaries because Americans did not experience firsthand the full and brutal destruction of World War II that Europeans did. I do not see that American quality as an actual shortcoming. I think, as Giantvalley has observed, that Horovitz's "sardonic vision of the world is leavened with compassion" because Horovitz is in fact genuinely American, caught up with often brutally relating truth but also idealistically hoping for change and improvement of the human condition.[2] It is this hope that prevents him from being "European" and marks him as genuinely "American." Often, even within his brutal depictions, Horovitz falls short of the brutality of his European contemporaries. For example, in his Obie-winning 1968 play, *The Indian Wants the Bronx*, Horovitz has his street thugs merely knife the hand of their innocent victim. Harsher dramatization was certainly presented when in 1965 Edward Bond inserted the brutal murder of an infant child onto the British stage in *Saved*.

So although Horovitz was undoubtedly influenced by Samuel Beckett and Eugene Ionesco (even to the point of adapting Ionesco's *Man with Bags* [1976], translated by Ionesco's daughter expressly for Horovitz's use), and although the Beckett-Ionesco flavor may explain why Horovitz is so widely produced in Europe, there is something to Horovitz's struggles that make him uniquely American, even more American than Edward Albee, the playwright standardly held up as America's foremost absurdist of the 1950s and 1960s.

But we must accept that Horovitz is not as American as, say, Lanford Wilson. In a 1982 article entitled "Images of America: Wilson, Weller, and Horovitz," Barry Witham focuses on the use of the Fourth of July by three playwrights to make connections between their dramatic protagonists and the "American condition" after the 1960s.[3] While Wilson's *5th of July* and *Talley's Folly* are consummately American plays, it is difficult to see Horovitz's *The Alfred Trilogy* in quite the same way. With its connections to Aeschylus' *Oresteia* and Sophocles' Oedipus myth, Horovitz's work presents something quite ambitious but ultimately less specifically applicable to the American condition than Lanford Wilson's or Michael Weller's plays, despite the fact that in *Alfred Dies* the final execution/suicide scene is presented on July 4 under a town park bandstand.

While Witham asserts that in *Alfred Dies* "the American success is put on trial on the 4th of July,"[4] Giantvalley is perhaps correct in asserting that although playwrights like David Rabe and Sam Shepard give their plays "mythic or sociological resonance," most of Horovitz's work "is more potent when presenting the psychic violence people inflict on one another."[5] In other words, Horovitz is more successful at presenting highly personal dramatic predicaments, less successful at elevating the personal to metaphoric statements of universal conditions. The dilemma is that it appears that Horovitz does in fact attempt to reach such a plane; perhaps the most one can conclude at this point is that Horovitz currently lingers at the stage where one can see the effort (despite the shortcomings) to reach this level, but from the current output one hopes he will eventually achieve his ends.

That Horovitz presents violent responses on the part of citizens of a dysfunctional society is incontrovertible. That the violence of these citizens is directed at equally impotent members of society rather than at the failed social institutions is equally incontrovertible. In Horovitz's first New York theatrical success, *The Indian Wants the Bronx*, two youths figuratively lost in the inner-city slums confront a Hindu Indian who is literally lost, a stranger in a strange land trying to find his son's apartment but unable because he cannot speak English. The two boys, Murph and Joey, are friends, but having lost the means to create a meaningful relationship—because they likely had no model—their bonds have decayed to little more than macho efforts to assert dominance over the other. They begin their encounter with the Indian by harmlessly taunting him, but the encounter slowly escalates. Momentarily left alone with the Indian, Joey reveals his essential humanity by trying to communicate, showing his prized knife to the Indian, who misinterprets the action as a threat. When Murph returns, so does the effort at macho one-upmanship. The result is an escalation of events that leads to the Indian's aggressively defending himself which in turn leads to Murph's using his own knife to slice the Indian's hand. As Harold Clurman observes:

The boys' malevolence is "play": a consequence of their idleness in an environment empty of any fulfilling contact or purpose. They are not evil: they are stinging bugs produced by the dry rot in the wide fringes of the social structure. They produce shivers because their menace and violence are part of the greater beastliness inherent in our society, which, because it does not inspire creative action based on humane thought and energy, turns to wanton and senseless destructiveness.[6]

Neither youth is inherently violent, but a fundamental lack of communication—literally between the youths and the Indian, and only slightly less literally between the two youths—leads to a reversion to primitive behavior that inevitably leads to gestures of aggression.

Similar aggressive behavior occurs in *The Honest-to-God Schnozzola* (1969), again predicated on a fundamental sense of personal impotence in the face of overwhelming odds against expressions of humanity. Two business colleagues traveling to Germany engage in sexual power plays while trying to win over two prostitutes, one of whom turns out to be a tranvestite. The play reveals that both men are in failing marriages and are reduced to securing human contact in this most superficial of ways. The men are even incapable of being humane to each other, openly revealing their mutual contempt. The play moves listlessly until the final scene, when, as Clive Barnes notes, "like a well-oiled guillotine, the play clicks sickeningly into place."[7] When one of the two men sexually "triumphs," the other reveals the trick of conning the "victor" into relations with the drag queen. In a ferocious final gesture, the transvestite is beaten up despite pleas for mercy and understanding.

That competition—the cornerstone of American capitalism and so the ingrained primary trait of American culture—reverts to violence in contemporary society is at least implicit in the two above works. In *Line* (1967), competition is reduced to its simplest form, and attendant aggression/violence is once again revealed. Fleming, described in the stage directions as a "war-vet," is accosted by Stephen who asks, "Is this the line?"[8] Though there is no line, and no reason for there being a line, Fleming plays along. Three others enter the scene, and the group proceeds to struggle to assume and hold the front of this bogus line. Aggressive behavior turns into group rape inflicted against the sole woman participant, carried out as her husband struggles to keep his place in line. Stephen reveals at the end of the play that he had been searching for an occasion to induce his own murder. His efforts here, however, are thwarted because everyone ultimately becomes more concerned with convincing themselves that they in fact have wound up first despite the fact that there is no longer an actual line. Perhaps in this play Horovitz offers an answer to the fundamental problem of American culture, which has put into practice the impractical and naive ideal that every citizen can end up "first" if he or she simply tries hard enough. The impracticality of such a cultural dream is revealed in Arthur Miller's *Death of a Salesman*, a play that asserts the obvious truth that every individual success is achieved ultimately at the expense of numerous other failures. For every one that ends up first, there is a dime-a-dozen mass that ends up runner-up. What each competitor in *Line* ultimately achieves is a personal interpretation of what it means to be first; each has finally devised his or her own vision or definition of "line," definitions that establish each one first within his or her personal vision. Although the play's mood is undoubtedly gloomy, it does offer a halting,tentative vision of hope. The hope, however, is not necessarily a positive one, for the price paid for this resolution is isolation. Community is destroyed by this resolution, but then the price to be paid for community as defined by our competitive culture is itself self-destructive, demanding payments of aggression and hostility.

A much later play, *The Widow's Blind Date* (1981; revised 1989), picks up on the thread of competition transformed to rape and abuse, relating a reunion between a recently widowed woman and two local boys with whom she attended high school. The two boys, now struggling working-class men, are friends who exhibit aggressive traits of male bonding, verging on overt hostility toward each other throughout the play. Margy returns to this home town and calls one of the men for a date, which sparks even further aggressive behavior. When Margy enters the play, she eventually forefronts past events that the two men have obviously chosen not to confront until this moment. The key event is a graduation night gang rape of Margy, the reason she has returned, in search of revenge. Margy's nightmarish recollection of the events reveals her long torment and also the two men's lack of awareness of her suffering through the years. In fact, throughout the play, the two men continue to jockey for her favors, realizing the extent of their past crimes only when Margy forces them to see the event from her perspective. Margy's goal, of highly questionable virtue, is to induce a deadly struggle between the two men, destroying the tenuous friendship and in fact leaving one of the men dead, and the other certainly heading to prison for the death. Revenge is served, necessitated by a cultural failing on numerous levels, forcing a primitive justice that is perhaps justified but at a terrible price to everyone, including Margy.

Horovitz's dramas have hit upon a sort of resolution that reflects a postmodern American condition revealed in the works of the late 1960s and 1970s, a solipsistic turn that pays dearly for its triumph because it has given up on community. A potent reason for this solipsistic turn stems from a quite accurate realization that the roots from which to feed community have been destroyed by our cultural worship of competition. Playwrights such as Sam Shepard, David Mamet, and David Rabe have all diagnosed the same condition. Performance collectives such as Richard Schechner's Performing Garage have similarly documented the condition. But often, as in the cases of Richard Foreman, Robert Wilson, and Spalding Gray, theatre turned its back on the dilemma by addressing aesthetic concerns or focusing on highly personal issues, often utilizing autobiographical material that resulted in intriguing theatre but at the price of abandoning issues of culture and community. Horovitz has eschewed such tempting options, choosing to search for models that have historically overcome the impasse, challenged the solipsism, and worked to mend what has been damaged.

Horovitz's 1979 *Mackerel* attaches interpersonal hostility to a global catastrophe by first presenting a dysfunctional American family whose various failures place it on the verge of self-destruction until a storm avails them of financial doom in the form of a gigantic mackerel that they surreptitiously begin to market for incredible profit. When the fish's flesh turns out to be deadly poisonous, the family continues to sell the product, with genocidal results. Greed, under the guise of capitalist enterprise—the family becomes a well-oiled machine—takes precedent over respect for life. When the world community arrives outside the family dwelling, personal betrayal results in the family's demise, though even then the family absorbs the blow by accepting their roles as infamous, genocidal case studies. No remorse ever results. A sense of self prevails over any feelings for communal well-being. So even a decade after Horovitz's first dramatic successes, he presents a diagnostic analysis of the travails of those who pursue the American dream, cashing in on a bankrupt system that howls at atrocity resulting from its moral bankruptcy but offers no clear resolution to the current condition and attendant horrors.

Horovitz appears to be citing two levels of dysfunction: the material/social and metaphysical. In *Rats* (1968), the rat race is literally presented for what it is, dramatizing two actual rats—one the established hero of the ghetto who has chosen to withdraw from the viciousness of the rat race and the other an ambitious young climber. The older rat has retired to a baby's crib, seeking peace and in the process caring for the human child with whom he shares a home. The younger rat insists on pursuing his nature, trying to convince the other of the propriety of attacking the baby. The play's climax involves the older rat's killing the younger one to protect the child, but the skirmish frightens the baby, causing it to scream and triggering the doom of the rat protector, who will doubtless soon meet the baby's parents. The play presents a near-classic tragic paradox: Pursue one's social Darwinian nature and die in the struggle for survival of the fittest, or challenge the social order and meet one's doom (at the hands of a higher order) while defying the prevailing social hierarchy.

That Horovitz continues at this stage in his career to howl at the injustices individual constituents inflict upon their neighbors is an indication that Horovitz, too, much like his dramatic and literary colleagues, remains unable to secure his much-sought-after resolutions. But his plays are written in the midst of his sincere efforts at resolution, though they produce admittedly mixed results. Barnes, for example, notes of Horovitz that "the eloquence with which he says something at times still outweighs the value of what he is saying."[9] What Horovitz tries to tap into, however, are two historical patterns of resolution and conciliation, represented by the patterns of revenge/brutality-turned-mercy/conciliation in the classic Greek tragic and Elizabethan history play traditions. The former appears to find its model in the *Oresteia* of Aeschylus and the latter in the War of the Roses history cycle of Shakespeare. Both dramatize a process wherein a primitive order of revenge and retribution is replaced by a new order of mercy, conciliation, and grace—one reflecting a religio/mythic establishment of a new world order where the Eumenides, or spirit of Humanity, take control of human destiny, the other where national civil war and the shedding of brotherly blood from an old order, the Plantagenet dynasty, results in a purging of sin and the establishment of a new order, the Tudor dynasty. While the former works in the realm of something like a divine comedy, the latter plays itself out in the political—and therefore social—arena. Clearly, American culture needs to confront itself at both levels, spiritual and political. But Horovitz's modified vision succeeds incompletely, if for no other reason than that both Aeschylus and Shakespeare were manufacturing creative fictions that were never quite realized in the real world as presented and that Horovitz was and is confronted with attempting to effect a vision that must actually be achieved. Such an effort as Horovitz, and so many of his contemporaries, is working toward will ultimately be judged not in the isolation of noble intentions from the perspective of art but from a perspective more pragmatic and less aesthetic or even philosophical and visionary. Such pressures placed upon our contemporary playwrights (especially American playwrights) regularly result in critical conclusions of their being foolish idealists if they choose to be apocalyptic and pessimistic realists if they choose to document actuality. Horovitz and others have chosen the latter condemnation. Consider Clurman's advice to Horovitz in his review of *Indian*:

[L]ike other playwrights of his generation (those between 21 and 30), he should not dwell too long or too lovingly within that sphere [that which is presented in *Indian*]; it is narrow and shallow for lack of a more complete understanding of the world outside it. That world may be equally ferocious, but it is the world, and all of it must be explored to make art splendid and life worth the strife.[10]

Later works by Horovitz seem to attempt to unearth the larger picture, as evidenced by his efforts to use Aeschylus and Shakespeare as allies, but the risk of idealism must always be managed.

Horovitz's 1970s *Alfred Trilogy* is essentially his *Oresteia*, though a more direct sense of his interest in Greek tragedy can be found in his *The Good Parts* (1983). By Horovitz's own admission, *The Good Parts* "was written by me as a sort of relief—a rest-period, of sorts—from more serious writing." He observes of the play, "For me, the play is about a man who is in love with a play [*Electra*]. And while 'The Good Parts' satirizes Greek tragedy, it also, frequently, mirrors this high form of drama, as well."[11] Set in Greece, two American males are on an adventure wherein one of the two seeks to fulfill his ambition of acting out the role of Electra in Athens' Parthenon. While pursuing this dream, the two men learn something of the irreconcilable conflict confronting Electra and Orestes and in the process kill a Greek guard, bringing down the wrath of the Furies. Though the play's resolution is highly unsatisfactory in that the innocent guard's death is forgotten, the lessons the men learned seem to create a tenuous peace for them in their efforts to save their various relationships between themselves and their significant others. Experience does not bring on a new order necessarily (as in the *Oresteia*), but they gained a knowledge of existence and an appreciation of the dangers that likely await them in the future.

This appreciation of the dangers ahead seems to be what Horovitz selects as a focus in his *Alfred Trilogy* and *Gloucester Plays* (his Shakespearean work). *The Alfred Trilogy* (*Alfred the Great*, *Our Father's Failing*, and *Alfred Dies*) is an American *Oresteia*, as Martin Esslin once observed, with one significant exception: It fails to offer a revised cosmology as is found in the last part of the *Oresteia*, *The Eumenides*. Aeschylus transforms a world driven by primitive vengeance—personified by the Furies—into a world of grace and forgiveness—personified by the Eumenides (read "Humanities"), themselves formerly the Furies. The cycle of unrelenting and unending violence and revenge ultimately finds a resolution, a new world order that offers an answer to the question of how to put an end to the cycle. The old order is shattered by a new vision. Horovitz does not offer such a solution, in part, one presumes, because even Aeschylus' visionary resolution succeeded only in art and not in the real world order. So, too, Horovitz could at best offer a visionary dream and risk ridicule as a hopeless idealist. Or he could do what he did: document a predictable inevitability of a continuing cycle eliminated only by wholesale eradication. The metaphyical composition of contemporary American society shows no signs of alteration, so Horovitz can at best suggest by implication (attaching a classic echo to his work) a changed vision, but he finally must document the unlikelihood that the echo will sufficiently reverberate so as to create a change.

Alfred is the American success story, making millions from selling swampland, an appropriate symbol of the tenuous foothold he (or anyone else) has on the elusive pursuit of happiness in American culture. The curse of matricide haunts Alfred (echoes of Orestes), and virtually every character is guilty of incestuous relationships.[12] Alfred's father allows himself to be placed in an asylum in order to hide the secret of Alfred's past. Trying to recover the past is apparently the reason Alfred returns to his home town, a past that he has willed out of his consciousness but that his wife is determined to act upon, because Alfred had in fact killed her mother the moment he killed his own (they are siblings). The central curse upon this inbred community is nondeath and stillbirths—that is, no one any longer dies of natural causes, and this generation has not produced offspring since it has matured. Nature allows nothing to leave this unending degenerating line or to enter into a regenerative cycle.

All the characters seem aware of some part of the various secrets, but none chooses to reveal what they know. Instead, the bits of knowledge are used as power tools to allow each character dominance over the other. In fact, self-delusion itself allows each character to control his or her self-image. So the knowledge utilized is a selective part of knowledge accepted and applied for purposes of control over others and self. The attendant isolation results in obvious hostility and destructive (and self-destructive) tendencies, all of which feed into an "American" competitiveness smothering any feeling of cooperation that may momentarily arise.

In *Alfred Dies*, Emily, Alfred's wife/sister, imprisons Alfred under the town square's gazebo and forces an unfolding of Alfred's guilts upon him. In a final speech, before she commits suicide, she pronounces: "I forgive you, Alfred I do. [*Pauses.*] Forgiveness is all I have for which to be proud . . . of me. Forgiveness is my last and final right on this habitable earth." Referring to the need to end the series of violence that has become their family line, she adds, "Someone has to stop it, here and now. There's always a possibility that one child might make it all the way . . . be born . . . start it again."[13]   She dies, leaving Alfred sure to perish in his cell and ending the line of the house of Alfred as Fourth of July fireworks explode over the grounds above.

Presumably the town will now find new life, a resurrection from its living death and an end to the violence and aggression that had engulfed it.   But this hopeful resolution is not guaranteed in any manner parallel to the *Oresteia*. Admittedly, Alfred closes the play by assuming a "hopeful" aspect, as the stage directions indicate.   But what is there to be hopeful about?   Though his death may bring life back to the town, nothing has been put in place to replace the operating cycle of revenge.   Alfred, Emily, and others must die first.   All guilt must be paid for.   Unlike the *Oresteia*, in which the survivors are forgiven, in *The Alfred Trilogy* violent resolutions are the only offerings provided—resolutions that weave into a continuing cycle rather than offering an alternative to the unending process.   Horovitz is still stuck with the pattern of violence begetting violence, competition never giving way to cooperation, and forgiveness, when offered, only being a formality proffered before blood is let in payment for guilt.

If Horovitz cannot quite arrive at an American *Oresteia*, cannot quite present a vision of an altered metaphysics, neither can he provide a sociopolitical alteration that moves beyond cycles of violence. *The Gloucester Plays* have as their second play a work directly modeled after the English War of the Roses material Shakespeare used in his history plays. In the first of Horovitz's "history," *Henry Lumper*, Henry Boley (read "Bolingbroke") and Thomas Percy share control of a trade union they took over after murdering a corrupt labor boss. Though this "regicide" may have been just, it is a murder nonetheless, so the new reigning family may never hold control with ease.   The two men's sons, ("Prince") Hal Boley—a spendthrift youth—and Harry Percy—a true Hotspur character—vie for control of the dynasty as their fathers, growing old and ineffectual, must step down.   Hal eventually triumphs over Harry, killing the corrupted rival and assuming leadership of the union.   Hails of victory and cries of hope surface, leading to hopes that the travails of *2 Henry IV* will move onto the triumphs of *Henry V*.   However, if there is a *Henry V* sequel to *Henry Lumper*, we do not see it.   The violent cycle begun by the fathers and continued by the one son can promise nothing more than a continued spiral of violence. If the regicide in Shakespeare's *Richard II* could lead to momentary triumphs in *Henry V*, Shakepeare was fully prepared to remind us of the sins of regicide in the three *Henry VI* plays.   But Shakespeare would also conclude his history plays with his own *Eumenides*, wherein *Richard III* would turn to a breaking of the cycles of violent revenge by establishing the Tudor dynasty out of the Plantagenet turmoil.   Horovitz, however, only offers us his *Henry VI*, in that the hopes of *Henry Lumper* are turned into despair in the sequel. *North Shore Fish*, thematically related to *Lumper* though none of the characters reappear, documents the dying spasms of the world Hal had promised to defend and rebuild, much in the same way the *Henry VI* plays document England's self-destruction following Henry V's brief triumphs. Though set in a fish-processing plant, the play is more general in applicability, as Gussow observes: "Without pressing the point, the author makes a provocative statement about the state of the American economy. This could be an automobile factory in Michigan or a steel mill in Pennsylvania instead of a small, home-grown Massachusetts business, soon to be replaced by a fitness center." He adds, "Individualism is at an ebb and profits, when they exist, go far away from the source."[14] The result is predictable. Emotional assault and interpersonal divisiveness resorting in physical violence are again present, again the result of fierce competition for individual survival as the community itself is self-destructing. If Hal's promise to unionize—to communalize—the old order will ever be fulfilled, it has not occurred in *North Shore Fish*. The same ingredients for violence and abuse exist, and the same violent responses to aggressive competitiveness result.

One is hopeful that Horovitz has his own *Eumenides* or *Richard III* yet to be produced, or at least yet to be written. If that means that he must first probe even more deeply into human depravity and despair, then it should be encouraged if, like Shakespeare in *Richard III*, he will eventually envision a national resolution to the cycles of violence he sees and documents. If there is no resolution, then perhaps Horovitz's future products will indeed be absurdist (or neoabsurdist) dramas of the European sort, which may then depict even more radically the random insignificance of existence unforeseen even by the European absurdist of the 1950s and 1960s. But to date his dramas are perilously on the verge, clinging to a hope that a positive turn will soon come into sight. Because he appears to resist naively optimistic solutions while so clearly longing to be able to provide a hopeful picture, perhaps Horovitz's future work can serve as a barometer for American culture, an indicator of where we are but also a sign of where we might be going. The sad truth today is that Horovitz the barometer, while looking for signs of hope, speaks with a great deal of concern and worry that hope is not on the horizon.

Although *Uncle Snake* (1976) is perhaps too inconsequential a play to be given much attention here (it is only a twenty-page street pageant piece), in it Horovitz has a clear sense, though only in the abstract, of what he wants to see in American culture. *Uncle Snake* retells the signing of the Declaration of Independence and summarizes the "imperfections" and petty concerns of the various document signers. All are seriously flawed men; all have self-interests that are not fully satisfied in the Declaration. The fear is that none will sign. But the Union is, of course, established, and Ben Franklin's image of the colonies as a snake hanging together almost by a mystical force of will becomes the final image of the piece. Surely Horovitz is saying that we can—and must—find a way to hang together. Surely we can unite to break the cycle of violence symptomatic of so much else that is at heart wrong with the country.

But at this point, apparently, we are not deeply enough in trouble to create the necessary revolution.

NOTES

The title of this article is taken from *Uncle Snake* (New York: Dramatists Play Service, 1976), 8, a U.S. Bicentennial pageant play performed on the streets of New York, in which the debates leading to the signing of the Declaration of Independence are given revisionist interpretations that reveal the human pettiness of the individual signers who must overcome their individual urges before they can "hang together"—or otherwise, as Ben Franklin remarks, "It'll be separately we hang" (16).

1. Scott Giantvalley, "Israel Horovitz," in *Crtitical Survey of Drama*, ed. Frank N. Magill (Englewood Cliffs, N.J.: Salem Press, 1985), 3:958.

2. Ibid., 964.

3. Barry Witham, "Images of America: Wilson, Weller, and Horovitz," *Theatre Journal* 34 (May 1982): 223-32.

4. Ibid., 231.

5. Giantvalley, 964.

6. Harold Clurman, "Theater," *Nation*, 12 February 1968, 221.

7. Clive Barnes, "Theater: 'Honest-to-God-Schnozzola,'" *New York Times*, 22 April 1969, 40.

8. Horovitz, *Line*, in *First Season* (New York: Vintage, 1968), 10.

9. Barnes, "Theater," 40.

10. Clurman, "Theater," 221.

11. Horovitz, *The Good Parts* (New York: Dramatists Play Service, 1983), 6.

12. Page 307 of Horovitz's *The Wakefield Plays* (New York: Bard/Avon, 1979) contains a complex outline of the interrelationships of the Webber-Lynch family lines, too complex for easy delineation, but once sorted out, it proves to be quite accurate.

13. Horovitz, *Alfred Dies, The Wakefield Plays*, 249.

14. Mel Gussow, "StageFish by Horovitz," *New York Times*, 12 January 1987, III:20.

3

Ins and Outs: The Ethnic World of Israel Horovitz

Robert Skloot

Despite his extraordinary prolificacy, Israel Horovitz's plays, produced worldwide for more than twenty years, maintain a low profile in the halls of modern American drama. He remains, in the mid-1990s, a playwright uncanonized and largely unheralded, though not without his articulate enthusiasts, including Horovitz himself. Yet Horovitz is virtually without peer among Americans in the range of his theatrical writing and represents the kind of playwright whose work needs consistent championing (by others than himself) to maintain his visibility in an artistic landscape where the struggle for attention is relentless and for respect frustrated. It may be that his steadiness of purpose and concern for craft consign him to the nearer margins of contemporary playwriting, but he is a playwright of great accomplishment nonetheless, whose work over a quarter century requires evaluation and assessment.[1]

Recently, Horovitz was quoted as quoting one of his own characters from *Park Your Car in Harvard Yard* (1983) to the effect that he has continued to develop as a playwright over a quarter century of tireless effort.[2] I would argue that Horovitz's development as a playwright is better characterized as artistic restlessness; the evidence for a straighforward linear pattern is elusive. Only when his playwriting is assessed in its totality will the clearer patterns emerge. From absurdist comedy to naturalistic tragedy and touching on a number of stylistic places in between, Horovitz is on the move as a writer as well as a person (he is well known as a competitive long-distance runner). In addition, the erratic artistic course includes the revisiting of his plays and commenting on them, sometimes even revising them.

Of first importance, however, is to note that Horovitz's coming of age as a playwright was achieved in the 1960s (he was born in Wakefield, Massachusetts, in 1939), and his vision of America comes from that time. He possesses a modernist, socially oriented vision of theatre that values community and humane behavior and expresses that vision in a mixture of tones and a variety of forms. In a note to the 1971 text of *The Indian Wants the Bronx* (1968), Horovitz alludes to this issue:

I should note that on rereading this early play, I do find it very much representative of my attitudes during the 1960s. Curiously, in a period of instant vogue, the 1960s signaled the end, really, of American naturalism: the formal factor which seemed to make this play popular in its first decade. Inversely, as its naturalistic form died, its theme of irrational violence zoomed with new life into the 1970s.[3]

Although the disappearance of American naturalism is a dubious claim, Horovitz is correct that each of his plays contains an idea that precedes and determines the impression or effect each play produces. The idea becomes the writer's primary contribution to the production, and Horovitz works hard to make the idea clear before and while shaping it with actors. (What is not clear can be made so later in a revised text.) As a result, his plays seem, in the 1990s, somewhat behind our postmodern culture, a popular culture whose arts embody self-referentiality and self-conscious style and whose artistic themes, at their most extreme, assert a self-obsession and self-doubt in the context of critical indeterminacy.

In this chapter, I trace briefly one of Horovitz's themes that is particularly and consistently his own: the pervasive concern with the newcomer-outsider that makes his work a theatrical commentary on the ethnic condition of America. Because one of the salient features of Horovitz's work is its concern with broad social issues, even when they are presented in the most assuredly of comic ways, exploring this theme is one way to appreciate the range of Horovitz's talent and to judge his attitude toward the country whose continual "remaking of itself" poses inescapable and complicated problems for all those caught up in that enterprise. The plays under scrutiny come from three different (culturally and otherwise) decades: *The Indian Wants the Bronx* and *Morning* (1968; 1969), *The Primary English Class* (1976, revised 1984), and *Today I Am a Fountain Pen, A Rosen by Any Other Name*, and *The Chopin Playoffs* (published together as *An Israel Horovitz Trilogy*, 1987).

One of four Horovitz plays produced in New York in 1967–68 and published in the collection *First Season, The Indian Wants the Bronx* brought critical acclaim and popular attention to Horovitz. Its compelling idea is summed up in the epigraph attached to the text:

There is no crime greater, more worthy of punishment, than being strange and frightened among the strange and frightened . . . except assimilation to the end of becoming strange and frightened, but apart from one's own real self. [4]

The declaration is strong and aggressive, if overstated, just as Horovitz overstated the formal naturalism of the play in 1971. But the statement's ethical purpose is never in doubt. (The identical point is made by LeRoi Jones/Amiri Baraka in his 1960s essays and plays, which are also important cultural and political artifacts of that decade.) With such a creed at its center, this early play of Horovitz carries a number of issues he will develop in later ones, in particular, the conflict of outsider challenging insider over the possession of both turf and self.

Horovitz's special gift, shown early and well in *Indian*, is to display the issue of geographical and psychological displacement comically, at least for much of the play. The two young thugs, Murph and Joey, possess urban esprit and energy, as well as menace. The comedy develops primarily from Horovitz's rhythmic patterns of action and language, patterns that propel the play forward in time even as they retard its motion. Murph's first line, after the play begins with the two toughs singing badly together, becomes particularly ironic in the light of what will come later: "I've got a knack for harmony" (*Indian*, 128).

The singing is also comic, and the comedy is sustained at least through the first half of the play, until, as the stage direction instructs us: *"Now that they sense his [Gupta's] fear, the comedy has ended"* (*Indian*, 147).[5] Until that time, there is horseplay and bravado, and ignorance that seems mostly foolishness in the light of its inconsequentiality. The great cleverness of *Indian* is Gupta's speaking entirely in Hindi, making his dialogue incomprehensible to Murph, Joey, and us, the audience. Lurking behind the conflict is the issue of strangeness—of how the inarticulateness that comes of displacement can draw violence to itself if conditions are right. Of course, Gupta is completely articulate—to himself and to anyone who speaks his language. And that is Horovitz's point: Even the most eloquent would be lost outside their context and at risk when confronted by deeply held intolerance and racism.

For the first half of *Indian*, the ignorance of Murph and Joey is comically turned, nowhere better than in their ethnic confusions, racist slurs, and even homophobia. Gupta is called a Turk, a Turkie, a fairy, a "commie slob," and confused with "a chink," and later with an American Indian. His answer to Murph's first direct question is translated in the text (as are all his lines) but is incomprehensible in performance to a non-Hindi-speaking person: "I cannot speak your language. I don't understand." Here, the audience is placed identically to Murph in not understanding what Gupta is saying, and our response takes its cue from Murph's comic reaction:

Murph (To Joey, <u>does a terrific 'take,' then speaks, incredulous</u>): He's got to be kidding. (*Joey and Murph laugh.*)

In the moments before the comic business ends, in what the playwright calls "the transition scene," Murph and Joey *"dance a war dance around him*

[Gupta], beating a rhythm on the trashcans, hissing and cat-calling for a full minute. Murph ends the dance with a final 'Hey!'" (147). From here to the play's conclusion, the comedy of misunderstanding will be entirely turned to the ugly results of ethnic disharmony. And, as in a later Horovitz play concerned with a primary English lesson, a major theatrical moment occurs when a character (here Gupta) *"makes one last effort to escape and runs the length of the stage, screaming a bloodcurdling, anguished scream."* In the final seconds, Gupta, abandoned on the stage, turns to the audience, and, with badly bleeding, outstretched hand, speaks in his new country's language: "Thank you!" (171).

In his discussion of *Indian*, John Lahr remarks that the central insight of the play lies in Horovitz's understanding "that violence partakes equally of ignorance and fear."[6] As we will see, it is precisely this insight that informs many of Horovitz's plays, including the comic violence of *The Primary English Class*, in which the ethnic and linguistic confusions are no fewer than in *Indian*, though ultimately more benign.

The comedy of ethnicity, as well as the tragedy, is well displayed in Horovitz's ferocious satire *Morning*, a one-act play produced with two others, *Noon* by Terrence McNally and *Night* by Leonard Melfi.[7] The play is a representative piece of 1960s theatrical history, not only for the conditions of its collaborative production but for its similarity to a number of other works of the time that also addressed social issues with a mixture of excessive profanity, flaunted sexuality, satirized hypocrisy, and male hegemony; Douglas Turner Ward's *Day of Absence* (1966), Sam Shepard's *Tooth of Crime* (1972) and David Mamet's *Sexual Perversity in Chicago* (1974) come to mind.

Morning is a one-joke play about the consequences of racial prejudice. It relies heavily on the brash use of ethnic language to make its point about the evils of racism. Here, a black family of four is turned suddenly white after swallowing pills from God (who is black) sold to them by "a small fat Jewish man who runs a pawnshop on East 126th Street." (The fat Jewish man never appears.) Horovitz creates a comedy that parodies and ridicules racial and cultural (including biblical and musical) shibboleths in a deliberately confrontational performance that, additionally, satirizes the normative style of theatre production through its exploitation of non-naturalistic staging techniques. Gertrude's first words, spoken to her "white" husband, are spoken *"fiercely"*: "Come on, Updike. You worthless white nigger! Get your black ass out of that fucking black bed" (429). Thereupon, *Morning* gets raunchier and more abrasive.

The story of the play concerns the attempt of the white racist Tillich to find Junior, the black (now white) teenager, who, Tillich says, got his daughter Alice pregnant. In a series of scenes intended to show the stupidity and cowardice of the family and its accuser, Tillich is disarmed, threatened, and revealed to be black also, his white condition the result of swallowing one of the two remaining of God's "antidote" pills. Tillich's fury derives from his humiliation that Alice will give birth to a black child. At the end, the family, brushes in hand, paints him black on the outside to match the truth of his inside. Then the lights go out and pistol shots are heard. The concluding image of *Morning* is extraordinary:

Gertrude and Updike throw buckets of black fabric at the audience. Precisely when the fabric leaves the buckets, the lights switch from the stage into the audience's eyes again. During this blackout on the stage, Tillich turns on his back, dead, with his head over the lip of the stage, his face, upsidedown, facing the audience with a hideous stare . . . Blood slowly trickles from his mouth. Junior walks calmly to Tillich and photographs him with a flash camera. Then the family poses over Tillich's body as hunters with a slain lion. They are photographed. Then they all photograph the audience. There is a pinspot on Tillich.

The ferocity of this image summarizes the rage of blacks in a society that has historically subjugated them, though their condition in the play is "photographically" reversed. Black and white become their opposites in *Morning*, with lethal results in the "play," and, of course, lethal results in the world the play comments on. The dire consequences of racial oppression, described in identical terms to the situation of the victimized Gupta (though here in a theatrically more complex and sprawling manner), is the important connection to make in assessing Horovitz's central idea of his comedies of ethnicity. In *Morning*, the desire to implicate the audience by including them "in the photograph," in a like manner to the Indian's wanting the audience to hear his "new" language, is, one could say, pure Horovitz in the morning of his career.

A last connection between *Indian* and *Morning* is instructive. As in the earlier play, language and how it is used is at the center of the comedy. Among the moments that stand out are Updike's speaking in "British" English to Tillich to convince him he is white (scene 3) and Gertrude's astonishing song (accompanied by rock band and the family as chorus) "White Like Me," when *"she begins the song very 'white'. Slowly, she goes through the gradations of gray, from white to black, and completes the song as a soul singer"* (scene 8), which is followed by the family's conversing *"in dialogue and accent . . . very 'Amos and Andy'"* (scene 9). *Morning* is Horovitz's crudest and loudest ethnic comedy, and, in performance, may still be his most dangerous, though it is wholly a "60s" kind of play in its outrageousness and overt display of aggression.

The Primary English Class represents Horovitz at his most theatrically daring. The play is a mad farce of linguistic misunderstanding that makes itself perfectly understandable from the moment it begins. Smiednik, the night janitor in the school building, is seen mopping the classroom floor while singing "I Can't Give You Anything But Love, Baby" in Polish. Horovitz assumes, correctly I think, that the song's tune is immediately recognizable to the audience, though incomprehensible in its lyrics, except, of course, to speakers of Polish. The disjunction of sound and meaning, and the laughter it provokes (the familiar jostling the strange), is a major source of the play's comedy. Further, the comic situation is an entirely human one, familiar to anyone who has traveled "abroad" (even in one's own country) where someone else's language dominates and where attempts at communication create only frustration and confusion. The commonality of this experience should not be underestimated in an assessment of the cleverness or impact of *Class*; enormous numbers of us know what it is like to be "lost in the translation." And judging from the solid connection audiences made (and make) to the play, Horovitz has succeeded again, though in a benign, nonconfrontational way, in making the audience feel connected to the plight of the newcomer-outsider.[8]

One by one, the classroom is visited by persons of differing nationalities: Polish, Italian, French, German, Chinese, Japanese, and American, none of whom speaks the others' language but all of whom join in a quest to make English understandable. Horovitz's thematic point is made early in the play as all the characters come to realize they have the same last name regardless of what language they speak: Wastebasket. The teacher's name is (or is close enough in English to) that universal receptacle: Debbie *Wastba* (pronounced, she says: Wah-stah-ba).[9]

Although Horovitz has admitted that the play "was written by me as a sort of relief—a rest period, of sorts, from more serious writing," it is appropriate to see the play as another example of his continuous inquiry into the predicament of outsiders in a society closed to them, linguistically and otherwise.[10] The play deliberately emphasizes the image of a closed society by being set in a single, overheated classroom from which departure may be risky and, on occasion, impossible. Several times the room becomes a kind of fortress to keep out the "threats" that prowl the (literally) dark corridors of the "out there," at least in the overripe imagination and repressed sexuality of Wastba, the teacher who refuses to let her students leave. The "invading forces" she conjures up are the result of previous comic misapprehensions, but the precise central scenic image is important to Horovitz's serious concern for the welfare of the human family as the world at large lurches into chaos. When he is in a hopeful mood, as in *Class*, the chaos subsides and the promise of understanding survives. Thus Wastba, momentarily abandoned by all her students as the play ends, is surprised by the return of Mrs. Pong, and the two of them resume the interrupted lesson. The last stage direction reads: *"Wastba smiles, hopefully, happily, into Mrs. Pong's hopeful, happy smile"* (79, 1984).

Getting to the end of the play, however, requires moving through a time and space of great violence, a crucial element of all farce comedy. Wastba's taking of Mulleimer's eyeglasses, for example, provides the opportunity for tirade, hysteria, and physical humiliation. The overheated environment, the urgency of the students' desire to learn and to please, the fragile authority and overbearing personality of the teacher, the outside urban setting, and, above all, the group's inability to understand the many languages spoken provide countless occasions for humor, physical as well as linguistic. Importantly, the audience understands everyone, through the work of the two translators who "narrate" the dialogue. They know, through the narration and the translation of the dialogue, that the comic premise of the play will not be violated. Thus, in this ethnically diverse and ethnically divided world, no permanent harm will be done, save to the seemingly utopian idea of a harmonious planet.[11]

The Primary English Class is not merely a spoof on language education like *The Bald Soprano*, the famous "anti-play" of the 1950s by Horovitz's mentor, Eugene Ionesco. It also partakes of the seriousness of Ionesco's murderous *The Lesson* when the story of miscommunication among the ethnics (and the United States is, in this context, ethnic too) conveys trenchant criticism of America as seen in the character of Debbie Wastba: inept, insecure, racist, repressed, and prone to hysterical outbursts.[12] Hers is the "bloodcurdling scream" referred to earlier, and it is her admission late in the play that her "heart is filled with such loathing for all of you!" that momentarily and riskily throws us off the wild comic ride we are enjoying.

Horovitz's meanest and truest observation concerns the intolerance at the heart of humanity. In *Class*, it is the teacher who possesses prejudice most clearly (though some of the others exhibit "cultural superiority" too), and it is only her inability to make herself understood that protects her from the immediate negative responses of her students. Horovitz is wise to have the two translators "on our side," objective observers who speak "our" language and can protect against the disgust that would come from recognizing ourselves in her. Only by avoiding this recognition and the real primary English lesson she teaches (which is easy to do) can we believe that the playwright cannot give us anything but love.

The Horovitz ethnic masterpiece is his trilogy: *Today, I Am a Fountain Pen, A Rosen by Any Other Name*, and *The Chopin Playoffs*. The plays were inspired by a book of autobiographical stories of the Canadian novelist Morley Torgov, *A Good Place to Come From* (1974). The stories provided Horovitz with the perfect stimulus to explore his own Jewish upbringing in Massachusetts. Using Torgov's geographical home, Sault Ste. Marie, Ontario (the "Soo"), as the location for his own speculations, he writes about the ethics and ethnics that inhabit his history and his imagination. The three plays cover six years (1941–47) in the lives of the Rosen and the Yanover families, sharing a structural and spatial similarity and a spiritual and musical affinity.

The character who binds together the three plays is the old Jew, Ardenshensky. He introduces each play, connects them together in a running narration, and plays a dozen other characters, including an Italian caterer, a Ukrainian priest, a British-Canadian judge, and a Chinese restaurateur, in the course of the trilogy. In other words, Ardenshensky embodies a diverse ethnicity in and of himself, though it must be said that first among ethnic equals is his identity as a Jew. In fact, Horovitz calls the trilogy "Growing Up Jewish".[13] Ardenshensky is important for an additional "ethnic" reason: by his age, he represents the maintenance and resistance of the "other" to the dominant society. His disputes with the two Jewish families are decades old, and part of *The Chopin Playoffs* tells the story of his pride in being "the oldest living man in the Soo." Ardenshensky represents the value of continuity, the wholeness that history awards our future, and he functions as a (Jewish) stand-up comedian too. In *Today*, his promise to "be back later" is more than an offhand remark; it is the indisputable evidence of the rhythm of long-term ethnic survival.

Plays about Jews and their struggle to assimilate into larger, ethnically diverse cultures of the "new world" are a staple of American drama. From before Elmer Rice's *Counsellor-at-Law* (1931) and Clifford Odets's *Awake and Sing!* (1936) to after Mark Harelik's *The Immigrant* (1985, set in Galveston in 1909) and Shelly Berman's *First Is Supper* (1989–90, set in Chicago in 1919), European-American Jews have used the theatre to describe their confrontation with the non-Jewish "new" world. Like other immigrants in our own time, their stories combine and comprise an experience of settlement, confrontation, and validation that is told and retold in each succeeding generation. Horovitz chooses to tell his saga with humor and affection, and thereby share some of his own genuine enjoyment in growing up Jewish in a small New England town. It is this pleasure, first and foremost, that he wishes to share with his audience, although, being Jewish, it is mixed with sentimentality and sadness.

Each of the three plays involves some kind of a crisis in the relationship of Jews to the non-Jewish world, and all the plays locate the crisis primarily in the experience of youth. The effect of this decision is to diminish the trilogy's sense of tragedy, making the "lessons" Irving Yanover and Stanley Rosen learn a part of their natural maturation and ethical growth rather than experiences of irreparable harm. In *Today*, ten-year-old Irving must deal with the problem of keeping kosher (adhering to the Jewish dietary laws) and confront his consuming passion to taste bacon. His mother, Esther Yanover, has vowed to keep kosher "so there'll always be Jews" (27). In *Rosen*, Stanley struggles to decide for himself what kind of bar mitzvah celebration he will have. In *Chopin*, both boys, now seventeen, must confront the issue of marrying outside their religion. Thus, the underlying idea of the trilogy becomes how can the things (customs, rituals, etc.) we know and love be preserved and passed intact, and with meaning, to those who come after, in the face of the pressures to divest and assimilate.

Horovitz intends his conflicts to be generational as well as ethnic, and his visual and linguistic demands must be taken seriously. In his "Note to the Director and Designer" appended to the text of *Chopin*, he specifies:

A stern note on casting this play. It is my intention that the Rosen parents and Yanover parents be cast with youthful, attractive actors. Stereotypes are to be avoided, entirely. Additionally, Yiddish or Eastern European accents—or stereotypically "Jewish" intonation—are also forbidden in the casting of the parents. By contrast, Ardenshensky should be cast authentically old, optimally with an experienced Yiddish theatre comedian; certainly with a European-born actor. It is my intention to contrast the parents and Ardenshensky as modern vs. ancient world figures. (8)

As Irving and Stanley grow up, they stand in uneasy contrast to two generations, questioning the values and traditions of their elders once and twice removed.

Yet, despite Horovitz's statement, the "parents" are not ethnically neutral. They reveal a catalog of traits, habits, and experiences that identify them as both Jewish and universal. As children of immigrants to Canada, the second generation of Yanovers and Rosens struggles for economic self-sufficiency as middle-class merchants. Reflecting on their own experience, they want their children's lives to be better than their own: better educated, better employed, and better able to control their lives. But these hopes are reflected in a specific ethnic context, for their names are recognizably Jewish, their speech laced with ironic, self-deprecating humor, their concerns specifically Jewish, their supplications occasionally addressed directly to God, and they love Chinese food. And, most important, they are anxious about their religious-cultural status in a frequently hostile social environment.[14]

Of the three plays in the trilogy, *Rosen* presents the strongest expression of the social and familial tension brought about by ethnic struggle. As a result, its emotional subtext is deepest and its resolution most satisfying. Horovitz achieves this in two ways: He keeps uppermost in our attention the fact that there is a war raging in Europe (it is 1943) in which the enemy is dedicated to destroying Jews, and he features prominently the terrible results of antisemitism.

In *Rosen*, there are several air raid drills, and Irving's cousin, a shellshocked war veteran named Manny Boxbaum, comes to live with them. During one of the air raid drills, Manny goes berserk. The greatest threat to the Rosens' happiness comes when a window in Barney Rosen's store is broken by a rock (thrown, it is suggested, by Catholic school children). The incident precipitates a crisis for Barney who decides, against all contrary arguments, to change his name to Royal:

Barney: This family has suffered enough for its Jewish name.
Manny: (*Screams*) Uncle Barney, listen to me! I have just come from a War that is being fought, in part, over Jews . . . Jews who are proud to be Jews . . . .

Barney: (*Outraged, screams*) *I am a Jew!* But, I see no reason to print it on my forehead, or on my wife's forehead, or my innocent son's forehead! And that is my decision . . . <u>my decision</u>.
Manny: My God, I thought *I* was confused . . . .
Barney: Manny, do you think I'm some kind of an idiot? Do you think I've given this no thought? I see what's coming. Today, in Canada, it's rocks through the windows. Tomorrow, in Canada, it's going to be rocks through skulls. (48-49)

Because Barney's fear is genuine and deeply felt, his response to the provocation is a terribly violent one within the context of the play. Appearing in court (the judge is played "knowingly" by the actor who plays Ardenshensky), Barney insists that his name change be made legal. And in response to Judge Brown's request for objections, it is "eloquent" Stanley who rises to confront his own father. The boy proclaims:

I want to be Bar Mitzvahed as Stanley Rosen. That's who I am, a Jew with a Jewish name . . . .
        This is my name! Mine! I am proud to be a Jew and I want it stamped all over me . . . . I, Stanley Rosen, am a person and I have rights!!! I . . . am . . . not a victim! (56)

When Stanley refuses to retract his objection, Barney becomes furious, tyrannical and abusive. Yet the boy courageously holds to his decision and administers the most terrible rebuke a child can make to a parent.

(*He yells at his parents.*) I don't want to be your son! You hear me? You hear me? I wish I weren't your son! (*Without thought, without warning, Barney slaps Stanley's face. It is a sudden, shocking blow. The boy reels backwards, trips, falls, stands immediately. Stanley's moves should be awkward, graceless, touching. Pearl [his mother] is astonished. She spits a whisper at her husband.*)
Pearl: How dare you? *How . . . dare . . . you?* (57)

The comic resolution of the story is hilariously contrived, and the play ends with two bar mitzvahs and, of course, the reappearance of the narrator Ardenshensky to bridge the gap into *Chopin.*
        In the trilogy, and especially in *Rosen,* Horovitz creates a comic world disrupted by the violence that comes from ethnic tension. It is a stage world upon which the playwright has lavished great love, a historically distanced world but one filled with contemporary insights. Seen together, *The Indian Wants The Bronx, Morning, The Primary English Class,* and the three plays of *An Israel Horovitz Trilogy* display Horovitz's great concern with the dire state of the world and suggest how we may be brought together in a condition of peace and cooperation. Our differences can divide us or they can heal us, a point aptly illustrated in *Chopin* when the Yanovers and the Rosens are

reconciled under the auspices of the Chinese restaurateur Mr. Wong of the Ritz Cafe who, not surprisingly, argues like Reb Brechtman of *Rosen*, both of whom are played by the actor who plays Ardenshensky.

The presentation of the problem Horovitz describes in these six plays, and his solution to it, seems somewhat distanced from the 1990s, but it would be a grave mistake to underestimate the range or skill of these plays, and a tragedy not to accommodate his vision into our understanding of the contemporary world. If we remember that these six plays represent only a fraction of Horovitz's total output and that the artistry of his playwriting is enlarged further still when the entire body of work is considered, we can begin to be in touch with his extraordinary achievement.

The ins and outs of Horovitz are many and varied, although I have chosen to concentrate on only one aspect of his work: how being in and being out is a comic and serious thematic preoccupation of his work, often expressed through the agency of language. An even more extensive assessment of Horovitz's work will prove him to be one of our best contemporary American playwrights.

NOTES

1. To a degree, I am returning Horovitz's own favor. In a review of the 1983 London season, with generosity and brevity, he assessed the careers of a number of writers, including Tom Stoppard and Brian Friel. He also revealed, as all critics do, the kind of theatre he prefers. The short overview he provides to others is certainly due him. See "London Night Out," *Village Voice*, 26 July 1983, 78-79, 89.

2. Patti Hartigan, "Horovitz's Life as a Town Bard," *American Theatre* (December 1989):58-59.

3. "Author's Note" to *The Indian Wants the Bronx* in *Famous American Plays of the 1960s*, ed. Harold Clurman (New York: Dell, 1972), 277.

4. *The Indian Wants the Bronx*, in *First Season* (New York: Vintage, 1968), 125.

5. In the Preface to *First Season*, Horovitz says of his play *Line*: "The horror is the comedy" (xxi).

6. John Lahr, *Showcase 1: Plays from the Eugene O'Neill Foundation* (New York: Grove, 1970), 91.

7. All three are found in *Best American Plays: 1967-1973* (New York: Crown, 1975), edited by Clive Barnes. Barnes, in introducing the plays, offers a peculiar though relevant biographical observation: "Horovitz is a Jew. McNally is an Irishman; it [the evening] needed something else to round out this ethnic trio. Leonard Melfi is Italian, of course" (428).

8. In the Introduction to the Book Club edition of the trilogy, Horovitz writes that up to the late 1970s, *The Primary English Class* was the longest-running play in Canadian history. (Garden City, N.Y.: Nelson Doubleday, 1986), vii.

9. In an important revision of the play made in 1984 for the Dramatists Play Service acting edition, Horovitz declares his theme earlier and more pointedly, through the use of a comically farfetched intervention. Prior to Smiednik's song, the translator's voice explains how the human race is descended from a single ancestral family named Nachsart (a German kind of word with the meaning of "resemblance" or "relatedness," e.g., *Nacharten*). The translator describes how the descendants of the wealth family were expelled from their Mesopotamian homeland by the "filthy janatorial class," dispersed worldwide, and reassembled for the first time on the evening of the play's performance "to give us great insight into the true possibilities of World Peace" (83-84). Without question, here the translator is speaking for the playwright.

10. In a note to the acting edition of *The Good Parts* (New York: Dramatists Play Service, 1983), 6.

11. "It is a microcosm of confusion and prejudice, where the incomprehensible parley of strangers is gibberish or suspected insult to baffled ears. And the myth of Babel that underlies the comic situations, show how absurd a punishment language can be." Keith Garebian, "Benediction and Babel," in *The Canadian Forum* (May 1980): 39, cited by *Contemporary Literary Criticism* (Detroit: Gale Research, 1989), 155.

12. In an addendum to the text, Horovitz specifies that the teacher in the play (the Wastba character) should always speak the language of the country *Class* is being performed in, and the students obsessed with learning that particular language. Thus, the "authoritarian pedagogical personality" is made a feature of *all* societies, not just the American, though the play, of course, originated in an American milieu (80).

13. In a Note in the Dramatists Play Service acting edition of *Today, I Am a Fountain Pen* (1987), 58. Because these texts of the trilogy are the most readily available, I will cite them parenthetically (by play and page number) in the remainder of this chapter.

14. The Yanovers of *Today* are contrasted to the Ukrainian Ilchak family, whose aspirations (especially those held for the daughter, Annie) are considerably lower than those of their Jewish acquaintances. Still, Annie has her higher dreams, father Emil Ilchak loves music (though he does not realize—or like—that the operas he loves are Italian) and, importantly, all the Ilchaks experience the effects of a proud but isolating ethnocentrism. See pp. 53–55.

4

O'Neill and Horovitz: Toward Home

Robert Combs

Eugene O'Neill casts a long shadow across American drama, not only because of his greatness, but, more simply, because of his subject: the unfulfilled promise of America. In the following famous quotation O'Neill prophetically announces his theme, and it has been a theme of American drama ever since:

The United States, instead of being the most successful country in the world, is the greatest failure . . . because it was given everything, more than any other country. Through moving as rapidly as it has, it hasn't acquired any real roots. Its main idea is that everlasting game of trying to possess your own soul by the possession of something outside it. This was really said in the Bible much better. We are the greatest example of "For what shall it profit a man if he shall gain the whole world and lose his own soul?" We had so much and could have gone either way.[1]

To the face of American optimism, O'Neill held up a mirror that revealed a betrayal of soul. At the same time, his dramas were invigorating because of their insight, tough-mindedness, and tremendous sense of frustrated hope. In a word, O'Neill's plays were passionate.

Singlehandedly, O'Neill modernized American drama. Superimposing Ibsen, Strindberg, and Freud on American melodrama, O'Neill took the family as his special province. It became the place where individuals were thrown back upon themselves as they struggled with large forces of their outer and inner worlds. For O'Neill—and for Tennessee Williams, Arthur Miller, Edward Albee, and numerous others who followed him—the American family took on great dramatic interest. Momentous individual struggles were enacted at home, the price paid there for the great American failure. The regeneration of hope was sought, if not found, there by prodigal sons and daughters repeating the Judeo-Christian pattern of turning again to God. Surely the ultimate hope—perhaps O'Neill's hopeless hope—was that this family would turn out to be the family of humankind and so finally mitigate the national sins of greed.

The continuity of these themes within contemporary American drama is remarkable. Israel Horovitz, John Guare, Sam Shepard, Wendy Wasserstein, Marsha Norman—to name only a few—are masterful diagnosticians of various forms of American malaise. August Wilson, Ntozake Shange, Larry Kramer, and Mark Medoff focus on people victimized by stereotypes. All of these playwrights have a keen eye for what O'Neill saw as the failures of prosperity. They find the individual voices who speak with human warmth in a world where devastating struggles for power are transpiring. And they have a strikingly accurate ear for caricature. Furthermore, they express the struggles of their characters in the context of family or in a social environment that tries to be a family. Domestic realism, or surrealism, is most often their medium for intimately pondering the challenges faced by society and individuals alike in their day.

In the prolific career of Israel Horovitz, we see a robustly engaging celebration of humanity in an age that has tended to glamorize business, especially business as usual. Horovitz seems to use the theater itself as an occasion to rehearse the saving human graces of playfulness, mockery, and self-affirmation. His plays take place, to be sure, in that wasteland of unfulfilled dreams first charted by O'Neill. But Horovitz's comedy, sometimes quite dark, concentrates on making the best of things. Just as O'Neill used Ibsen, Strindberg, and Freud to find depth and grandeur in what was becoming increasingly banal American middle-class life, so Horovitz has revitalized himself with the help of Samuel Beckett and Eugène Ionesco. He has found sympathetic common ground in the midst of deadly economic realities by focusing on their attendant human absurdities. Following O'Neill, Horovitz reaches through American loneliness toward a greater kinship of spirit.[2] His *mise en scène*, like O'Neill's Monte Cristo Cottage, is a space that is trying to domesticate itself, a space where people might live together in peace and mutual respect, a space trying to become a home.

O'Neill began his career in earnest when he found a symbol large enough to contain his feeling for American loneliness: the sea. The sailors in his *S.S. Glencairn* plays have no homes and wander the world like Wagner's *Flying Dutchman*, as if enchanted. Yank describes the sailor's life to his friend, Driscoll, in *Bound East for Cardiff*, as though to console him as Driscoll lies dying:

This sailor life ain't much to cry about leavin'–just one ship after another, hard work, small pay, and bum grub; and when we git into port, just a drunk endin' up in a fight, and all your money gone, and then ship away again. Never meetin' no nice people; never gittin' outa sailor town, hardly, in any port; travellin' all over the world and never seein' none of it; without no one to care whether you're alive or dead. [*With a bitter smile*] There ain't much in all that that'd make yuh sorry to lose it, Drisc.[3]

Reminiscing about their pipe-dream of one day buying a farm together, Yank and Driscoll are typical of O'Neill's sailors. They have been separated from their original families and try to bond with each other. Yet they remain isolated orphans, sharing only a mystical mother, the sea. The sea is a symbol of the boundless life they have embarked upon, the maternal embrace that holds them, in life and then in death, and their fate, whatever it may turn out to be.

Paradoxically, the sea suggests both the sailors' human commonality and their strangeness to each other, their otherness. Each character represents a different cultural type; the only thing they share intimately is their alienation. And the sea cannot teach them how to make of themselves a new family. This they must do for themselves if they can and will. So the individual visionaries of O'Neill, one after another, express their melancholy homesickness as an inarticulate longing for forms of community or relationship not yet successfully imagined.

Several forms of alienation are examined in O'Neill's early Sea Plays. In *The Moon of the Caribbees*, sailors are exploited economically by sea captains and shipowners, who treat the men like children or slaves.[4] In turn, the sailors exploit the island native women for rum and sex. The men are profoundly unaware of the social and economic conditions of their own lives, moving from dream to dream, only momentarily stirred by violence and death to notice that the world they inhabit cares nothing for them. They journey through cyclical patterns of mechanical routine and Dionysian excess. This addictive syndrome has shattered their sense of family while it both revives and frustrates their hope of restoring it, just as the alcohol and morphine addictions described in *Long Day's Journey Into Night* carry each member of the Tyrone family off into their own worlds where they look back, as it were, on the family they both love and resent.[5]

O'Neill develops his characters by alienating them. He pushes them to the point where their prior identities—the premises of their lives—no longer support them. In *Beyond the Horizon*, for example, two brothers tragically exchange destinies, one going to sea, the other staying to tend the farm.[6] In this way, O'Neill dramatizes powerfully the incompleteness of life on this side of any horizon. And in *Anna Christie*, a prodigal daughter disrupts the peace of her retired sailor-father by shattering his idealistic view of her and forcing him and her future husband back to sea in order to maintain the only relationship she will accept, one in which she remains independent.[7]

The dramatic conflict of alienation lies between possessiveness and the creative freedom of relationship. In O'Neill, characters often cannot accept themselves without external confirmation, which, ironically, can only be a false confirmation. In *The Hairy Ape*, Yank has always felt his human worth through his job as stoker.[8] But when Mildred, daughter of the shipowning industrialist, expresses her revulsion toward him, he no longer has any way of justifying his existence to himself, of knowing that he is something other than an extension of the industrialist's capital and machinery. Similarly, in *The Emperor Jones*, Brutus Jones would have ample proof of his own inner resources, having made himself Emperor by his wits.[9] Yet he cannot resist the coercive power of the ways others see him. Like a character out of Poe, Brutus defeats himself by trying not to think of himself in the one way that will destroy him. And in *Desire under the Elms*, Eben Cabot cannot believe that Abbey might actually love him for himself even if she did have their baby partially in order to gain a home.[10]

The self is radically insecure in these protagonists because outer, historical processes have usurped virtually all ways the self could represent itself to itself. The alienation of labor in *The Hairy Ape*, racism in *The Emperor Jones*, and the corrupting power of ownership in *Desire under the Elms* blind characters to their own real worth. These characters fail to affirm the self by affirming the values of others or of an other—someone with an individual existence as valid as theirs but unlike them. And they fail to accept the confirmation another could offer them—through love, for example—until it is too late. These plays express the felt need to create a way to be, a way to belong in a world of others, a world feared to be, and possibly really, filled with threatening agents. The challenge faced by an O'Neill character is to relate instead of to possess or to be possessed out of fear. O'Neill is still dramatically alive for us because we still face these challenges, more than ever in our international, intercultural age.

The positive power of this dramatic conflict inspired O'Neill throughout his creative life. As strange as it may seem initially, the dedication of *Long Day's Journey into Night* expresses not only the meaning of this play but the hope that lies within this darkest of American dramatists:

For Carlotta, on our 12th Wedding Anniversary

Dearest: I give you the original script of this play of old sorrow, written in tears and blood. A sadly inappropriate gift, it would seem for a day celebrating happiness. But you will understand. I mean it as a tribute to your love and tenderness which gave me the faith in love that enabled me to face my dead at last and write this play–write it with deep pity and understanding and forgiveness for *all* the four haunted Tyrones.

These twelve years, Beloved One, have been a Journey into Light–into love. You know my gratitude. And my love!

GENE

Tao House
July 22, 1941[11]

Simply put, it means that the past is unchangeable and inescapable. And although one must struggle with it again and again, wisdom finally lies in making the best of things, in accepting the grace of second chances.

The Iceman Cometh is O'Neill's American *Götterdammerung*, in which he expressed unreserved pity for the fate of common humanity at the time of the emergence of the modern superpowers, capitalist and communist possessors on the grand scale.[12] In *Long Day's Journey into Night*, he made a full confession of his own sources of despair.   And in *A Moon for the Misbegotten*, he imagined a moment of peace for one of his most important "others," his brother, in understanding and forgiveness, given not by himself but by another, Josie Hogan, the very soul of self-acceptance and dignity.[13] The emotionally wrenching character of these late plays testifies to the possibility of moving beyond the past by paying the full cost of doing so. And finally, in making his own life the subject of a play to be produced after his death, O'Neill affirmed quite unforgettably the possibility of moving beyond the past into an indeterminate future with courage and, as the dedication to Carlotta clearly says, with love.

In the early plays of Israel Horovitz, the depth psychology of O'Neill has yielded to a postmodern surface of moment-by-moment experience that cannot be transcended. Instead of facing a conscious crisis of identity, Horovitz's characters struggle reactively in a tragi-comic landscape of metaphors that mirror pervasive conditions of everyday urban life. In *Line*, four men and one woman want desperately to be "first"; they struggle to identify themselves in relation to an almighty strip of white tape on the floor.[14] As the farcical strategies of one-upmanship accelerate, the audience begins to recognize themselves. They are watching, very probably, their own behavior in coming to the theater.[15] And they are forced to think philosophically about what meaning the never-ending struggle to dominate or displace others might or might not have.

An unanticipated commonality results when the audience starts to enjoy the struggle. On the stage, no one can win for long, so a certain camaraderie of defeat (or victory?) evolves for the witnesses. The isolation of privilege and power is acknowledged. And not only does the struggle to lord it over others appear futile, it also appears to be an inescapable condition and a strangely satisfying one. At the end of the play, Stephen, a *puer aeternus* identified with Mozart, youth, genius, joie de vivre, and early death, eats the line and transforms himself into a machine that dispenses lines for everyone else who wants one. Now everyone can be first. The childishness of this "solution" is touchingly satisfying. It is as if everyone were finally getting, with the help of the artist, their fifteen minutes of fame promised by Andy Warhol. The play has generated a commonality that is simultaneously an irreducible pluralism. And the conditions of competition, so often degrading in reality, have been provisionally humanized by being held up for serious, if comic, attention.

In *The Indian Wants the Bronx*—more realistic event than parable—cultural difference is expressed as a barren space that attracts violence.[16]   Two street kids in New York happen upon a fifty-year-old East Indian named Gupta, newly arrived in America and lost.   He stands near an outside telephone booth, which, like the line in the previous play, creates the only sense of reality—a possibility, but only a possibility, of communication. Speaking Hindi, Gupta is trying unsuccessfully to reach his son in the Bronx. The boys bully and tease him in an effort not to appear unmanly in each other's eyes and because they are at a loss how else they might treat him.

In Gupta's terror and incomprehension, the audience recognizes their own fear of anonymous urban violence.   And in the boys' also sympathetic plight, they see the underlying powerlessness and frustration that creates it.   Wards of a social worker, living at home with single mothers, these boys use language—with impressive virtuoso bravado—to deny their own social obscurity and isolation. Gupta continually apologizes to them, saying, "I can't understand your language," but it is the boys who are at the mercy of their own language.[17]   Their crude slang, peppered with racist and sexist abuse, represents a failure at communication and a failure to express their lives to themselves in a satisfactory way.   Like the sailors on O'Neill's *S.S. Glencairn* and like Yank in *The Hairy Ape*, the boys cannot communicate with others because they would be required to become conscious of their own unacceptable and perhaps unbearable social realities.   Horovitz mercifully spares the audience having to witness a murder.   Gupta escapes with only a cut to his hand.   And the playwright avoids victimizing the boys—"people like them"—further.

An effective treatment of the paranoia sometimes indigenous to diverse cultural situations, poised again just on the edge of violence, is *The Primary English Class*, a masterpiece of black comedy.[18]   Here a motley assortment of bright-eyed immigrants attend their first night-class in what might be called basic communication. Like Gupta in *Indian*, they speak their native languages, variously Italian, French, German, Chinese, and Japanese, throughout the play. A translator's voice assists the audience occasionally.   But their gestures and vocal inflections convey most of their responses.   The young American instructor, impatient with—really contemptuous of—these "foreigners," but also understandably insecure in her new role of authority, is determined that both she and her students will succeed at their appointed tasks. Hilariously, she does not speak any language other than English.   And it is the students, all adults and probably older and more sophisticated than she, who try to put her at ease and encourage her in her efforts to teach.   Like the street kids in *Indian*, she effectively communicates only her own desperate isolation within her predetermined role, one of unquestionable authority.   And she becomes increasingly violent when the students do not confirm her as a success. Convinced that a mad rapist lurks in the hallway—a result of another failure to communicate, this time with the Polish plumber working in the bathroom—she holds her class hostage, forcing them to attempt a linguistic exercise: "to reach the negative through the positive," to respond spontaneously, "I cannot," before an appropriate verb.[19] This depressing task is finally achieved at the end of the play, proving only the absurdity of the effort all along, except that momentarily some basic human regard is ultimately expressed, through the nonverbal medium of a kiss.

What better image of a diverse social group trying to become a family in a wrong-headed way than the classroom, especially one populated by adults in roles traditionally assigned to children. Obviously, teachers are not improved parents. And students must ultimately take the responsibility for their own education. The play further suggests that the idea of having one privileged language, whether English or any other, and an imperialist attitude toward indoctrinating it is ridiculous. The rich diversity of cultures and personalities that could have been brought together in this classroom has only been further dispersed.

Dispersal and reunion belong to the dynamics of family. Reunion, particularly, seems to be a naturally dramatic occasion, exhibiting both the failures and the persistence of togetherness of all kinds. New or unexpected combinations of people, reassessments of the past, and confrontations about old grievances inevitably arise, questioning what people have in common. *The 75th*, a one-act play of great charm, takes a look back at the cultural givens that seemed so important in another time.[20] Physical appearance, marital status, social position, and measured intelligence are subjected to the thorny memories of two former classmates, now in their nineties, who are the only arrivals for their seventy-fifth high school reunion.

Amy Chamberlain and Arthur "Cookie" Silverstein try to recall images of their deceased classmates in terms of who was tall, short, academically or sexually legendary, bald, or "normal." They take these classifications with a grain of salt now, the classifications having become as ghostly as the people themselves. Searching the jukebox menu unsuccessfully for "Don't Fence Me In" and "Those Wedding Bells Are Breaking Up That Old Gang Of Mine," they settle for whatever is contemporary. And they accept their own cultural differences, still very much alive—Jewish/Christian, rich/not so rich—as amicably as they do conditions of age and biology, as parts they must play gracefully. The theatrical metaphor, employed often by O'Neill, in *The Emperor Jones*, for example, and by Horovitz in *Line*, is central to the sense of reality created by this play. Trying to remember their parts from a now-distant past, Amy and Cookie must make the most of this scene, improvising if necessary. Their effort to relate to each other, which represents no less than an affirmation of life this late in the day, depends upon their willingness to connect with each other amid the vagaries of cultural costume and spectacle.

At the same time, they accept their separateness realistically. Amy is not only being coy when she says, "I can't promise you we'll meet next week, but we can discuss it . . . the possibility of our meeting . . . when you call."[21] She is being straightforward about uncertain conditions. Just as her refusal to allow Alfred L. Webber, "the gentlest man I have ever known my entire ninety-three years of knowing men," to be mocked testifies to the health of maintaining her own version of the past. What her experience has been is a part of who she is; there is no reason she should falsify it in order to please someone else. These characters have survived enough of their lives to relish the freedom of being who they are and still enjoy good company. The absolute recalcitrance of the other must be one of the most fundamental themes of all drama. O'Neill invokes it throughout his works to suggest the legitimacy of struggle as a form of relationship, even a form of love, as in *Anna Christie* and *Long Day's Journey*. And Horovitz revels continually in the comic failures of his characters who try to dominate or psych each other. Their frustration renews hope for relationship, even when, as in *The 75th*, the real basis for connection seems virtually lost in the past.

Another reunion play, *The Widow's Blind Date*, is not so gentle.[22] Initially, we accept the rough banter of Archie and George in the wastepaper warehouse where they work. But when their former classmate, Margy, arrives for her date with Archie after all these years, we begin to see this territorial violence, mocking cruelty, and abuse of women for what they are. Archie and George have never evaluated their past actions, which include, we come to learn, the gang rape of Margy at a drunken high school party years ago. They are continuing to act out essentially the same attitudes and values they experienced as adolescents but with increasing self-deception. Margy, on the other hand, has left this small town and her own tough beginnings and started a second life, which has included education and marriage. Now widowed and attending her brother as he dies, she finally feels strong and free enough to return to the scene of her violation and confront it. The men, faced with their own evil, turn upon each other, and George is killed. This is only the beginning, we are told, of Margy's revenge.

Yet this powerful play is not actually about revenge. It is a portrait of the necessarily double consciousness—a brokenness bound together but not healed—that has developed in a woman surviving a past that cannot and should not be accepted. Violence functions in the play on a number of levels. It reflects Margy's understanding of what has been done to her. "You know what I was doin' while you was doin' it to me? Huh? Huh? HUH?" she laughs. "I was thinking that I was getting run over . . . by a bus . . . by the *Hudson* bus. That's what I was doin' I swear ta Christ! That's how much *I loved it*!"[23] It dramatically balances the merciless condition that still prevails in the consciousness and world of Archie and George, who mock Margy's efforts to "come back to town and be new" in a place where "nothin' changes, not around here."[24] And it challenges the audience to accept the seriousness of what they have seen as real.

The play addresses blindness, or willful ignorance in the form of self-serving assumptions about the irresistible nature of sexual desire—mocked by Margy when she bares her breasts and rejects the demonic sexualizing of women; about the pastness of the past—which returns to condemn Archie and George; and about the isolation of people within their own worlds—refuted in the figure of Margy's dying brother, asking and receiving forgiveness for also being one of the gang who raped her. At the end of the play, Archie "*stares out into auditorium. His eyes are dead, hollow. It is the stare of a blind man.*"[25] Reversing the catastrophe of *A Streetcar Named Desire*, Horovitz has made Stanley Kowalski the figure of pity and Blanche Dubois the figure of strength.[26] And he has made the audience see what the protagonist cannot: a world that brutalizes people in the name of love.

Henry Lumper makes a fitting conclusion to this discussion of the unfinished business of America.[27] It tells the story of a Massachusetts fishing village being corrupted by big money from real estate and drug deals. What had been a family-centered world is breaking apart into factions. Modeled on Shakespeare's *Henraid*, the play features a modern-day Prince Hal who comes into his own when he realizes how bad things will get if he does not take up his life again in all seriousness after a period of dissipation and depression.[28] The characters double, illustrating archetypal aspects of his struggle. Hal and his nemesis Harry struggle for control of the union; Hal's father dies after giving his deathbed blessing, while Harry's father commits suicide. The moral victory requires fighting the same old corporate-style evil again and again instead of living in complicity with it and refusing to allow the Lillies, a local religious group, to be turned into scapegoats.

Paradoxically, the source of Hal's strength is that he, like O'Neill's Edmund in *Long Day's Journey into Night*, has been to the gutter and back. Rather than nurturing illusions about life, he has tasted its bitterness; in fact, he has nearly drunk himself to death. But he has found courage with Patty to try again. He expresses his new humility, interestingly, in terms of the ocean: "Many's the time I've looked at the ocean and said, 'I never could drink that much. I am humbled'."[29] The frustrating vastness of life itself, symbolized for O'Neill by the sea, cannot be contained by self-pity. One might as well live.

Indeed, the sea is equally the image of abundant life, spanning cultures and generations. Thus, *Henry Lumper's* vision is stated by Hal's father:

Listen to me, Henry. When the Italians first came to Glossop, everybody said they were gonna' ruin the fish business. The same with the Irish, the Finns, too. The same with the Portuguese, when they came. The Lillies are no different from any of us. They're just people come to fish . . . Nature is supply and demand. When a mother stops nursing her baby, the milk dries up in her breast. As long as she keeps nursing, the milk keeps flowing. That's what life is Hal . . . somebody's got to fish, Hal. If there are no fisherman, the fish themselves will die.[30]

Yet Horovitz sees the personal struggle against despair mirrored by political realities. A measure of Hal's ability to accept himself is his determination to acknowledge the rights of others. Fittingly, then, it is Hal who asserts with finality the play's Epilogue: "No matter if they are Portuguese, Irish, Finnish, Italian, Korean, Protestant, Catholic, Jew, hard-working people will have their chance. I promise this."[31] *Henry Lumper* ends with a public declaration of personal commitment by a man on his way to establishing a new home. He will now be at home in public life, and his home will be a refuge for all hard-working people of goodwill.

NOTES

1. Croswell Bowen, *The Curse of the Misbegotten* (New York: McGraw-Hill, 1959), 313.

2. Israel Horovitz, "The Legacy of O'Neill," *Eugene O'Neill Newsletter* 11, no. 1 (Spring 1987): 6. Horovitz has described his debt to O'Neill as a "legacy": "What I have learned from both Ibsen and O'Neill, as well as from Beckett—three fathers of choice—is an utter seriousness of self. I am simply human. My experience is simply human experience. What is for me is for humanity, no more, no less."

3. Eugene O'Neill, *Bound East for Cardiff*, in *Seven Plays of the Sea* (New York: Vintage Books, 1972), 46.

4. O'Neill, *The Moon of the Caribbees*, in *Seven Plays of the Sea*, 1-29.

5. Eugene O'Neill, *Long Day's Journey Into Night* (New Haven: Yale University Press, 1956).

6. Eugene O'Neill, *Beyond the Horizon*, in *The Plays of Eugene O'Neill* (New York: Random House, 1955), 3:79-169.

7. O'Neill, *Anna Christie*, in *Plays of O'Neill*, 3:1-78.

8. O'Neill, *The Hairy Ape*, in *Plays of O'Neill*, 3:205-54.

9. O'Neill, *The Emperor Jones*, in *Plays of O'Neill*, 3: 171-204.

10. O'Neill, *Desire under the Elms*, in *Plays of O'Neill*, 1: 201-69.

11. O'Neill, *Long Day's Journey into Night*, 7.

12. Eugene O'Neill, *The Iceman Cometh* (New York: Vintage Books, 1957).

13. Eugene O'Neill, *A Moon for the Misbegotten*, in *The Later Plays of Eugene O'Neill*, ed. Travis Bogard (New York: Random House, 1967), 295-409.

14. Israel Horovitz, *Line*, in *Acrobats and Line* (New York: Dramatists Play Service, 1971), 17-58.

15. Cf. Emily Dickinson, poem 1206, in *The Complete Poems of Emily Dickinson*, ed. Thomas H. Johnson (Boston: Little, Brown, 1960), 532.

The Show is not the Show
But they that go—
Menagerie to me—
My Neighbor be—
Fair Play—
Both went to see—

16. Israel Horovitz, *The Indian Wants the Bronx* (New York: Dramatists Play Service, 1968).

17. Ibid., 19.

18. Israel Horovitz, *The Primary English Class* (New York: Dramatists Play Service, 1976).

19. Ibid., 53.

20. Israel Horovitz, *The 75th*, in *Hopscotch and The 75th* (New York: Dramatists Play Service, 1977), 28-61.

21. Ibid., 58.

22. Israel Horovitz, *The Widow's Blind Date* (New York: Dramatists Play Service, 1988).

23. Ibid., 64.

24. Ibid., 67.

25. Ibid., 69.

26. Tennessee Williams, *A Streetcar Named Desire* (New York: Signet, 1947).

27. Israel Horovitz, *Henry Lumper* (New York: Dramatists Play Service, 1990).

28. William Shakespeare, *Henry IV, Parts I and II*, in *Shakespeare: The Complete Works*, ed. G. B. Harrison (New York: Harcourt, Brace & World, 1952), 613-96.

29. Horovitz, *Henry Lumper*, 57.

30. Ibid., 75.

31. Ibid., 85.

5

The Influence of Aeschylus's *Oresteia* on Israel Horovitz's *Alfred Trilogy*

Dennis A. Klein

The name of Israel Horovitz often evokes images of experimental plays, such as *Trees*, *Acrobats*, and the recently revived *Line*, plays that place him within the avant-garde movement and in the company of such writers as Samuel Beckett and Eugène Ionesco. And although Horovitz dedicated *Alfred the Great* to Beckett, the plays that compose *The Alfred Trilogy—Alfred the Great*, *Our Father's Failing*, and *Alfred Dies*, (completed in 1978)—approach classical lines in subject matter and technique. The trilogy treats adultery and matricide, revenge and retribution, all subjects in Aeschylus's *Oresteia*, the common title given to his dramatic trilogy of *The Agamemnon*, *The Libation Bearers,* and *The Eumenides* (completed in 458 B.C.E.). This chapter focuses on the elements of plot, theme, and characterization, as well as imagery, and technique, that appeared originally in Aeschylus and that Horovitz has reshaped into his own masterfully paced trilogy of revelation of past events and the net into which those events trap the characters.

While it is hardly necessary to write plot summaries of the plays in the *Oresteia*, some brief notes on those works will serve here as a point of departure. Orestes is not present in *The Agamemnon*, the first play of this trilogy that dramatizes the title character's triumphant yet doomed return from the Trojan War accompanied by King Priam's captured and prophetic daughter, Cassandra. During Agamemnon's absence, his wife, Clytemnestra, who has never stopped brooding over Agamemnon's sacrifice of their daughter Iphigenia, began an adulterous relationship with Aegisthus, her husband's cousin and long-time enemy. Clytemnestra awaits the return of a husband, "this woman's man-strong heart / With all a female's longing" (31) not to resume their marriage, but, as she later reveals, to take revenge on him for their daughter's death, as well as for having degraded her by being "petted ... by every gilded girl at Troy" (87). She also wants to be free to marry Aegisthus. In addition, Aegisthus has his own reason for wanting to kill Agamemnon. He must avenge his father, Thyestes, to whom Agamemnon's father, Atreus, long ago served up his (Thyestes') children at a banquet, in reprisal for Thyestes' having seduced his brother's wife. It is the motive of vengeance that has brought Aegisthus back to Argos. He feels responsible to avenge his father and thus adds another link to the chain of family crimes. While Clytemnestra realizes Cassandra's prophesy of Agamemnon's death with her long-premeditated fatal blow against him, as well as the murder of Cassandra herself, in the second play, *The Libation Bearers,* she lays part of the blame for the murders on fate, an unspoken but implied element revitalized in *The Alfred Trilogy.* Although this play is complete within itself, the Chorus anticipates the second play of the trilogy and virtually reveals its plot in a single sentence: "But if Orestes lives, / Is somewhere in the sunlight still, / May fortune speed him home, oh graciously! / To kill the pair of them—completely kill" (97), thus setting the stage for *The Libation Bearers.*

The trilogy's name, *Oresteia,* is drawn from its central character, Orestes, whose revenge overshadows Clytemnestra's acts of adultery and murder that set the work in motion. At their father's tomb, where Electra, Orestes' sister, is offering up libations, the siblings plot to kill their mother, Clytemnestra, and Aegisthus, her new husband, for which purpose Orestes returned to Argos accompanied by Pylades. Realizing his mother's disturbing dream that she gave birth to a serpent, the traditional symbol of treachery, Clytemnestra is murdered by Orestes, whom she considers the traitorous son she bore. Although she warns him about the mother's curse that will be on his head if he kills her, Orestes fears the guilt by which he will be haunted if he fails to avenge his father's death and regrets only that he was not present to prevent his father's murder. And so with Pylades he carries out the double murder. Initially he feels no remorse for his actions, but he is later pursued by the Furies, visible only to him. The stage is now set for *The Eumenides,* in which Orestes goes on trial for matricide. The last lines of the play may well be the theme of both the *Oresteia* and *The Alfred Trilogy:* "Oh, when shall it finish, when shall it sate— / lie down to sleep this fury-bound hate?" (153).

The relentless pursuit by the Furies forces Orestes to flee from land to land until he finds sanctuary in Delphi; he hopes that Apollo, who instigated the crime, will intercede on his behalf in the world's first court of justice. Orestes' trial results in a tie (six votes in his favor, six against), and he is exonerated on the charge of matricide. With this foundation laid, it is now possible to examine Horovitz's trilogy and speculate on Aeschylus' influence on it.

Before analyzing the themes of Horovitz's plays, it is appropriate to comment on their structure. There is a danger of being anachronistic since Aeschylus's plays predate Aristotelian theory. Be that as it may, *The Agamemnon* appears to conform to the classical unities, while *The Libation Bearers* and *The Eumenides* have changes of place. Horovitz observes the unities of time, place, and action in *Alfred the Great* but departs from the unity of place in *Our Father's Failing* and from the unity of time in *Alfred Dies*. It is important to keep in mind that the plays are as much about what happened in the past as about what happens in the present, and what happens in large measure is the gradual revelation of the past events, which provide the motivations for the present reactions. In that sense, Horovitz's works parallel Aeschylus's in the technique of gradual discovery.

The structures of the two trilogies are parallel to the extent that both begin with triumphant returns and end with the protagonists on trial. Even the title of Horovitz's first play indicates a heroic presence: *Alfred the Great*, a title more appropriate to the king of Argos, who has returned from performing heroic acts, than to the unheralded return of a Wakefield, Massachusetts, wealthy son. Alfred has been away from Wakefield for fifteen years, during which time he has become rich and famous, if only by local standards.

His first stop on the surprise visit is to the home of Will and Margaret, in whose living room the entire play transpires. In high school, Alfred and Margaret were romantically involved, and since Alfred left town, Margaret has kept a scrapbook of all of the items that have appeared about him in the local newspaper. For a long time she wrote to him every night. Those activities have inspired jealousy in Will, who views Alfred's presence in his home with suspicion, especially since his entrance in the play takes place while Alfred and Margaret are staring into each other's eyes. It is with good reason that Will feels hostile toward Alfred. Despite Margaret's declaration that her marriage is solid, it is no stronger than any of the other marital unions in *The Alfred Trilogy*.

A major theme throughout is that of children, often with some mystery about their origins. Margaret wastes no time in bringing up the subject to Alfred. Although Margaret and Alfred avoid the subject of a "little girl," for no apparent reason, she begins their conversation by mentioning that Will has become a model father to Will, Jr., who was born out of wedlock, the issue of Will's impregnating a cheerleader named Ruby, during his senior year in high school. Margaret assumes responsibility for the fact that she and Will will never have children, introducing the theme of infertility and impotence prevalent throughout the trilogy. Whatever bond there is between Will and Margaret is the result of their upbringings: Will was a foundling, and Margaret never knew who her father was.

Another theme that begins early and permeates the trilogy is that of death. Alfred has been to the cemetery and noticed that someone has been putting flowers on his brother's grave. Within moments, Alfred makes another reference to death: He wants Margaret to quit smoking before it kills her. The fact that his wife, Emily, smokes does not bother him: "Emily's a big girl. If she wants to kill herself that's her concern, not mine" (65). The first scene ends with a threat of death: If Will catches Alfred touching Margaret, he will break his head.

The opening segment of the second scene is between Alfred and Will. Will wants to know when Alfred is planning to visit his father; Alfred, however, speaks of his father in the past tense and insists that he is dead. Will expresses the same hostility and perhaps jealousy about Margaret's stepfather that he feels toward Alfred, resenting the fact that for ten years he practically lived in Will's house and then ran off and became involved with a widow. The person Alfred remembers is Roxy, Will's stepmother. Unfortunately, her life, as so many other lives in Wakefield, was riddled with scandal. She now lives in the nursing home, as does a man named Sam about whom Alfred inquires, and apparently Alfred's father.

During the moment that Will is out of the room, Alfred returns to the subject of making love to Margaret. Not only does Margaret not discourage such thoughts, but after an obligatory slap, she and Alfred kiss, as Will and Emily enter. Alfred dismisses what they saw as "grade-school sweethearts reminiscing and kissing. There is absolutely nothing to worry about" (85). Will reminds Alfred that he almost killed a man over his wife, a woman who has no shame. That incident took place a long time ago, before they were married, and yet the image of Margaret with another man still haunts him. As the act comes to a close, Alfred chastises Emily for following him to Wakefield.

Act 2 presents images that will become important in the next play. As it opens, Emily is holding a knife, the instrument that kills both Agamemnon and Clytemnestra. Despite its menacing appearance, it functions here only for cutting an apple. Margaret wants to know how Alfred's father is feeling, but he keeps insisting that his father is dead, as well as his mother and brother. Later, Will puts on a baseball cap, which upsets Alfred ostensibly because it belonged to his father. Alfred admits that something is wrong with his mind and memory and suspects that it has something to do with the murder of his brother, an act that he believes Will committed.

In the second scene of the act, the conversation shifts to the Greasy Pole Contest, an event fraught with phallic symbolism and whose meaning does not become fully clear until the last play of the trilogy. In the midst of talk about greasy poles, Emily insists that she was Alfred's first woman: "Alfred never had a girl before me. I was his first. Can you imagine" (93)? Will corrects her by saying that Alfred had in fact "had" Margaret in high school and made her pregnant. They had a daughter, whom they gave away, and that incident ruined Margaret's life. This revelation makes clear the embarrassed reference to the little girl at the beginning of the play. Likewise, Will admits that he got a cheerleader "in trouble." Then, during a moment when they are alone, Emily tells Will how attractive she finds him. The shoe is now on the other foot: Alfred enters to find *them* kissing.

It is Emily's turn to reveal some information or misconceptions about her past. (It is important to remember that what is presented as factual in this play are fragmented memories and mysteries, to be explained later in the trilogy.)

As Emily remembers her parents, her father was "a sainted man" and her mother a virgin at the time she married him and when she died. She also remembers having spent her first ten years in an orphanage and then attended a boarding school for gifted children in California. Emily, who insists on facts, also wants a clear answer to the mystery of whether Alfred's father is dead or alive. It appears that he is alive and residing at the asylum to which Alfred had him committed. There is also a reference to Alfred's dead brother, Bruce, whose funeral—not his father's—Alfred attended. Bruce, who grew up in Woburn, Massachusetts, was a half-brother, by a different mother from Alfred. Will interjects that fifteen years ago he almost killed Margaret's boyfriend—a man from Woburn. Emily puts two and two together and realizes that Will murdered Alfred's brother. Will remembers watching Alfred and Margaret "doing it" on the sofa in the living room. And now Emily wants to have sex with Will and seemingly wants to be caught. But instead of sex with Will, as the second act ends, Alfred insists that Emily strip Will for another purpose.

As act 3 opens, Will is stripped to his underpants and socks, gagged, and bound to the stairway. What takes place is something like a mock trial, a foreshadowing of the main event in the final play. Emily accuses Will of murdering Alfred's brother. Margaret refuses even to comment on that distasteful event, and it is she who summarizes Alfred's return to Wakefield for truth and beauty: Margaret is the beauty, and Will is the truth; now all they have to do is punish the criminal and go home. Alfred's point of view on vengeance is right out of Aeschylus: "The murder of my brother needs avenging" (107). Furthermore, he wants Will to confess to the murder so that he can be punished. Before the trial can continue, however, Margaret denies that she ever had a lover. But Alfred remembers that his brother used to go to her house almost every day after work, that he loved her, and that he wrote to Alfred about her. Margaret cannot keep her silence when Will—now relieved of his gag—calls Alfred's brother a "falling-down wino." She is quick to say that he was a fine and understanding man, who made her feel clean and beautiful—although never so exciting as Alfred.

What becomes clear in the course of this play is Emily's dominant personality. Claiming that she literally owns Alfred, Emily makes him admit as much. Alfred makes an assessment of his present situation:

I am slightly more than forty years of age . . . And here I am, sitting in a room with my dead brother's mistress, her husband the killer, my wife Emily, who has been unfaithful to me in ways known only to scholars of ancient tribal unfaithfulness. I am told that my late, great, dead father is not only alive, but is, by reputation, the most promising pervert of this town. (113)

As the evidence against her mounts, Margaret finally confesses to her sexual involvement with Bruce Webber. She claims that he forced himself on her and then he thought that she was too easy; Will insists that she enjoyed it and could not get enough.

In the final moments of the play, important secrets are revealed. First, Margaret and Will were married before the birth of the child, whom Margaret had by Alfred. Margaret and Will put the baby up for adoption in New Hampshire because Will could not tolerate having Alfred's child in his house. Second, Margaret and Will, in addition to being husband and wife, are sister and brother; they did not know for certain until after they were married. Third, Will admits to the unpremeditated murder of Alfred's brother. In fact, he claims that Bruce died of a heart attack while Will was strangling him. When Will caught him and Margaret engaged in sex, Will just went crazy. Having admitted to the crime, Will insists upon being punished by Alfred: "You've got to kill me, Alfred. You promised . . . You said you'd punish the killer" (12). Emily agrees that there must be a punishment for the crime. Even Margaret wants her husband to die. Surprisingly, there are two gunshots offstage; both Will and Margaret are dead, and Alfred assumes responsibility. Although this play is complete in and of itself, Alfred's admission that it is now time to visit his father anticipates the next.

Our Father's Failing is a logical extension of *Alfred the Great*. Although it can stand alone, it provides answers to some of the mysteries planted in the first play of the trilogy; others are not explained until the final play. Whereas the first took place at the start of fall, *Our Father's Failing* takes place at the end of fall, a reasonable question is, What kept Alfred from visiting his father for as many as three months? The situation is further confused by a reference to a newspaper article that appeared just three weeks earlier, allegedly right after Alfred's arrival. Another indication, this in the list of characters, suggests that more than three months have passed between plays. In *Alfred the Great*, Alfred is precisely forty years old, handsome, and elegant. Now he is in his forties, thin, and receding in his elegance. The same description also applies to Emily. The work transpires partly in the backyard of the asylum, where Alfred's father, Tommy Webber, has been for thirty years, and in the living room of the first piece. There appears to be unity of time: The play begins at dawn and ends just before the following dawn. Tommy and his companion, Sam, both "ancient, white-haired, thin," provide the information and are thus more important players than Alfred and Emily, who learn it.

Pa (Tommy) is uneasy about Alfred's sudden arrival in Wakefield after so many years and perplexed by what his motives might be. Sam's guess is that Alfred is coming for Pa's money (which Sam calls "our" money), but Pa assumes that Alfred still blames his father for his mother's death. As Sam remembers the events, "You [Pa] found Sophie [Tommy's wife] and Willie-Boy [Will's and Margaret's father as well as Sam's brother] sacked up together in your big bed and that you lost your marbles and went into a terrible crime-of-passion state" (135). Pa then "remembers" that he killed both of them with Alfred's Boy Scout knife, to which there was a reference in the first play. Now the baseball cap mentioned in the first play takes on significance; it was stained with blood after the two murders. To hide the evidence, Pa and Sam burned the room. The police and newspaper let the event go unresolved, and Sam and Pa agreed to go into the asylum. Sam brings up yet another old scandal in which Pa was involved. Pa lived and had a daughter with the Widow O'Brien, a piece of information that will become important later in the play.

Although Emily tells Margaret and Will why Alfred returned to Wakefield in *Alfred the Great*, in *Our Father's Failing*, Alfred is vague about his reason for returning. He says that he does not forgive and does not forget and that there is "a very large debt owed to me . . . that wants to be collected . . . an old debt" (143). He never says that money enters into that debt; in fact, he has no interest in his father's money. Sam is concerned that Alfred is going to take his father away with him, but Emily assures him that such is not her husband's motive. *Her* motive is simple: She wants a financial payoff to leave the past behind them. She is also willing to trade Sam fact for fact. Emily reveals that her name at birth was Emily Marie O'Brien, of unknown parents. Since Alfred suffers from loss of memory, Emily is trying to uncover certain "juicy facts" for him. She remembers watching Alfred spending a week badgering Will into confessing to a murder that he probably did not commit. Emily believes that Alfred killed his own brother and that crime drew him back to Wakefield. Ignoring Sam's advice to get out and stop reviving old problems, Emily is a woman with a motive. She wants to destroy Alfred.

Pa's concern is that Sam may have revealed a secret and thereby betrayed him. In fact, Tommy himself will reveal the secret before the play is over. He makes a reference to a small detail that ties the first two plays together. Pa claims that his wife's body was burned by a cigarette, despite his begging that she give up the filthy habit. The incident occurred when Alfred was ten years old, but in his recollection, the fire was really a cremation, an attempt to destroy the evidence of Sophie and Willy-Boy in bed together. Alfred vows that the murder of his mother will be avenged, and he is correct but it will take another play. As in *Alfred the Great*, he steps back and assesses the situation:

I am forty. I am standing in an insane asylum with my mother's killers; my old pa and his best friend, Sam, two major-league lunatics. I see that my charming and python-like wife, Emily, is here, too . . . The murder of my mother will be revenged: absolutely and completely. I stake my life on that fact. (171)

Finally, there is Sam's version of the murder. He believes that he was an accomplice to a fire but to no more than that and that Sophie and his brother were dead before he started the fire. Pa insists that he killed his wife and then makes a statement belying his confession: "A father has an obligation to protect his son. No matter what" (173).

Act 3 takes place in the same living room as *Alfred the Great* and brings to a conclusion the mystery surrounding Sophie's murder. It also adds some information on Roxy, who was mentioned briefly in the first play and will be prominent in the third. Sam recalls that Roxy hated both Pa and Alfred and Emily reveals Alfred's motive in returning—to see his father die. With this revelation, Pa ceases protecting his son, thereby forcing him to remember what happened so long ago. Similarly, Alfred gives vent to the resentment, which he harbors against his father, who had run off four months before Alfred was born.

The baseball cap holds the clue to the mystery. It was Alfred who killed his mother and her lover. He wrapped the Boy Scout knife, which he used for the murder, in the cap. Alfred now understands that his father has been protecting him from the truth all these years. Emily swears that "Alfred dies" and thereby anticipates the third play. Now that Alfred knows that he committed matricide, the parallel with the *Oresteia* is established. Like Will in the first play, he wants to be punished. It will be Emily's pleasure to oblige him in the final play of the trilogy.

As in the *Oresteia*, the first play of Horovitz's trilogy involves adultery, and the second concerns matricide. It is therefore fitting that the third be a trial for murder. This play will substantiate the words of the Chorus in *The Agamemnon*: "The gods have eyes: / The multimurder is marked, / And in the end / The black Fates overturn and batter down / The lucky but too lawless man– / His life a shadow / Where arrivals in oblivion are most lame. / Overreaching glory is a ruin" (46). The "trial" in *Alfred Dies* is far less conventional than even that in *The Eumenides*, which, like our own judicial system, involved the votes of twelve jurors. As the play opens, Alfred is in his third day behind bars in a makeshift prison in an underground storage room, where the three acts take place. The author specifies the time of the play as the end of June and the start of July, but indications of changes in time from scene to scene are limited throughout to the word later. Yet when Emily appears she seems older to Alfred. As in the other plays, once again there are four characters, two of whom are Alfred and Emily—now described as "once elegant." The play's title eliminates any element of mystery about how it is going to end, and yet the playwright is able to maintain suspense through the details of the personal lives of the characters and by making revelations, which come as bombshells, however logically the conclusions follow from the evidence.

Alfred's "jailer" is Lynch, Margaret's brother, Will's brother, Sam's nephew, and the son of the man Alfred murdered. Lynch's resentment of Alfred goes beyond the fact that the latter killed his own mother and extends into Will's realm: Alfred became rich, and Lynch became nothing. Alfred used to be Lynch's ideal because he had his picture in the newspaper and was on television. That remark links Lynch to Will and serves to give a circular action to the trilogy. Lynch is acting under orders from Emily not to talk to the prisoner and to poke him with a pole on her command. Reasonably enough, Alfred's anger at—and even hatred of—Emily is at least as strong as Lynch's resentment of him. Lynch does have to admit that Alfred was his ideal because he became famous and had his picture in the newspaper. Lynch believes that Alfred ruined his life and that this is the day to even the score: "By the time we're through with you, Alfred, you are gonna wish you never set foot back here in Wakefield, Massachusetts, again . . . I give you my word" (215). Similarly, Emily is determined to fulfill the threat of the Chorus in *The Eumenides:* "When there falls on a man the reckless sin / Of self-destroying his kin, / We dog him down under the earth / To his minikin freedom of death– / Hardly excessive" (173). As the Chorus says in *The Libation Bearers*, "The anvil of Justice is firm" (133).

In the fourth scene of the first act, Roxy, mentioned in the two previous plays, finally appears. She acts as the court reporter and through the technique of reading back the record of the proceedings allows the playwright to let the readers or members of the audience know what transpired before the play began. She reads the charges against Alfred: "He has murdered his mother, causing the curse that fell upon the people of his town" (219). The Furies, too, the very embodiment of revenge, threaten to curse Athens, and only justice can turn the curse into a blessing. Additionally, he is charged with the murder of his father (who must have died between plays), his friends, and his children. Roxy adds her own charges: "All of my husbands, several of my children, and, of course, me. Alfred killed us all" (224). Emily holds him responsible for her four stillbirths and for all of the shame that they have caused her. The penalty is death, and all three of his accusers seem quite satisfied with themselves. Emily feels no remorse for her actions or for the charge she gave to Lynch and Roxy, in Clytemnestra's words, "You and I this house masters / Now shall order things right" (99). Although she does not specify the terms, Emily reveals that she, Lynch, and Roxy have entered into a pact.

As the "trial" progresses, Roxy reiterates information that the readers-viewers of the previous play already know, but Horovitz needs to explain in order to make this play independent of the others. Roxy recalls that at the age of ten, Alfred killed his mother and Roxy's boyfriend Willie-Boy. Lynch is furious at the suggestion that his father would have gone near a prostitute like Roxy unless he was paying her. In fact, Roxy did have two children by Willie-Boy. He recalls, too, that it was Tommy Webber who was nuts over Roxy. And Roxy is responsible, according to Lynch, for turning his sister Margaret into a hooker. While Lynch is attempting to choke Alfred with his belt, Roxy kills Lynch with the gun already in Emily's hand. Roxy's motive echoes Pa's words in the second play: "A mother has an obligation to protect her daughter. No matter what" (239). And so, apparently one of the two children whom Roxy had with Willie-Boy was Emily. Furthermore, Roxy blames Alfred because she has nothing to show for her life. She has been "sunk" since the age of fourteen, and now at the age of nearly one hundred has not seen any reward for all of her suffering.

Alfred pleads with Emily that he cannot be held responsible for what he did when he was ten years old. He acted, he says, because his father was a great man and he wanted to do something on his behalf, as well as to punish his mother for adulterous behavior. Emily accuses Alfred of letting his father rot in an asylum for thirty years, an act for which he does feel responsible. Alfred is shocked and shaken by Emily's next revelation, that they, like Will and Margaret, are brother and sister as well as husband and wife; Tommy Webber is *her* father, too. Emily claims that Alfred knew that they were brother and sister even before they were married, blocking out the knowledge as he has done with his other evil deeds in life: killing his mother and sequestering his father in the asylum. And now he, like Will before him, wants to be punished. There is a gunshot offstage, but it is Roxy killing herself.

Now Emily must die to complete the pact. She knows that she does not have the courage to kill Alfred but that her death will kill him and thereby complete the pact that nobody may leave the room alive. After Emily puts a bullet through her breast, where Clytemnestra was stabbed, Alfred puts the gun in his mouth, but he cannot pull the trigger. Instead, he shoots himself in the hand and will allow himself to bleed to death. In *The Eumenides*, Orestes says, "For the blood on my hands is sleeping, paling. / That horrid spot of mother's gore now washes out" (171). Similarly, Alfred watches the guilt of his mother's blood symbolically on his hands for some forty years pour from his body in his lifeblood. Indeed, in a fine essay Marty Roth contends that blood is also the controlling symbol in *The Eumenides*. For the first time, Alfred feels hopeful. His death may then be a heroic act; in the words of Another Old Man in *The Agamemnon*: "And yet there's grace for man to die heroically" (80). However, the outcomes of the two trials are quite different. Orestes is found innocent and lives; Alfred is found guilty and dies, but both are hopeful as the trilogies end.

Of the eight characters who appear in the trilogy, Alfred and Emily clearly derive from characters in the *Oresteia*. Alfred, though no hero, suggests both Agamemnon in the play of that title and Orestes in the other two works of the Greek trilogy. Alfred, like Agamemnon, begins the play with a triumphant return to his native city after a long absence. In *The Agamemnon*, a Herald hails: "He comes worthy of honor beyond all living men" (49). Such words may be befitting of a Greek war hero but also apply on a small scale to Alfred, a local hero. The Chorus welcomes Agamemnon as "great King," the adjective that found its way into the title of Horovitz's play. If nothing else, he is rich and famous, he gets his name and picture in the newspaper, and he has endowed a scholarship at the local high school. Alfred falls victim to his own pride and into a situation about which the Chorus advises in *The Agamemnon*: "Sooner or later Pride- / The-Old makes Pride-the-New, / Sporting in the wicked / (When its birth is due) A frenzied thing: / Infatuate, unwholesome, strong / insatiate, obsessive, black / curse upon the house– / image of its parents" (57). Could it be under the influence of these lines that Roxy talks of the curse that Alfred brought not only to his family's name but upon the entire town? There certainly is the suggestion of a curse perpetuating itself from generation to generation. In *The Alfred Trilogy* the cause may be less matricide than adultery and incest.

Alfred's shared traits with Agamemnon are less important than those he shares with Orestes. The essential element in any comparison between the two trilogies is the dual crimes of matricide and murder: Alfred kills his mother, Sophie, and her lover, Willie-Boy, as his Greek predecessor killed his mother, Clytemnestra, and her lover, Aegisthus. Apollo would have to argue that Alfred's crime was worse than Clytemnestra's because he spilled kindred blood, and she did not. Both sons shared the motive of wanting to avenge either their fathers' murder or shame. Orestes acted with the sole motive of killing the persons who killed his father after disgracing him with their adultery. Alfred thought that he was doing what his father would want. Orestes believes that he is doing what he had to do, and at the time the Chorus approves of his actions on behalf of his dead father. Apollo voices an opinion in *The Eumenides* that makes the role of the mother less than that of the father, a view unpopular in today's politically correct world: "The mother is not parent of her so-called child / but only nurse to the new-sown seed. / The man who puts it there is parent; / she merely cultivates the shoot— / host for a quest—if no god blights" (186).

Alfred has the flaw of shutting out anything that he does not want to remember and it falls to other characters to call his attention to his refusal to see. Several times it is his father who tells Alfred to open his eyes, but Will does so too. In effect, Alfred is as psychologically blind as was Oedipus physically blind, to evoke another Greek tragedy. Alfred could have kept his eyes metaphorically closed and gone through life that way, but he succumbed to returning to Wakefield and to his past.

Emily may well be the motivating force behind Alfred's actions and the character, like Clytemnestra, who sets the trilogy in motion. She takes credit for insisting that she and Albert make the trip to Wakefield. She echoes Clytemnestra, who proclaims, "My famous husband coming back?—is my design" (52). Both Emily and the possible source of her inspiration, Clytemnestra, are hypocritical and insincere. In fact, the Herald's words about Clytemnestra in *The Agamemnon* apply equally well to Emily: "Highflung words indeed— / if not freighted with the truth / And proper to a highborn lady's mouth" (52). Emily's importance grows throughout the trilogy. She is of only minor importance in *Alfred the Great*, overshadowed by Alfred, Margaret, and even Will. Her function is at first limited to walking in on Alfred and

Margaret while they are kissing and then turning the tables on Alfred by making a play for Will. She may be responsible for Will's death, because it is she who observes that a crime was committed (the murder of Alfred's brother) and that someone has to pay for it. If Emily does not pull the trigger on Will (or Lynch or Alfred, for that matter), she does declare about him, "This man *deserves* to die!" (121). She is the kind of monster of whom Cassandra speaks prophetically in *The Agamemnon*: "Ah! that unleashed female beast to kill a man. / What monster shall I call her? What abomination?" (76). The context is Cassandra's prophesy of Agamemnon's death; in *The Alfred Trilogy*, the deaths of three men occur. It is in the character of Emily that the pervasive theme of revenge is embodied, but Lynch and Roxy, Margaret and Will are also motivated by that impulse.

The second play, *Our Father's Failing,* reveals her greed. She demands an offer of money from Sam to stop her snooping and leave town. In a manner as prophetic as Cassandra's, she knows that something awful is going to happen. She reveals the real reason she wants to destroy Alfred. She also shows how domineering a woman she is through her interaction with Alfred, presents the notion that it was he and not his father who murdered his mother, and makes Alfred admit that he wants to see his father die. And she anticipates the final play by vowing that Alfred too will die.

Emily not only anticipates the final play; she literally dominates it. She has Lynch construct the prison and act as jailer and engages Roxy as court stenographer. She knew who had the strongest reasons in town to hate Alfred and who would be willing to enter into a fatal pact with her. Emily allows Lynch to give vent to his hate for and resentment of Alfred by having him jab the prisoner with a long pole. Her desire for revenge extends to committing suicide, at least in part to provoke Alfred into killing himself.

The motivating themes common to both trilogies are those of justice and revenge. Just as Clytemnestra wants the Furies to "pursue him [Orestes] to the bone" (164), Emily gives that charge to Lynch and Roxy. Roth views *The Eumenides* as dramatizing the institution of a new form of justice in Athens and believes that by the time the trial begins in the third play of the *Oresteia*, Orestes is already as good as having been declared innocent, absolved through expiation and sacrifice. It is a kinder and gentler form of justice than existed previously in Athens. Athena renames the Furies the Eumenides, or Gentle Ones, and the chorus sums up the new spirit of Athenian justice:

The dark of the people's blood
(Gulping vendettas down):
Slaughter for slaughter and ruin
Raging over the town.
Reciprocate graces instead
with mutual notions of love

And a single one of hate:
Such is the cure for much among men. (199)

(This attitude is a change from that in *The Libation Bearers*, in which the Chorus condemns Orestes.) In contrast, Alfred is perceived as guilty before his hopelessly unfair trial begins.

Adultery occurs in both Aeschylus's and Horovitz's trilogies; the latter contains related sexual matters, such as promiscuity and incest, impotence and barrenness. It is not only Clytemnestra who is guilty of adultery with Aegisthus but also Agamemnon with Cassandra. While Agamemnon never says so directly, he makes a statement that is oblique—and poetic—on their sexual liaison: "She came to me, choice flower: / Prize of an empire, present of an army" (64). Clytemnestra is no fool about her husband's behavior and, on meeting Cassandra looks "challenging" at her, as one might at a rival. There might be a clue here to Sophie's motivation for a sexual affair with Willie-Boy, who was Tommy's (Pa's) friend and partner. It could well have been a situation of what's good for the goose is good for the gander: Tommy's sexual prowess was well known. Tommy did think that his wife "hated his guts" and that she carried on sexual liaisons in their own home. Indeed, he claims not to have known when it was safe to go home. It is sexual promiscuity coupled with adultery and incest that make for such complicated family trees and husbands and wives who are also brothers and sisters, or who at least shared one common parent in *The Alfred Trilogy*. Tommy did not have to tell Alfred that Emily, his wife, was also his sister from Pa's union with Roxy. The son knew as much from a photograph that his mother, Sophie, had forgotten to take off the wall. His mother let him know that Emily was his father's daughter, given away to a home in Boston. Alfred lived in fear after that moment of being given away, too.

Then, of course, there is Roxy. She had child after child and gave them away. She was fifty-seven years old when Emily was born. Reluctant though he is to do so, Alfred admits that his father had a fling with Roxy. Similarly, Lynch does not like acknowledging the fact that his father, Willie-Boy, ever went near Roxy, except when he had the fifty cents that she allegedly charged other men for her services. And yet Roxy and Willie had two children together, one of whom was Margaret. At the same time that Willie-Boy was Roxy's boyfriend, he was also having an affair with Sophie. Alfred admits to having had a "high school indiscretion" with Margaret, as a result of which she had to leave school and have an abortion in New Hampshire. There is a further reference, which indicates that Alfred got Margaret pregnant a second time while she and Will had broken up. She was married by the time the daughter was born, and Will could not live with the girl in his home, so Margaret put her up for adoption in New Hampshire. Margaret and Will did not find out that they were brother and sister until after they were married. Just as Lynch tries strangling Alfred to shut him up, so Lynch's grandfather hanged one of his own sons in an effort to stop the incest.

Masculinity is an important issue in *The Alfred Trilogy*, and Will's is as much a source of pride for him as his intellectual inferiority is a source of self-consciousness. While Will claims "kids make me want to puke" (80), he had another reason for not wanting to raise Margaret and Alfred's child: It is not manly to do so. Nor does he cry as Alfred does because "it ain't manly" (111). He would never give a child of his own up for adoption, because that is not manly either. If sexual prowess is any measure of manliness, Tommy takes the prize. According to Will, Tommy Webber is the same sex maniac now that he was sixty years ago and according to Sam, Tommy has had every woman he has ever wanted. Pa claims that Sam has been trying to kill him by putting six drops of strychnine in his water every day, but the effort has not only failed to kill him, it has heightened his potency and made a real lover out of him.

In contrast, Sam has been impotent for the past sixty-one years; a failed attempt on a beach turned Sam into a sexual cripple. There is humor in the way he tells the story:

Her name was Susan. Little dark-and-darting-eyed Congregationalist. Slim and very wealthy. Just got ourselves ready. . . . Just mounted her . . . when the biggest fuckin' wave you ever seen . . . washed right over us . . . like a ton of wet bricks. . . . Drug me right off of her . . . Hoisted me up and catapulted me more'n a hundred yards. Slammed me right down on the beach, like a clean but crazed human bomb, bareassed, right beside a nun. . . . She was, at that point, just minding her own business, cooking weenies on an open fire . . . Landed almost on top of her. Knocked the poor sonofabitchin' nun face down in the sand . . . I haven't had a hard-on in sixty-one years. (148–149)

As a result of that experience and its consequences on him, Sam seems to have channeled any feelings that he might have had for women into an emotional companionship with Pa. Sam calls him a saint and states that he never married because of him. In a moment of affection, "Sam*'s hand is on* Pa*'s cheek, his thumb near* Pa*'s mouth.* Pa *bites* Sam*'s thumb*" (186).

Sam's impotence may in fact be a bond with Alfred, about whose virility Emily raises doubts. At the opening of the trilogy, Emily tells Will that Alfred is an unhappy man because he is impotent. Later she tells Margaret, "Alfred isn't excitable. He doesn't . . . get excited. That's why he had to see you, Margaret: you're Alfred's stiffest memory" (116). Again in the second play, Emily refers to Alfred's lovemaking as a laugh: He was once a laugh a minute but has not given her even a "chuckle" in years, to the point of having lost his "sense of humor" altogether. Impotence is a touchy subject from the start. Alfred does confess to Margaret that he was impotent twice with Emily and is terrified that it will happen again right now—with Margaret. Of course, there is always the possibility that he is trying to get sympathy from Margaret or to put her in a position—on the sofa—that she can prove to him that with the right woman, his masculinity is assured. Emily may even have spoken of the subject to Lynch, who asks Alfred early on in the third play and à propos of nothing, "How's your pecker?" (200). Could the inclusion of this trait be traced back to Orestes' remark that Aegisthus is a woman at heart? The Chorus says of him, "So you could not kill the king yourself / But had to let a woman do it" (97).

Will has trouble believing that Alfred is impotent because he watched him and Margaret on the sofa for thirty-five minutes, as long ago he watched Alfred's brother with her. The two incidents make Alfred think that Will is no more than a "keyholer." Will claims not to have any problems with impotence and is therefore more of a man than Alfred. Alfred is surprised that Will and Margaret never had children together, for which Margaret takes the blame. Will, however, places the blame elsewhere—squarely on Alfred. Margaret's experience of having given away a child—Alfred's—for adoption has left her "psychologically barren," and Will says that "barren women get boring after a while" (77). Is he saying that he has lost sexual interest in Margaret? Is that why she lies to Alfred about how solid their marriage is? Is it why she ends up on the sofa with Alfred? And is sex, not money, the real cause of Will's jealousy of Alfred?

Alfred's and Emily's visit to Will and Margaret is little more than a game of switching partners. While Emily claims at one point to hate sex, she does initiate the moves with Will, because he supposedly can keep going for an hour. But her motive may be revenge on both Alfred and Margaret. She makes no attempts to go off secretly with Will and appears to want to be caught in a reciprocally adulterous act. If Alfred can want nothing more than to be at home making love with Margaret, Emily can want the same with Will. Neither the men nor the women have sexual problems as long as their partners are not their own spouses. Like Alfred who got Margaret pregnant, Will had a child with Ruby long ago. And he is nothing short of playing coy with Emily about how she could never be interested in a "townie" like him. Will has no qualms about committing adultery with Emily, however, since he reasons that Margaret "would flop every man in Wakefield on my sofa if I didn't stop her" (116).

From her side, Emily holds Alfred responsible for the past twenty years of her life, during which she had four stillbirths but no children. All of Alfred's money cannot erase the shame he has caused her, especially during the loss of her last pregnancy, from the blood stain she left in a taxi cab to the dead body left in her "broken stretched-out bleeding body" (225). She feels the kind of shame that Clytemnestra described among the dead for having been murdered by her son. Emily's situation is similar to Clytemnestra's: The former holds Alfred responsible for killing their unborn children, just as Clytemnestra has never forgiven Agamemnon for sacrificing their daughter Iphigenia. She goes around the living with the shame that the ghost of Clytemnestra goes around the dead: For having killed her husband and having been murdered by her son, Clytemnestra is "a reproach that never stops wandering in my shame" (163). All of the pieces of the puzzle fit together for Emily: "I know why you had to marry me, why you forced me, why you held me down. I even know why my babies died" (190). It all stems from the Widow O'Brien scandal involving their father. At the moment of that realization, she experiences feelings comparable to those Clytemnestra expressed after having murdered her husband: "Why not pretend / I'm *not* Agamemnon's / Wife, but the ruthless ever-old wicked / Spirit of Atreus, barbarous feaster, / Adopting the semblance of corpse's consort / To pay him with primest of victims / The price of babies dead?" (90).

The series of Wakefield plays consists of seven works: *The Alfred Trilogy* framed by four one-act plays, whose characters and subject matter relate to the main body of the text. The references to characters from the trilogy give the complete cycle of Wakefield plays an aspect similar to that of Balzac's *Comédie humaine*. The first play is called *Hopscotch*, and the two characters are Will and Elsa, who calls herself Lorali. Will bears the name of Margaret's husband; he is associated with Alfred through his past actions. Long ago, when he was seventeen and Elsa was sixteen, he got her pregnant and ran away. Elsa claims alternately to having given the child away and to having killed it because the child had its father's face and she could not stand looking at it. The daughter whom Margaret gave away was also named Elsa and whom she called Lorali. Elsa reveals that her father died of a heart attack but is as mysterious about the circumstances surrounding her mother's death as Pa is about revealing the secret about the death of Alfred's mother. She shares Emily's interest in money and Roxy's interest in men. She specializes in baton twirling, the event that is taking place above Alfred's prison on the day he dies, the Fourth of July. There is a phallically symbolic connection between the batons and the Greasy Pole Contest. Will, in *Hopscotch*, finds the batons sexually stimulating: "Maybe it's the way you fingered the aluminum stick" (13). In the Greasy Pole Contest, "A long hard stiff pole sticks out from a wharf" (93). Men have to walk the length of the pole, and Emily finds the event "quite stimulating." Willie-Boy was twice champion. It was during one such contest that Emily, who allegedly has always had "a certain curiosity" about craggy old men, found herself in trouble with the locals of Magnolia, Massachusetts, who did not take well to her "*kind.* . . . A youngish woman, naked, a craggy old man, also naked, and a gaggle of locals chasing after" (97). Alfred watched as the men beat up Emily, just as Will once watched as Alfred's brother, as well as Alfred, had sex with Margaret. The pole reemerges in *Alfred Dies* with Emily and Lynch in control and Alfred the victim. At one point during the "trial," Lynch gets upset with Roxy and threatens to shove a greasy pole into her. A final element that ties *Hopscotch* to the trilogy are words that Alfred quotes from his father about

Wakefield, Massachusetts, U.S.A., North America, Western Hemisphere, Earth, Universe, Infinity, New England. (They are also close to Thornton Wilder's words in *Our Town*.)

The remaining three plays require far less commentary than the first. The second play to precede the trilogy is *The 75th*, involving the only two alumni who show up for a seventy-fifth high school class reunion. Its sole interest in this study is the references to characters who appear in the trilogy. For example, Amy refers to Alfred as the gentlest man she has ever known, and she regrets his untimely death; the poor man drank too much and had no close friends, but he did take walks with Amy. Cookie (as Arthur refers to himself) found Alfred to be "as weird as they come" (5). The reader learns that Alfred's brother, Bruce B. Webber, was valedictorian but then failed out of MIT. Cookie, like Alfred, owns a great deal of land. There are references, too, to the late Wilbur Lynch, to a girl who married another Lynch and had fourteen children, and to a girl "in a family way" who had to drop out of school. There is talk of the death of Amy's husband and of a teacher, for which Cookie feels responsible. Neither Cookie nor Amy ever had children. The two plays that follow the trilogy are *Stage Directions* and *Spared*. The first refers to the death of the characters' father and of a "family curse," and the second is about a man who attempts to commit suicide sixty times.

Both the *Oresteia* and *The Alfred Trilogy* deal with revenge. Aeschylus allowed his to end on notes of hope and triumph: Orestes is a free man, and the Furies are renamed the Gentle Ones. Not so with Horovitz. While Alfred feels hopeful as the final play closes, all he can hope for is a relief from the misery that is his life.

The message in *The Eumenides* is recited by the Chorus after Orestes wins his trial:

Slaughter for slaughter and ruin
Raging over the town.
Reciprocate graces instead
With mutual notions of love
And a single one of hate:
Such is the cure for much among men. (199)

The men and women who populate Horovitz's plays never got the message.

WORKS CITED

Aeschylus. *The Orestes Plays*. Trans. Paul Roche. New York: New American Library, 1962.

Horovitz, Israel. *The Wakefield Plays*. New York: Avon Books, 1979.

Roth, Marty. "'The Blood That Fury Breathed': The Shape of Justice in Aeschylus and
Shakespeare." *Comparative Literature Studies* 19, no.2 (1992): 141-56.

6

Double Mixed Memories

Liliane Kerjan

L'esprit n'est que sensibilité et mémoire.
Helvetius

The tricks played in our mind by our memory provide the starting impulses of the *Quannapowitt Quartet*, placing Israel Horovitz on a line with the American theatre of the same period that has also been represented by Edward Albee's *All Over* and *Listening* and even more obviously by Arthur Miller's double bill *Danger: Memory*! In four terse one-act plays, Horovitz offers various codes of representation, several layers of reality, oscillation between rage and frustration, but very little nostalgia, if any, building on the recollection of tragic events and visceral spasms sometimes counterbalanced by comic trivia, keeping his audience spellbound by his surgical and musical delicacy.

The quartet written between 1975 and 1977 is composed of *Hopscotch, The 75th, Stage Directions,* and *Spared,* four pieces framing *The Alfred Trilogy*, the quartet and the trilogy forming a seven-cycle meant to be performed over five evenings. This ambitious modern reference to Mystery cycles is known as *The Wakefield Plays* after the name of the playwright's home town in Massachusetts; to complete the onomastic and geographical identification, the alliterative title of the quartet comes from Lake Quannapowitt on the border of the small town of Wakefield. This "American Oresteia," to quote Martin Esslin's appraisal, therefore immediately disposes of the three unities of time, place, and action, each play concentrating on the acting out of the fantasies or emotions simmering in couples, in close-knit trios, or in a solitary individual's hot blood. If the Wakefield cycle has been described as "Horovitz's most extended treatment of American Guilt," the quartet combines mixed moods, melancholy being attached to youth, levity to old age, and double entries to memorabilia.[1] Although the four plays cover one century, there is no attempt to present the history of a rural or suburban New England: the perspective is private, narcissistic, and confessional, to a point. Resilience, reticence, absence: the tripod of memory will be the material of the playwright.

In *Stage Directions*, the only trinitarian play of the quartet, one character remembers the overlapping of the news on a radio program—a death announcement—and the notes of a Bach concerto for *Three Harpsichords in D Minor, alla Siciliana*, thus offering the listener the literal and metaphorical contours of the play in terms of key, measure, and ensemble. The three players, however, are not vocalists, but the playwright is vocal. Three siblings, named Richard, Ruth, and Ruby—as if they were the basic three R's of Victorian education—bereaved and sharing the common loss of both their parents, are at this point totally unable to communicate verbally due more to long-standing hatreds and quarrels, rather than their common emotional shock. Since the family reunion has become a meeting of mutes, Horovitz soon transforms it into an apologia of the acting progress, a brilliant game in which body language and mime are sustained by stage directions.

Samuel Beckett immediately comes to mind with the creation of the theatrical feast through self-contained injunctions, running commentaries, inverted messages, obsessional monodies. This systematic emphasis on stage directions, quite original in 1977, was tremendously well received some twenty-five years later at the Lucernaire in Paris, all the more so as in the same season the production of *Desire under the Elms* made full use of Eugene O'Neill's stage directions incorporated in the soundtrack. Such an interest for the peripheral indications of the playwright was no doubt initiated by such plays as *Stage Directions*. Occasionally the "dialogue" needs directions, playfully called "notes" by Horovitz: "[Note: The following speeches are to be spoken as though interruptions, often overlapping, as often blending. No considerable movement wanted during this section]," thus achieving an interpenetration with the rules of the game.[2] Choosing the private altar rather than the public ceremony, the intimistic ritual of the family get-together after the funeral rather than a grander, more spectacular scene by the grave at sundown according to the Jewish custom, Horovitz gets to the more trivial as well as the more moving moments of confrontation with the icons of the dead. Most of all, he uses the technicalities of the theatre in a totally instrumental way, creating life out of stage directions the way Beckett triggered life out of flashes of light.

The resonance of Bach in *Stage Directions*—just as *Line* was under the auspices of Mozart—is sustained with arithmetic precision. The mourners, Richard, Ruth, and Ruby, are in fact part of a quartet of siblings, originally two pairs: the sisters, Ruth and Ruby, and the brothers, Robert and Richard. These two equal groups provide a double perspective of presence and absence, Robert having died three years before. Similarly the life-and-death opposition is carried out by two threesomes: the siblings briefly united in the family mansion after the funeral and confronted with the loss of three missing members: their parents and brother. Furthermore, past, present, and future have the same milestone, a burial, with three different causes: disease, accident, and suicide, the spectator being left with the anticipation of a composition *en abyme of souvenirs*, like a series of Chinese boxes full of souvenirs.

The memory of past endearments explains and revives present antagonisms: Ruth and Ruby were obviously very fond of their brother Robert—Ruby "loved her brother, Robert, deeply. Mourned his death, not forgotten" (263)—while they dislike their brother Richard. Ruby misses their father, while Richard and Ruth relate to their mother. The play is a series of confrontations with one's alliances and constitutive knots and frames, a revelation made apparent by the unveiling of draped mirrors and portraits, which adds another variation to the interplay of appearance, representation, and make-believe. The disclosure of the parental image reiterated to remain each time a personal ordeal, betrays the emotional turmoil without words:

Ruby: Ruby exposes twenty-four-by-thirty-six-inch tinted photograph of their parents, posed, taken on occasion of their fortieth wedding anniversary. Ruby stares at photograph . . .
Richard: . . . Richard carefully, silently, removes black fabric veil from photograph, allowing fabric to fall to floor beside his feet (. . .), stares intently at the photograph, reaching his left hand end up and forward, touching the cheek of the man in the photograph. He rubs his finger gently across the face of the man, through the void between the man and the woman, finally allowing his finger to stop directly on the chin on the image of the woman in the photograph. (265, 267)

The contrasting attitudes of the brother and sisters, motionless with heads bowed, will never lead to a communion; the spiritual contact between the living and the dead seems easier to achieve in some egotistic moment of bereaved wonder. The three siblings in the living room of their parents' home, ironically enough, remain so strained that they are unable to touch one another because they are "frozen," "stopped," "quenched," and have not been on speaking terms for several years:

Ruth: Ruth stands, moves toward Ruby, tentatively: painfully slow, frightened. She plans to embrace her sister, but will not have the courage to do so. (266)

Richard, full of contempt for his sisters, "smiles, seeing Ruby's pain" (264), and so does Ruth in spite of exchanged acknowledgments.

The confrontation offers another thread of irony attached to the social evolution: Whereas the parents are immortalized in a conventional pose on the celebration of their fortieth wedding anniversary, the siblings, self-conscious in all their attitudes and very fidgety during this brief visit, are unattached. The son is single, the daughters divorced. Ruby left her husband "first to door, first to street, first to forget" (263), and no descendent can be expected—"Engendered nothing, ovaries broken at birth" (263), as she remarks. Consequently, the original potential and strength is dissipating, gradually oozing out, dried up like the drinks spilled on the carpet, leaving nothing but stains and broken glass. The impression of emptiness and doom settles in as the family reunion turns into a meeting of the dead with living mutes and as the initial combination of three males and three females is reduced to Richard and Ruth when ultimately Ruby commits suicide, as if to top the funeral pile. Hence, the two "hawklike" (255) siblings survive; the "wrenlike" (255) figure is defeated. The family curse hits once again—men being caught by an incurable disease, women by violent death.

With the last pair of survivors, Horovitz shifts the focus on one of the cardinal motifs of the Wakefield plays: incest. As soon as Ruth enters the family living room and sees Richard already there, she is determined to force his attention. Noticing that he "adjusts his underwear, discreetly" (257), she immediately picks up the clue:

Ruth: Ruth pretends to be removing her overcoat while never removing her stare from the back of Richard's head she slips her hand inside her coat and discreetly adjusts her brassière. (257)

From then on their tentative striptease will overlap competitively, the overlapping effect being used a second time when the three characters recall the breaking of the news of their parents' deaths in their respective surroundings, linking each time fragmentation and reunion:

Ruth: Ruth removes her gloves . . . and hat . . .
Richard: [overlapping] . . . placing it precisely beside his first shoe . . .
Ruth: [overlapping] . . . tossing them in a heap on the sofa . . .
Richard: [overlapping] . . . He then peels off his other sock . . .
Ruth: [overlapping] . . . She then hoists her skirt and unhitches her stocking-top from the front and back garters on her garter-belt. (258)

An unfading mimetism will bring the three siblings to similar gestures: Ruth and Ruby adjust their skirts and brassieres one after the other, while Richard "scratches his chest" (264), or again:

Ruby: Ruby moves to Richard's chair, sits, allowing her skirt to remain pleated open, high on her leg.
Richard: Richard notices her naked thigh.
Ruth: Ruth notices Richard noticing Ruby's naked thigh.
Richard: Richard notices that Ruth has noticed him. (268)

Now in his forties, Richard plays not only master of ceremonies but messenger of death. He has not spoken to Ruth or Ruby for four years, to his father for five years. Yet he is the one who arranged for his mother to collect her husband's body and fly it home, and he is the one who summons his sister for the funeral of both parents. The sinister brother is alive: the dead brother was lovable. Nevertheless, the two sisters never said good-bye to their beloved Robert: Ruth was never reached by her parents, and Ruby arrived too late. Consequently the two sisters mourn their brother "silently," "endlessly." After a final bow and sob in front of his parents' photograph, Richard "stares at Ruth, arm outstretched in her direction, fist pointing accusingly . . . watching to see if she will have the strength to cross the room to him" (269).

A similar gap and complementarity crops up in connection with languages. Richard is an academic working in the Department of Asian Studies of the University of Vermont, where, according to Ruth, he is "employed as nobody, researching nothing, touching no one" (261). Ruth, in spite of her total ignorance of its languages, has always loved Asia; even when she found herself surrounded by Cantonese, she managed to survive just as she had previously in Northern China, although she could not speak a word of the dialects. The interest of Horovitz for languages as demonstrated earlier in *The Indian Wants the Bronx* or *The Primary English Class* is beyond the point here, yet once more absence of words will breed disaster.

Stage Directions is a play of entrances and exits. Coming in stealthily, one by one, the three siblings depart abruptly, one by one, respecting the order of seniority. As always, Horovitz is at his best in brisk, violent denouements: Richard drops his armband, thus signaling the end of commitment and the funeral ceremony. From then on, the acceleration betrays an irrational fear of being left the last and all alone in the family sanctuary:

Ruth: Ruth finds shoes, slips quickly into same, moves to sofa, rapidly collecting her outer clothing.
Ruby: Ruby, suddenly realizing she might be left alone in room, moves quickly away from photograph, sees Ruth; stops, frozen.
Ruth: Ruth races to redress herself in her coat, jamming hat on to head, stockings in coat pocket.
Ruby: Ruby has her outer clothing now in her hands but realises she is too late.
Ruth: Ruth has moved quickly and successfully, assuming an exit position at the door, coat buttoned closed. (269)

Exactly like Jerry on his bench at Central Park in Edward Albee's *Zoo Story*, Ruby will impale herself on the sofa. She was the perfect scapegoat from the start; shocked by her absence at Robert's funeral, her family never forgave her. Yet this young girl banished from the family circle was once a cheerleader and a promising young scholar; today she is perceived only as the sum of the drawbacks of her elders, afflicted with her brother's "studied pomposity: his gravity" (261), her sister's "unfathomable lack of courage" (261). She crystallizes the decadence of the elders, too heavy for her "rich girl's shoulders" (261), too cumbersome for her "small Vuitton weekend case" (264). She will drop objects accidentally, always caught unawares, always late and blundering. The allusion to *Zoo Story* would place Horovitz in the absurdist vein of the sixties and at the same time close to Sam Shepard or Tennessee Williams: Ruby, a cheerleader, and a Ph.D. fascinated by Joyce and Woolf is reminiscent of Blanche Dubois in love with British literature and finally destroyed by a world to which she no longer belongs. Ruby is ultimately trapped alone in the family mansion where she decides to join her parents in death; softly caressing their images, already "frozen, sad eyed" (270), she reaches her last stage.

The twin piece, *Spared*,—same place, the vicinity of Lake Quannapowitt, and same time, the present—switching from the hysterical to the obsessional mode brings a perfect counterpoint. There the recurrent suicidal sprees of a man always fail, and although he is suspended in "infinite blackness and space" (274), his memories seem to keep him well and alive. While the last tableau of *Stage Directions* offers Ruby bleeding herself to death with the jagged neck of a glass decanter, at the first curtain of *Spared,* an old man pulls the trigger of a pistol pressed to his temple and gets no gunshot. This nonevent is the starting point of the unraveling of the story of his life summed up at the opening: "I have tried to destroy myself more than sixty different times" (274).

A persistent, incurable guilt colors both plays: black space, black armbands, black garments, black drapes. If Ruby feels she has never been forgiven for her absence at her brother's funeral, the old man is intensely aware that for him there is "No pardon. No amen. No matter how I tried, I could not end it" (292). Faced with the same malediction, both characters will take similar steps, become wandering Jews, share literary inclinations—as a student the old Man was an expert on Blake's *Jerusalem*—and yet come to antithetical ends: the woman dies, the man survives. This sexual discrimination is interesting in itself. Horovitz, like Sam Shepard, draws powerful male characters and has not so far given as much attention to female parts, with the exception of his widow. The old age of the protagonist, another Krapp, is a pretext for copious memories, burlesque episodes piling up all sorts of male pranks or weird accidents: The old man, nicknamed "kiss of death"(286) when he was selling death insurance, survived eight incurable diseases, tied himself to the train track, tried to strangle himself and to perish by fire, always engaging himself in scenarios reminiscent of the silent movies: "No breath, no sound, no voice; no scream" (276), "Not a sound. No cry, no scream" (277). In spite of their nefarious contents, such evocations are happy memories and represent the survival kit of a lucky fellow. Similarly, the reminiscence of his early years sounds highly positive—"children happy, laughter all around, mother all ears, hugs abundant, sister wide-eyed adoring" (292)—as opposed to the blackout in the family of Ruby, Ruth, and Richard.

Whereas in *Stage Directions* the confrontation of memories and the memory of past confrontations generate a regression on the verge of autism leading to self-destruction and violent death, in *Spared* memories ensure construction and urgent life. An exercise in the vein of *Krapp's Last Tape* with four voices for a man at different ages and six speakers for his environment, *Spared* is also a mock-heroic version of the Wandering Jew turned philandering atheist, his memories retaining the branded traces of fleeting contacts with death and flimsy love episodes that he seems to be able to replay at leisure like so many mischievous pieces by Eric Satie.

Hopscotch, presented in Paris in 1993 on a double bill with *Stage Directions*, gripped and seduced the French public, who immediately recognized highly popular themes developed by Flaubert and Balzac: a young woman's life with the burden of her memories and fantasies. Elsa, alias Lorali—or Lorah-liar, as her afternoon companion puts it—is indeed the modern version of the much-admired literary *femme de trente ans*, some new Emma Bovary: *"Le coeur a sa mémoire à lui. Telle femme incapable de se rappeler les événements les plus graves se souviendra pendant toute sa vie des choses qui importent à ses sentiments."*[3] And this will apply all the more as the provincial Elsa never leaves Wakefield and totally misses out on the sophistication of world travel, just as she misses out on the political and cultural events of the sixties. Elsa is a prisoner of her childish grid, with its simplistic geometry of earth, heaven, and hell.

Sexual attraction, anger and fear, hopelessness, the weight of betrayals are slowly distilled, while lies, pretense, and painful memories gradually wind up into a pathetic interrogation:

Will: Listen! If you had a son . . . and he was seventeen . . . and he got a local girl knocked up . . . and he could either stay here and . . . be married to her . . . or he could get the hell out 'ta Wakefield! . . . which would you want him to do ??? (20)

The encounter of the former lovers, provoked by Will, is meant to smooth out the bitter years separating their college idyll from the empty present. Once more the intimate meeting is nearly a family reunion or funeral, Elsa's parents having died four weeks before, without forgiving the young man's sin. The twelve or fourteen years of waste have been filled with resentment, the young man has become a midlevel manager traveling extensively with an expertise in demolition, while the young-woman-turned-nymphomaniac is still playing hopscotch in their home town. Their analyses remain as unreconcilable as the gender gap that culminates in tragic outbursts:

Will: Elsa !

Elsa: There's no son! I killed it! I couldn't take his crying. I couldn't take his noise. [Pauses.] He had your face. That's what I really couldn't stand . . . He was you! [Pauses.] It's true!
Will: I didn't make a mistake at all did I? I did just the right thing didn't I? [Pauses, then suddenly] I think you're a *monster!* (21)

The hopscotch grid, just like the symbolic line, maps out the ambitions and strategies of an arrested mental development, since Elsa never recovered. Left weeping on the bench, confronted with her name and the heart and arrow drawn by Will, she is abandoned once more, hopelessly destroyed and immature .

Taking place on the territory "of a tribe that vanished" (6), introduced by the sentimental tune "Was a Sunny Afternoon" (5), with characters pretending that they have forgotten each other's name, *Hopscotch* strikes the keynotes of reminiscence and regrets so characteristic of the cycle of the Wakefield plays, announcing the family curses and *Buried Child* of Sam Shepard, denouncing the vulgarity and endemic prostitution of American suburbia with touches of black humor to temper the malaise of strained love ballads.

The September stance of *Hopscotch* is followed by a twin piece, *The 75th*, another September evening, another duet, donkey's years again, but this time the two characters, Amy Chamberlain and "Cookie" Silverstein, are both ninety-three and ready to celebrate their class reunion, the old boys and girls who studied together seventy-five years before at Wakefield High School. Whereas *Hopscotch* covers the grim ending of a college passion, *The 75th* closes with the first quiver of mutual interest and the hearty promise of a rendezvous, exchanged with exquisite tact and delicacy. The careful symmetry of the two plays is perfect as the confessions, the untangling of memories lead to opposite directions due to unabashed sincerity, emotional implication, and temporal distance.

Unable to identify the other at first, Amy and Cookie are nevertheless quite relieved from the moment they meet in this half-blind date. They try to guess, rather than remember, tossing names in a very playful manner. As they rediscover mutual friends, they trust each other:

Amy: I wish I could say I remember you. I don't.
Cookie: May I be truthful?
Amy: I wish you would.
Cookie: I don't remember you, either.
Amy: But that's just ridiculous!
Cookie: But it 's the truth! (34)

There is no shame, no embarrassment but the saving grace of amnesia leading to conjuring up of neighbors, classmates, relatives, warmhearted, talented people such as Miss Caswell: "Wonderful woman. Wonderful teacher and a wonderful human being to boot" (43). Avoiding altogether the historical evocation of Wakefield at the turn of the century, they concentrate on people, on flirts and infatuations, on boys' fondling girls, convinced that their memory has not failed:

Amy: Old age is supposed to dull it all . . .
Cookie: Blend it together . . .
Amy: Not I.
Cookie: Me, neither . . . (47)

Friendly though formal, they attempt a few steps of a waltz, pick up the words of a favorite song, mention their marriages with ease and detachment, visualize the group of cheerleaders of the school, comment upon their relatives very freely—"my entire family was flukish, genetically speaking" (30), or: "my sister, poor thing, she was incredibly short . . . nearly a legal midget" (30). Thus, a lifetime fresco full of movement is punctuated by laughters and smiles without ever trespassing on intimacy:

Amy: I'm a bit overprotective with my memories . . .
Cookie: I understand. (52)

Unlike Eugène Ionesco's old couple in *The Chairs*, Amy and Cookie do not spend the evening waiting for improbable guests as soon as they discover that they are the only survivors among a group of twelve classmates. They, too, have been spared, hence their propensity to enjoy life and retain positive memories, their youthful energy reflected in their kicking and whacking the jukebox. A perfect link between *Hopscotch* and *Spared*, *The 75th* takes stock of life as a privilege by showcasing the memories of love and the education of sensibility:

Amy: Seventy-five . . . [A pause] I remember being two.
Cookie: Two years old?
Amy: I do. I have a memory. My mum . . . cuddling me. (46)

Similarly, they remember their alumni meetings in terms of trophies—in other words victories—unlike Arthur Miller's dejected and jaded characters.

Horovitz, has become a classic in France and it is quite revealing that the theaters there that initially played Ionesco and once described Horovitz as a tender American hoodlum repeatedly recast his one-act plays; such a success, praised by the avant-garde press as much as by more classical voices, is best explained by Claude Roy in the preface for the adaptation of *The Widow's Blind Date*: "L'art d'Israel est à sa perfection dans l'économie: économie d'interprètes (avec trois personnages, il peut évoquer tout un peuple), économie de mots (l'arrière texte chuchote longuement comme les vagues derrière la plus brève réplique), économie d'action."[4] As Roy astutely observes, "The art of Israel (Horovitz) reaches perfection through economy, the economy of spare cast (with three characters he can call up an entire people) economy of spare words (the aftertext of which whispers endlessly like the waves behind the shortest line), and economy of spare action. Economy, the keynote of the quartet, does not preclude a capacity for wonder, a vulnerability best encapsulated in the interplay of loss and gain, the sifting and mixing of memories.

NOTES

1. Ruby Cohn, *New American Dramatists: 1960-1980* (London: Macmillan Modern Dramatists, 1982), 55.

2. Israel Horovitz, *The Wakefield Plays: Stage Directions, Spared, Hopscotch, The 75th* (New York: Avon Books, 1979), 261. All further citations from this volume will appear parenthetically within the text.

3. "Our heart has its own memory. A woman unable to recollect the most serious events will remember things of importance to her feelings for the rest of her life."

4. Claude Roy, *Le Baiser de la veuve* (Paris: Edilig, Collection "Théâtrales," 1984), 7.

7

The Widow's Blind Date: "A Shitload of Getting Together"

Leslie Kane

In his depiction of violence in America, Israel Horovitz has continually dramatized variations on the theme of violence—physical violence in *The Indian Wants the Bronx* and *Rats,* psychic violence in *It's Called the Sugar Plum, Line, Acrobats*, and *The Primary English Class,* and economic violence in *North Shore Fish.* Dramatizing how violence can and does spring from futility and frustration, Horovitz's theatre is an extraordinary study of the psychology of terrorism. Referring to *Indian,* Harold Clurman once observed that Horovitz's characters "produce shivers because their menace and violence are part of the greater beastliness inherent in our society, which, because it does not inspire creative action based on human thought and energy, turns to wanton and senseless destructiveness."[1] Horovitz's recent drama, the brilliantly imagined and chillingly executed *The Widow's Blind Date,* similarly derives its power from wanton destructiveness. Violence takes the form of a gang rape—at once realistic and symbolic—that is as violent as anything that Horovitz has ever imagined.

Until recently, the subject of rape and its effect upon women's lives and social status was subject to remarkably little discussion, research, or analysis. "Indeed," insists Susan Griffin in "The Politics of Rape," "the obscurity of rape in print exists in marked contrast to the frequency of rape in reality, *for forcible rape is the most frequently committed violent crime in America today.*"[2] But a significant sociological and psychological investigation of 646 rape cases documented in *Patterns of Forcible Rape* confirmed that sex offenders do not constitute a unique or pathological type—tending to be different from normal, well-adjusted males only in having a greater tendency to express violence and rage—nor is rape the consequence of impulsive behavior. Rather, Menachem Amir's study revealed that more than 85 percent of rapes were planned and executed by young men between the ages of ten and nineteen; that the gang rape (pairs or groups of men) constituted more than half of the 646 cases studied (with 43 percent pairs or groups of men); that the most excessive degrees of violence occurred in gang rape, with the presence of other men encouraging sadism; that the first rapist was more commanding and violent than the others; and that more than 90 percent of the victims, women between the ages of fifteen and twenty-four, knew their assailants and did not report the rape.[3]   "The theory that women have liked being raped," argues Griffin, "extends itself by deduction to the proposition that most or much of rape is provoked by the victim" who "asks for it" by dressing or behaving provocatively.[4]   But whether the victim exhibits outright or overt seduction, covert or suggestive behavior, the offender's interpretation leads to his action and legitimizes it for him. In other words, "teasers" are stereotypically women of low moral worthiness, and rape is viewed by the offender as a means of punishment and social domination.[5]

In the spectrum of male behavior, rape is the "perfect combination of sex and violence," what Susan Brownmiller in *Against Our Will* refers to as "a conscious form of intimidation by which *all men* keep *all women* in a state of fear."[6]   Thus, in our culture, where male eroticism is wedded to power, the startling increase of rape by teenagers may be explained in good part by the fact that it is viewed as a rite of passage and as an expression of adolescent male bonding.[7]   But if a male society rewards aggressive sexual behavior, such behavior is ultimately sexually schizophrenic in that the masculine man is also expected to prove himself a protector of women, suggesting a dichotomy between those who protect and those who rape. These roles, too, are confused in the light of the fact that chivalrous behavior extends to the chaste woman only. The fallen woman does not deserve protection, or more specifically, what has been defiled cannot again be violated.   "Presumably, then, the female victim in any case will have been sufficiently socialized so as to not consciously feel any strong need for vengeance," and "if she does feel this need, society does not speak to it."[8]

But in *The Widow's Blind Date*, Horovitz not only speaks to the issues of revenge; he exposes and explodes the myths associated with rape, extending that rape metaphorically to suggest personal and social terrorism, humiliation, hostility, and degradation. Transposing a friend's detailed confession to the gang rape of a high school student on the beach into a chance encounter years later between the victim, Margy, and two of the men "who savaged her adolescence," Horovitz sends the victim, as well as himself, on a quest into a painful memory. Even after more than twenty-five years, the playwright clearly remembers that the young woman, whom one of his closest friends had raped, possessed "the most frightened eyes I have ever seen in my entire life ... then or now or ever to come."[9]

Recalling the five people jockeying for first place on an imaginary line in Horovitz's early play, *Line, Widow's Blind Date* raises the ante to ten men who quite literally compete to be first in a realistic line to rape a seventeen-year-old woman. Although reminiscent of Durrenmatt's *The Visit*, in which a violated woman returns to the scene of her disgrace with a detailed plan for revenge, Horovitz envisions Margy as a woman whose only plan for this reunion is "an evening of apology and forgiveness."[10]   Instead, she nearly relives one of the worst nights of her life with two men stuck sexually in the second grade. As we witness what Horovitz terms her "'radicalization'—her trip from Forgiveness to Revenge," what emerges is not the anticipated revenge drama but a fascinating exploration of victimization—of victim and victimizer—in an evening notable for its vacillation, vilification, and vivisection.[11]

Paralleling Harold Pinter, Horovitz situates the action in the dark, confined setting of a baling pressroom, with its "metaphor of history compressed and recycled," its claustrophobia and intimations of menace, its seemingly aimless, colloquial speech laced with innuendo, its realistic props metamorphosed into instruments of torture, its intrusion of memory and betrayal, and its potential for theatrical surprise.[12]   Like Pinter, Horovitz establishes familiarity and strips it away: language functions as both weapon and defensive mechanism, characters are kinetic and quiescent, nightmares assume a striking resemblance to reality, and truth is unreliable and unattainable.   In this baling pressroom similar to one Horovitz worked in as a boy, where he claims to have learned about life "through the teachings of day-laborers, bums and wineos who philosophized on Work and Women"—the very same men who had gang raped a woman in a laundry adjacent to his uncle's shop whom Horovitz vividly recalls as offensive in their "'cat-calling' despite the woman's apparent terror"—the playwright counterpoints Margy's wit and syntactic polish with the rapists' faulty English, underscoring the elusive, wordless history that binds them together.[13] Structurally, the play is as taut as the bundles of paper bound by wire in the baling press, the play's central metaphor, that is at once an image of domination, a vise squeezing out confessions, and to use Kevin Kelly's term, "a slow guillotine."[14]

The playwright does some of his most sophisticated work in dramatizing the foundation of the men's friendship. In a world that has given neither of them a chance, these two high school classmates, Archie, a lumpish philosopher, and George, a razor-sharp "steel blade in search of the nearest soft underbelly,"[15] stuck in a dead-end job at an adolescent wage, cling to teenage bonding rituals such as reviewing events from high school, ranking women as "dogs," "rich bitches," or "pigs," swilling beer, and rough-housing that they sense will somehow empower them.[16] Archie alludes to "a kind of supper thing I gotta do" with Margy Burke, whom both have known since childhood, and who has returned to Wakefield for a death vigil for her brother, Swede (4). Despite an animated discussion about Margy and corroboration of shared reminiscences—the rape excluded—confusion and contradiction prevail, and by the time that Margy makes a much-delayed entrance, it is impossible to differentiate between truth and gossip: Was Margy the school's star scholar worthy of Archie's years of devotion or the school slut, one Bunny Palumbo, whom George remembers as a tease who allowed boys to look down her blouse?[17] While the men hope that the reunion will provide one or both with a sexual payoff, Margy immediately disarms and confuses them with behavior alternately flirtatious and condescending and language both patently sexual and erudite.

Throughout much of the first act, Archie, George, and Margy attempt to place people and events in their shared past through nicknames and anecdotes, although significantly, Margy is hard-pressed to remember George "Kermie" Ferguson. That which is initially casual quickly becomes caustic and confrontational, sustaining a crucial but delicate balance of provocation and humiliation. As the thirty-seven-year-old critic from New York University "mocks the men's hopeless English and they mock her schoolmarmish pretensions," it becomes increasingly apparent that their reminiscences camouflage a secret, erotic triangle of Archie's love and George's lust that binds them together.[18] Cumulatively, the psychosexual battle of wills and wits explodes the pretense of reunion with its implicit suggestion of communion and resolution. Thus, in the second act, in which both scene and subject darken, it is obvious that in playing one friend against the other, Margy has sought to disarm both men and empower herself. But humiliated by Margy's "smart remarks," enraged by what he perceives as her efforts to make them both look like "God damn fools" (88), and sexually frustrated and jealous of Archie, George, misinterpreting Margy's silence as weakness, violently seizes control of both the emasculating bitch and his spineless friend by fondling Margy's breasts in full view of a paralyzed Archie and countering with a few sarcastic "smart remarks" of his own:

You ain't in no hoity-toity *Worcester,* or no *Springfield*, or no *Nooo Yahwk*, or no *London*, *England* or no *Paris, France* . . . You're in none of those high-falutin, hoity-toity, swell places, now, Bunny Palumbo! You're home, *Home*! And when you're home, sis'tah, you are what you are. (*Pauses;* angrily) *What you are* !! (*Pauses*) Gangbanged at Fisherman's Beach. (93)

Although Archie threatens George, implores him to desist, and questions the purpose of bringing up old news, his lack of effectiveness in the face of George's unmitigated rage and Margy's eerie silence not only implicitly confirms the extent of George's hostility and authority but wordlessly conveys Archie's guilt and Margy's vulnerability. The point of this exposure, insists George, now lecturing on life as Margy previously pontificated on language, is that "this girl thinks she can come back to town and be new . . . and she can't . . . she can't. That ain't the way things are. This girl ain't no Princess Margaret . . . this is plain Margy . . . Bunny Palumbo . . . blind Swede's no-titted sis'tah . . . our stuck-up Salutatorian" (94). Unlike Stanley in *A Streetcar Named Desire,* George need not threaten Margy. Merely addressing her by her nickname, "Bunny," toying with his prey, and referring possessively to Margy as "*our* stuck-up Salutatorian," George telescopes twenty years back to Fisherman's Beach.[19]

Vividly conveying the motivation and savagery of the gang rape, George simultaneously justifies his psychological and sexual terrorism of Margy, both then and now. The disparity between Margy's personal and financial independence and George's entrapment in a low-paying, menial job in the same town in which he was raised is exacerbated by her refusal (or inability) to respond to him. Although Horovitz heightens our sensitivity to George's personal frustration and hopelessness, from George's perspective, his control of his world can be accomplished only by destroying Margy's. Thus, George's victimization by society is mirrored in his victimization of Margy.[20] Once again Margy is that seventeen-year-old woman, surprised by the attack and entrapped by her attackers, dehumanized and defenseless on the sand. Illustrating the surprise and concomitant paralysis of terrorism, Horovitz presents a victim linguistically and emotionally tied in knots.[21] Stripped of language, by which she has previously commanded respect and inspired contempt, Margy is again rendered powerless; she can neither fight, nor run, nor scream.

Margy's silence, palpable, even eloquent, in stark contrast to her former loquaciousness, is even more dramatic when contrasted with Archie's tears, into which he has now dissolved. Ignoring her anguish, George thrusts himself into Margy's mind, forcing her to remember the gang bang line-up and prodding her, as if by electric shock, with his torture by tirade: "You remember who went first? You remember?" he insists, striking terror into her heart. "*Do you remember? Do . . . you . . . remember?*" Her primal scream reverberates in the silence as she spits out the one word: "*You!*" but the triumphant Kermie, now finally recognized, is not yet satisfied. Pushing deeper and deeper into her psychic space, George commands: "What's wanted here is the memory and name of the man who went second . . . number two . . . sloppy seconds . . . *sloppy seconds.*" Receiving no reply and relishing every minute of her suffering, George commences chanting in a sing song cheerleader's rhythm:

Who? Who?
Who was number two!
Who? Who?
Who was number two!
Who? Who?
Who was number two? (94–95)

With Archie weeping openly, and the "acrid act of purification consuming the territory like napalm,"[22] George mercilessly squeezes the memory from both Margy and Archie, and then giggling, summarily condenses it in his own inimitable way:

I led off, Archie was sloppy seconds. Swede was *numero trez*, and Spike the Loon was the definite clean-up . . . I myself always knew Moose Burke was a complete shithead, but who woulda guessed he woulda gone for the town pump, huh? (To Archie) Married her. Jee-*zuz*! (97) [23]

Enraged by George's giggle, deprecating reference to her dying brother and dead husband, Moose, and to her as the "town-pump," Margy responds as two distinctly different characters: one, the teenage "toughie" who was raped at Fisherman's Beach; the other, the mature widow and mother of two who has attempted to build a life under the shadow of that rape.

   In her essay, "From Split Subject to Split Britches," Sue-Ellen Case offers an illuminating explanation for the dichotomy of Margy's character and speech, alternating between that of an articulate adult and a "toughie" from Wakefield, whose slang authentically conveys who she once was. She expands on Lacan's premise that the "split subject is constructed upon a development and a physiology that the female does not share . . . Because the subject of discourse or representation is gendered as male, [the woman] split[s] once as the male-identified subject [and] once more as the woman who observes her own subject position."[24] This split is dramatized and emphasized through discourse. Case argues that the woman "cannot appear as a single, whole continuous subject as the male because she senses that his story is not her story," a point clearly illustrated by differing versions of the rape.[25] The split is further dramatized through younger and older selves, as in Marsha Norman's *Getting Out*, where Arlie/Arlene are so out of touch with each other that they appear to be different characters, and in *Widow* by Margy seventeen and thirty-seven, respectively.[26] Furthermore, split subjects share a number of attributes: "Mature subjects must struggle with that earlier identification, both to overcome it and to retain its power," and "other characters become relegated as objects of the woman's affections, hostilities, losses and triumphs."[27] Hence, when George taunts Margy, "You can read all the books you want and speak all the languages goin', Marg, and you ain't *never* . . . *never* . . . you ain't never gonna live that one down. (*Pauses*) Ain't that a fact? Ain't it?" (98), he underscores his control of history by imposing his inarticulate discourse. For her entire adult life Margy has indeed tried to live "that one down," but inspired by George's giggle, for a brief moment Margy is that teenage toughie, spitting out her rage and taunting her rapist, "C'mon ya blow'ah. . . . Ya wanna hit a girrlll? Huh? Huh?" (98). Almost immediately, the mature Margy assumes control, presence, and speech, and the rage we hear is her own:

I was seventeen, George, seventeen. Do you know how old seventeen is, George? Not very. *Not God damn very* ! Do you have any idea what it was you stuck into my seventeen-year-old MIND, George? Do you? *Do you* ? (*Pauses*) " Why'd they pick me? Was I too provocative? Was it the way I smiled? Did I look available? Did I look like an easy lay? " (*Pauses*) What was it, George? What was it about me that you hated . . . so deeply . . . so completely . . . so absolutely . . . that made you want to *make love,* hmmm? (*Pauses*) Years, God damn *years* of walking around like a zombie, wondering was I really, deep down, underneath it all *lookin' for it* ? I remember, ya' know, George. I really do. I was kinda standing off by myself, pitch black out, moon at all . . . and alls'a' sudden somebody turns me around and kisses me. I pull back from him, tryin' ta laugh it off, I say, "No thanks, really . . ." And he's giggling this kinda' high-pitched girlish giggle. (*She imitates George's giggle, then suddenly moves to George, faces him, eyeball to eyeball*). Weren't you giggling, Kermie, huh? And you hit me. You took your hand and you hit me. . . . Seventeen years old, five-foot-one-inch . . . and you hit me. And I whack you back and you hit me and you hit me. . . . and then you and your kind did what they did. You line up . . . *LINE UP* . . . you know what I was doin' while you was doin' it to me? . . . I was thinking that I was getting run over . . . by a bus. . . . That's how much I *loved it*. (98–100)

Addressing the issues of provocation, guilt, abuse of mind and body of the rape victim, Margy is now prepared to seek revenge for her lost youth and dignity, though, significantly, she cannot yet articulate the savagery by its name.

The violence recalled sets off a series of explosions and repeated blows mirroring Margy's vivid memory—Margy's directed at George and George's directed at his rival, Archie—but as George unhitches his belt, signaling his readiness to use both sexual and physical weapons at his disposal, it appears that the nightmare remembered will in fact be reenacted—that George will rape her again, seeking the sexual payoff that he assumes Archie received while he was out picking up the Chinese take-out. As George rips open Margy's blouse—the same blouse she did or did not allow George or anyone else to look down—the act of violence simultaneously conveys the tearing rape of the seventeen-year-old Margy and the tearing of the fabric of lies that has been protecting them all. Margy's bare breast and "naked shoulders glisten against the filth of the old newspapers" and George's "leering, hateful stare" (104).

Although George initially profits from the psychological advantage, the element of surprise, and the disabling of his friend and long-time competitor, Archie literally rises to the challenge and proves himself a worthy opponent. Enraged by George's action, Archie finally pulls himself off the floor and kills George, gaining both his revenge for George's foxing him out of line in the first rape and his pride by protecting Margy from a second rape, as he did not twenty years earlier. George's bleeding body is flipped into the baler, his face exploding blood, his terrible giggle finally silenced.

In her review of *The Widow's Blind Date,* Laurie Winer suggests that the play's final moment is "most incredible" when "Horovitz asks us to believe that Margy masterminded the evening's bloody outcome, and that she is leaving to finish off the other men who violated her."[28]   On the contrary, the conclusion is entirely credible as is Margy's rejection of Archie's patrimony—his warning "run . . . run, Margy, run, run, Margy, run, run, run . . . Margy, run . . . run," with its implication of long-delayed protection and responsibility (107).   Notably, similarities abound in this play to Edward Albee's *The Zoo Story*, specifically in Jerry's summons to Peter: "You better hurry now, Peter. Hurry, you'd better go."[29]   Even more applicable are analogues to Albee's *Who's Afraid of Virginia Woolf.*   One may read Margy as Martha, afraid of the "big, bad wolf," read George as George, "the weasel," and view Archie, "the goat," as he is referred to, as Nick.   Similarly, *Widow* closely parallels the paradigmatic "Fun and Games, "Walpurgisnacht," and "Exorcism," but with the essential difference that Horovitz affords Margy, if not Archie, the possibility of transformation consistent with her refusal to be victimized.   Bearing what Case terms "the essential scars of 'getting out' of the old object position and 'getting into' the subject position," Margy struggles for independence from the judgments of society and provides an image of "women in transition from social and cultural repression to the liberation of self-definition."[30]

In this final moment we understand the full significance of the title *The Widow's Blind Date.*   Margy's date has been with herself, her past, and her nightmares, having had what she calls "a shitload of getting together" with these men for "365 nights a year for three and a half years" (101). Now, having faced up to her demons and faced down her rapists, Margy is ready to forgive herself. No longer is she content to lock herself up with these ghosts, as Lavinia Mannon does at the end of *Mourning Becomes Electra.*   Rather, running her hand through George's blood, Margy confirms his death and affirms her own survival with a stunning response: "I'll be back, Archie. It's a long list" (107).

Although violence has consistently been a recurrent theme in Horovitz's plays, the playwright maintains that while his use of violence has never been gratuitous, the escalation of violence in such plays as *Indian, Rats,* and *Widow* reflects his attempt to understand those forces that may have motivated the violent action.   Thus, at the end of *Widow,* Horovitz has sought to encourage the audience "to feel," in his words, "affection for the bad guys . . . a sudden realization that they are only people—and an understanding of the things that move them to do the terrible things that they have done."[31]   Increasingly committed to the dramatization of human frailty, Horovitz concludes this drama not with Margy's ominous warning, but with a poignant portrayal of Archie's attempting to revive his dead friend:

This ain't funny, Kermie, ya dumb blow'ah. . . . This is wicked awful scarey, Kerm !
Kermie! We gotta run, Kermie, *together*, huh? I don't want to run withoutcha . . . Oh,
Jesus! Kermie? Kermie? Don't be dead, Kermie, don't be dead! Don't be dead! (108).[32]

With a bloodcurdling scream of recognition, Archie stares straight out into the
darkened theatre, the chilling tableau revealing the dead, hollow eyes of a blind
man unable to visualize life without his life-long friend (108).

Not only is this the best play that Horowitz has written since *The Indian
Wants the Bronx,* but it has also gained in intensity and authenticity during
progressive rewrites over a period of ten years. Paralleling the play, *The
Widow's Blind Date* has a compelling history of its own. The first draft was
written quickly and easily in a span of two to three weeks in 1978 during
rehearsals for the New York Shakespeare Festival production of Horovitz's *The
Quannapowitt Quartet* directed by Jack Hoffsiss and starring Mary Beth Hurt
and John Heard. Under the direction of Hoffsiss, Mary Beth Hurt and John
Heard, whose North Shore accents "were letter-perfect," were joined by Bruce
Hyde to perform a reading for Joe Papp, who later offered constructive and
commendatory analysis of Horovitz's new play. Barely fifteen minutes into the
reading, Horovitz began noticing perspiration seeping through his pants. "I felt
as though I might faint," the playwright recalls, "when I heard what I had
written read back to me for the first time by professional actors."[33] After he put
the play away for nearly a year, a revised *Widow* had its first public performance
at the New York Playwrights Lab annual festival at the Actors Studio in May
1979 starring the then unknown Jill Eikenberry, Robert Fields, and Ebbe Roe
Smith. Although Horovitz remembers a "star-studded audience" appearing
nightly lending its overwhelming support to the play, nothing stilled his anxiety.
Something about *Widow* "scared" the playwright "beyond my [his] wildest
dreams."[34] Again, Horovitz put the play away for another year until director
Bill Bushnell requested permission to stage *Widow*. Horovitz completed yet
another revision. Staged by the Los Angeles Theater Center under the direction
of Bushnell in October 1980, *Widow* won awards for both the play and the
director, but Horovitz was still restless, uneasy, and agitated during
performances of the revised play, unable to watch for more than fifteen minutes.
On the rare occasions that he attempted to sit through a performance, Horovitz
found he could do so only when gripping his wife's hand "tightly from start to
finish."[35]

Widow was staged at the Gloucester Stage Company in 1983, a production
that precipitated a crucial exchange between Horovitz's mother and the
playwright that at long last provided a key to the playwright's anxiety. Although
Horovitz had continually refined his conception of Margy, he was forced to face
down his own demons, learning that his mother never knew—or asked—if his
father participated in a gang rape with other workers in his uncle's junk shop.
Finally capable of sitting through a performance, Horovitz perceived

immediately that the play needed " an enormous revision—not so much a change of words as a change of view," specifically, that Margy's "radicalization" from intended "Forgiveness to Revenge had to fester and grow before our very eyes. We, as audience, had to bear witness" to its power, potency, and paralysis with and through "the eyes of the woman" if we were to comprehend her experience and "learn from her dark triumph over her victim-past."[36] Ironically, Horovitz's notes to his *Henry Lumper* provide the most sagacious insight on the artistic process reflected in *Widow's* final revision: "It seems to me," observes Horovitz, "that the most and best we playwrights can do when life serves up unthinkably high drama is to write it down."[37]

Employing the theme of betrayal and techniques previously developed in *Line,* where five men forego morality to be first in line, in *Indian,* where a triad struggles for territorial and psychological dominance, in *The 75th,* where old schoolmates attempt to recover a common past, in *Our Father's Failing,* where repressed knowledge of a crime is dramatized within a realistic framework, Horovitz has written not only "a small-scale horror show [of] violence, abuse, hatred and revenge [set] within the subtle frame of class warfare," but his most powerful treatment of guilt, victimization, and degeneration in America.[38] Although the playwright strongly believes that drama about women should be written by women, he nonetheless feels compelled to address the victimization of women perpetrated by the myth that men "were [are] in first place."[39] A profoundly sensitive portrayal of victimization and empowerment, *Widow* has not only earned this play international acclaim, it has energized and empowered the playwright, suggesting a new direction for his future work.

Turning back to the issues of power and fear that occupied him in the 1960s, Horovitz finally seems to be fulfilling earlier promise by tackling serious issues of social terror and essential vulnerability with a verbal dexterity and control of character and plot that attests to his maturity.

NOTES

1. Harold Clurman, "Theatre," *Nation* (12 February 1968): 221.

2. Susan Griffin, "The Politics of Rape," in *Made from This Earth* (New York: Harper & Row, 1982), 40. Emphasis is Griffin's.

3. Menachem Amir, *Patterns of Forcible Rape* (Chicago: University of Chicago Press, 1971), 51.

4. Griffin, "Politics of Rape," 42.

5. Amir, *Patterns,* 261.

6. See Susan Brownmiller's classic study of rape, *Against Our Will: Men, Women and Rape* (New York: Simon & Schuster, 1975), in which she convincingly argues this point.

7. While the motivation for this article was a specific incident of "wilding"—the brutal attack and rape of a female jogger in New York City known as the "Central Park Jogger"—Elizabeth Holtzman's "Rape—The Silence Is Criminal," *New York Times* (5 May 1989): 8, has wider application. According to Justice Department statistics, rape is increasing at four times the rate of other crimes, but as many as half of all sex crimes remain unreported. (Quoted in "Women under Assault," *Newsweek* 16 July 1990): 23.

8. Griffin, "Politics of Rape," 52.

9. Israel Horovitz, "Addendum," *Widow's Blind Date,* Gloucester Stage Company Performance Text, July–September 1989, 2.

10. Ibid.

11. Ibid., 3.

12. Ibid., 4.

13. Israel Horovitz quoted in Sonia Taitz, "A Tantalizing Return to the Scene of the Crime," *New York Times* (5 November 1989), H5, 40.

14. Kevin Kelly, "This 'Widow' Is a Stunner," review of *Widow's Blind Date* by Israel Horovitz, *Boston Globe* (21 July 1989): 32.

15. Sylvie Drake, "*Widow's Blind Date* at the LAAT—Let Us Prey," review of *Widow's Blind Date* by Israel Horovitz, *Los Angeles Times,* 7 October 1980, VI: 6.

16. Israel Horovitz, *The Widow's Blind Date* (Garden City, N.Y.: The Fireside Theatre, 1989), 12–13. All subsequent citations to the play are from this edition and will appear parenthetically in the text.

17. See R. Howard Bloch, "Medieval Misogyny," in *Misogyny, Misandry and Misanthropy,* ed. R. Howard Bloch and Francis Ferguson (Berkeley: University of California Press, 1989), for a fascinating study of woman as that which provokes contradiction, deceives with words, and seduces with ruses of rhetoric, esp. 16–19.

18. Taitz, "Tantalizing Return," 40.

19. My emphasis.

20. On the subject of victimization of all three characters, see Horovitz, quoted in Taitz, "Tantalizing Return," 40: "If I'm successful with this work you will see all three of them as victims."

21. See Susan Brison, "Survival Course," *New York Times Magazine,* 21 March 1993, 20, 22, for a poignant essay on the range of emotions such as anger, fear, self-condemnation, and helplessness that she has experienced both initially and during a prolonged recovery from a brutal rape. Especially telling is her observation: "Denial also takes the form of silence" (20).

22. Drake, "*Widow's Blind Date* at the LAAT," 1.

23. *The Widow's Blind Date* has undergone repeated revision since its first public performance at the New York Playwrights Lab (1979). As recently as the Gloucester Stage Company Performance Text, July–September 1989, this line on p. 100 read: "Swede was *numero trez,* Spike the Loon was the definite clean-up. ... The Moose was number seven."

24. Sue-Ellen Case, "From Split Subject to Split Britches," in *Feminine Focus*, ed. Enoch Brater (New York: Oxford University Press, 1989), 130.

25. Ibid., 131.

26. See my essay, "The Way Out, the Way In: Paths to Self in the Plays of Marsha Norman," in *Feminine Focus*, 257.

27. Case, "From Split Subject," 132.

28. Laurie Winer, "A Variation on the High School Reunion," *New York Times* 8 November 1989, C23.

29. Edward Albee, *The American Dream and The Zoo Story* (New York: New American Library), 49.

30. Case, "From Split Subject," 133.

31. Israel Horovitz, interview in *A Search for a Postmodern Theatre: Interviews*, ed. John L. DiGaetani (Westport, Conn.: Greenwood, 1991), 146.

32. My emphasis.

33. Horovitz, "Addendum," 2.

34. Ibid., 2–3.

35. Ibid., 3.

36. Ibid., 4.

37. Israel Horovitz, "Author's Notes," *Henry Lumper* (New York: Dramatists Play Service, 1990), 93.

38. Kelly, "This 'Widow,'" 21.

39. Israel Horovitz, personal interview, 22 March 1993.

8

The Unkindness of Strangers: Violence and Homosexual Subtexts in Israel Horovitz

John Watkins and Andrew Elfenbein

This chapter examines Israel Horovitz's treatment of explosive relations between men in two plays, *The Indian Wants the Bronx*, perhaps his best-known work, and *The Widow's Blind Date*, a play originally intended for the Wakefield cycle. Violence in these plays stems from the uncomfortable tensions in sexual definition characterizing relations between men who think of themselves as being just friends. Horovitz links this violence to issues of social concern, particularly violence against minorities and women. Yet in making this connection, his plays become pretexts for more disturbing inquiries into the values of liberal America. In particular, the sympathetic treatment of representatives of marginalized social groups becomes a mask for expressing less liberal values about relations between men in a more acceptable form.

Although the New York premiere of *Indian* occurred in 1968, some aspects of its action are disturbingly close to more recent events. On May 27, 1991, a middle-aged black woman telephoned the Milwaukee police to report that a disoriented Laotian boy, a probable victim of criminal assault, was running naked down the street. When the police arrived on the scene, a white man in his mid-thirties persuaded them that the Laotian was his nineteen-year-old lover, that they had had a quarrel, and that everything was under control. The police left the scene, returned the Laotian to the white man's custody, and gigglingly reported the incident back to headquarters as a "boyfriend-boyfriend" thing. Milwaukee later learned that the Laotian, who was only sixteen years old, was disoriented because the white man, Jeffrey Dahmer, had bored holes in his head and funneled acid onto the surface of his brain. Shortly after the police left, Dahmer killed the boy, dismembered him, and stored his body parts in his refrigerator with those of other victims.

The torture and murder of Konerak Sinthosomphone at the hands of a deranged white man with a previous criminal history bears several striking analogues to Israel Horovitz's dramatization of an attack on an Indian man by two New York thugs in *Indian*. In each case, the commitment of an atrocity by whites on an Asian victim forced the dominant class to recognize and dismantle the racial stereotyping that pervades its apprehensions of urban violence. At a time when reports of Asian gangs from Los Angeles to Minneapolis to New York were adding yet another element to the popular construction of the inner city as a war zone populated by marauding bands of blacks and Hispanics, Sinthosomphone's murder precipitated, at least temporarily, a more sympathetic view of the Southeast Asian immigrant community in the American press. Twenty-four years earlier, the Broadway production of *Indian* similarly challenged the longstanding image of Indians as sinister outsiders of Western civilization. Both on Horovitz's stage and on the streets of a tough Milwaukee neighborhood, the racial tables were turned. The victim was no longer the naive kid from the suburbs who found himself on the wrong side of the tracks or the American tourist wandering by mistake in the wrong part of Bombay. Nor was the perpetrator the terrifying Oriental other; the predominantly white readers of the *Milwaukee Journal*, as well as the predominantly white audiences in the Astor Place Theater, witnessed a member of their own race commit an atrocity against a helpless Asian immigrant.

A complicated interaction between social constructions of class and gender allowed Milwaukee's white, middle-class heterosexuals to view the Dahmer case with a detached complaisance. Their perception of the homosexual Dahmer, as well as of the negligent police officers and their working-class supporters, as individuals outside their own social group mitigated any sense of collective responsibility that they might have felt for the fact of white-on-nonwhite violence. Reports of the atrocity tended to reinforce this effect by minimizing the alterity of Dahmer's victims; they appeared more often as members of model bourgeois families, the beloved sons, brothers, and fathers of adoring mothers, sisters, and even wives, than as frequenters of the gay bars and public restrooms where Dahmer actually met them. Suburban Milwaukee overcame its racism by seeing Dahmer's black and Asian victims as martyrs in a common bourgeois struggle for humanitarian decency and family values against the evils of the inner city. Those evils were now conveniently embodied in the person of Jeffrey Dahmer, a psychotic homosexual whose defection from suburban decency was marked not only by his deviant sexuality but by his current employment as a factor worker.

The strategies by which Milwaukee's predominantly white, bourgeois press diffused the shock of white-on-nonwhite violence through the simultaneous manipulation of homophobia and longstanding class prejudices recur throughout *Indian*. From the play's beginning, Horovitz heightens sympathy for Gupta by characterizing him as a middle-class, respectable white man in disguise: "Gupta is in his early fifties. Although he is swarthy in complexion, he is anything but sinister. He is, in fact, meek and visibly frightened by the city."[1] Despite his unintelligible speech and traditional East Indian garb, whose exoticism Horovitz partially neutralizes by noting it as "appropriately" light attire for mid-September, Gupta's response to the city is no different from that of many white, middle-class Americans. Indeed, even most of the New Yorkers in Horovitz's audience would share Gupta's fears if they found themselves in a similarly tough neighborhood.[2]

The more Horovitz reveals about Gupta's history, the more he bypasses surface dissimilarities to suggest an underlying kinship between the Indian and the members of the audience. Gupta's first long speech reveals that his family conforms perfectly to the American nuclear model:

I haven't had time to learn your language. Please forgive me. I'm separated from my son. He's been living in your country for six years. When his mother died two months ago, he sent for me. I came immediately. He's a good son to his father. I'm sorry I haven't learned your language yet, but I shall learn. (144)

Gupta may not have yet learned English, but his pride in his son's filial devotion marks him not as an alien but as a kindhearted soul whose values are readily assimilable to the best of American culture. Although probably a Hindu, Prem fulfills the Judeo-Christian injunction to honor one's parents by inviting his bereaved father to America shortly after his mother's death. When Murph telephones Prem and taunts him with hints about his father's whereabouts, Prem's hysteria assures us that Gupta has not exaggerated his son's love or protectivenesss. Horovitz invites us to identify completely with him in the nightmare of losing an elderly, vulnerable parent in an unfamiliar metropolis.

The love and concern that diminish the audience's perception of Gupta's exoticism by associating his family with the ideals of the American middle class contrast with the dysfunction of Joey and Murphy's inner-city families. Murphy's "old man took off years ago," and his mother is "a pro" who "don't even make a living at it" (155); Joey speculates that she "probably tries it" with her own son. Joey himself shows more concern for his mother, but his fear that she would starve if he were to move out suggests guilt more than the affection bonding Gupta and Prem.

Family dysfunction is just one of the negative traits that figures in Horovitz's characterization of Joey and Murph as members of an urban lumpenproletariat ultimately more foreign to the respectable members of his audience than decent, law-abiding Indians like Gupta. Their broken homes, as well as the absence of positive male role models, are presumably the source of an underlying anger that erupts in seemingly unmotivated violence, which Horovitz further associates with their exclusion from good schools and other bastions of social privilege. Their abysmal education manifests itself not only in their confusion of native American and subcontinental stereotypes but also in their recurrent solecisms, the double negatives, and case confusions that Martin

Gottfried praised as true to the "obscene style familiar enough to anybody who can read scribblings on subway walls."[3] Gupta's Hindi may be unintelligible, but it is grammatically correct; by contrast, Joey and Murph's native but substandard English continually marks their status as social and economic outcasts. Significantly, reviewers of the play condemned Horovitz not for reinforcing a pernicious association of criminal behavior with illiteracy but for occasionally making the boys' language sound too sophisticated. By complaining that "there are a few instances in which the lines seem too sharp or too bright for the speakers," Edith Oliver revealed her own bourgeois investment in maintaining rather than interrogating and dismantling the linguistic barriers that separate her from the lower orders.[4] What most bothers a middle-class audience about moments when Joey or Murph's lines seem too sharp is not a purely aesthetic lapse in verisimilitude but the suggestion that it might not be so easy to differentiate good whites from bad whites after all.

Nothing absolved Milwaukee's white dominant class from complicity in the deaths of Konerak Sinthasomphone and Dahmer's other nonwhite victims more than Dahmer's repeatedly evoked homosexuality. It was not Dahmer the white former suburbanite who was responsible for the murders but Dahmer the homosexual. Despite occasional disclaimers from the district attorney's office throughout Dahmer's trial that he was being prosecuted for murder and not homosexuality, the case triggered a wave of homophobia throughout the city and the rest of the nation.

At first, the parallel between the Dahmer case and *Indian* seems to break down over the issue of homophobia. Whereas Dahmer's gay identity offered bourgeois Milwaukee a convenient means of displacing its racial antipathies, Horovitz overtly characterizes both Joey and Murph as straight. The play opens with their lovesong for Pussyface, Joey claims to have "had" Murph's sister, and Murph brags about the time he once "had . . . a real French lady" (144). But these heterosexual encounters and attractions lose depth and significance as the plot unfolds. Pussyface turns out not to be a real object of desire but the boys' assigned social worker; their serenade expresses contempt toward her as a representative of middle-class conformity. When it turns out that Joey's "French lady" was actually his girlfriend when both were in the first grade, we begin to question whether both the boys' heterosexual experience is limited to bragging about imaginary encounters.

The truly significant relationship in their lives is their friendship, a homosocial bond that conforms strikingly to the patterns of mediated desire traced by Eve Sedgwick.[5] Like so many other British and American narratives, *Indian* foregrounds a rapport between two men that is charged with suggestions of homoeroticism. In the opening moments of the play, a serenade sung by two men to a woman who never appears begins to sound like a love song between the two men themselves. Beginning with their initial apostrophes to "Pussyface," their conversation resonates with references to oral and anal sex.

Fantasies of vaginal and oral, heterosexual and homosexual intercourse converge in potentially threatening ways when Joey's observation that the Indian is talking out of the side of his mouth recalls stories about "Indian broads" that "have sideways breezers" (143). A series of double-entendres on "butts" and "noogies" ("nookie") transforms Murph's demand for a cigarette from Joey into a punning plea for anal satisfaction.

As Sedgwick notes in her discussions of novels like *Our Mutual Friend*, a common interest in the same woman tends to mediate homoerotic tensions between male protagonists: competition for heterosexual favor forestalls the threat that homosocial attraction might progress to actual homosexual activity. But in Horovitz's play, such a woman never appears. Pussyface is somewhere in New Jersey, and Joey refuses to get involved with Murph's allegedly incestuous mother: "But it just ain't right screwing your best buddy's old lady, right?" (156). Maggie, Murph's kid sister who once joined them in a trio and whom Joey claims once to have bedded, is now dead; if she mediated the boys' homoerotic tensions in the past, she can do so in the present only as a fantasy.

Instead of discovering a woman to mediate their homoerotic tensions, Joey and Murph turn to the Indian. The moment Joey sees Gupta, he describes him as "just another pretty face" (129), quips that "he likes us," and considers winking at him. Their taunts quickly take the form of queer bashing. Murph asks Gupta if he is a "fairy" and then addresses him "with a homosexual's sibilant's'" (136). Murph not only shows him an obscene "Christmas card," a photocopy of his own bare buttocks, but describes how he stripped down his pants and underpants to make the photocopy in the first place. Explicit taunting begins to look increasingly like the manifestation of a semiconscious desire to entice and seduce.

At several points throughout the play, the boys teasingly accuse each other of wanting to sleep with Gupta: "*You're* a Turkie-humper" (132). But when Murph returns from an abortive trip to get Pussyface, only to find Gupta shivering in Joey's sweater, his accusations acquire a darker, less ironic character: "Jesus, you and your Chief are pretty buddy-buddy, ain't you? . . . You give him your sweater. Maybe you'd like to have him up for a beer." (160) This is perhaps the darkest, most overdetermined jest in the play. Several converging subtexts account for the bitterness of Murph's tone. He is enraged not only by the sheer spectacle of unmediated male-male affection but, on an even deeper level, by a sense of erotic betrayal. Both the tenderness that Joey feels for the Indian and the tenderness that the Indian might feel for Joey make him jealous. The moment casts Joey both as Murph's rival and his adulterous partner, and Joey himself, intentionally or not, provides an apt commentary on Murph's homosexual panic: "Drop it, Murph. You're giving me a pain in the ass." In describing Murph's aggression as a form of anal penetration, Joey foregrounds the extent to which Murph's violence grows out of the threatening eroticism that is always present in their friendship.

Precisely because Gupta is a man rather than a woman, he is incapable of neutralizing the threat posed to Murph and Joey by their mutual homoerotic attraction. His maleness only aggravates the problem by driving them to ever more explicit references to homosexuality. As was made all too clear when soldiers began to beat up or murder gay men as soon as President Clinton moved to permit gays in the military, homosexual panic manifests itself in physical violence. The play's first critics often commented on the motiveless character of the tortures that Joey and Murph inflict on Gupta: "There is no logical pattern to follow; we must slip inside illogic to hear hate's heartbeat."[6] But the logic of the play is hardly so elusive. Joey and Murph's violence marks a transparent eruption of frustrated and dangerously displaced eros that characterizes them in turn as sexual deviants incapable of normal, heterosexual experience.

Like the newspaper accounts of Dahmer's murders, *Indian* seems to offer the white dominant class a timely exemplum about the evils of white-on-nonwhite violence. But instead of purging its audience of social prejudice altogether, it recodes it as classism and homophobia. The play denies alterities of race to reinforce those of class and sexual orientation. It lures its audience into sympathizing with Gupta not because he is an Indian persecuted by whites but because he is a white person in disguise persecuted by thugs whose language continually betrays their proclivities to deviant sexuality.

At first glance, the tone and action of *Widow* seem far removed from those of *Indian*, especially because of *Widow's* relation to the Wakefield cycle. According to Horovitz's brief introduction to the 1981 publication, the play was originally planned as part of this cycle, yet "in spite of the Massachusetts setting and indigenous Middlesex County dialogue, [it] seemed to demand its own life."[7] By the time of the 1987 postscript to *An Israel Horovitz Trilogy*, *Widow* had become part of "a cycle of plays set in [Horovitz's] adopted home, Gloucester, Massachusetts," so the play's "own life" did not last very long.[8] However, in the play's "final" version as published in 1989, the setting returns to "a newspaper baling plant in Wakefield, Massachusetts," so if it is not part of the Wakefield cycle, it does belong to Horovitz's plays inspired by that region.

Horovitz is somewhat disingenuous to claim that the play is linked to the Wakefield cycle chiefly by setting and dialogue; in both versions (1981 and 1989), it manifests numerous narrative and motivic links to the Wakefield plays. For example, the setting, "Baling-press room, wastepaper company, Wakefield, Massachusetts," recalls the "West Side Waste Paper Company" that Alfred maintains was run by Pa and Sam in *Our Father's Failing*, the middle play of *The Alfred Trilogy*; the violent action in the room shares the same sense of frustration and misunderstanding that characterizes the action in the trilogy.[9] At the beginning of the play, George and Archie, the two male characters, mention "Cootie" Webber, the name of the brother whom Alfred may or may not have killed in the trilogy. The name of Margy Burke, the widow of *The Widow's Blind Date*, recalls that of Margaret Lynch, the victimized wife in *Alfred the Great*, the first play in *The Alfred Trilogy*. Both women are characterized as the "town pump," and Margy Burke's revenge in *Widow* might be thought of as a displaced version of anger caused by Margaret Lynch's death. Horovitz also seems to like the name *Margaret* because it demands to be spoken with a regional accent; he specifies that Margy's name is to be pronounced "Mahh-ghee" (1981, "List of Characters") and Will in *Alfred the Great* torments his wife in part by pronouncing her name as "*Maahhr*garet" (*Wakefield Plays*, 86).

These are only a few of the many connections between *Widow* and the Wakefield plays. Nevertheless, the Horovitz play that really underlies the action of *Widow* is *Indian*; pairing the two underscores the extent to which this later play reconfigures the classism and homophobia of the earlier one through the overt inclusion of gender difference. Most obviously, like the earlier play, *Widow* is about three characters in which the confrontation between two men and an outsider (Gupta in *Indian*, Margy in *Widow*) leads to a violent conclusion: Murph's stabbing of Gupta in *Indian* and Archie Crisp's murder of George Ferguson in *Widow*. As in *Indian*, much of the action in *Widow* consists of apparently random chatter that gradually reveals complicated networks of power relations among the characters. The character of the "other" in *Widow*, as in *Indian*, is sympathetic in part because she is closer to the upper-middle-class theater-going audience in terms of manners and even class. Margy works at New York University and is presumably a literary critic, although she does not teach; when George asks her what she does, she answers, "I criticize" (69).

Widow rewrites the violence of *Indian* as revenge. The explosive potential of male bonding explored in *Indian* becomes the vehicle through which Margy, having been gang-raped by Archie and George at the end of high school, returns in *Widow* to revenge herself upon them—and upon all the others in the rape—by manipulating their sense of sexual failure and frustration and turning them against each other. *Widow*, like a mystery, becomes a different play on a second reading or viewing, when it becomes clear that the widow is going on anything but a blind date. Although she does not hold the upper hand continuously throughout the play, George and Archie stand as little chance against her as she did against them when she was raped twenty years before the action of the play begins.

Initially, Margy's revenge seems like a welcome response to the rampant sexism of Archie and George. When he learns that Archie has a date with Margy, one of George's first comments is, "Hey, maybe you could send her over to my place later, huh? For old times sake" (5). Archie's estimate of her is hardly more flattering: "She's flatter'n a pancake . . . two raisins on a breadboard" (7). By the play's end, George is throwing up the rape to Margy and mocking her for seeming to want to forget the past: "This girl thinks she

can come back to town and be *new* . . . and she can't . . . she can't. That ain't
the way things are" (94). He revels in tormenting Margy by insisting on the
inescapability of the past (a favorite theme of the Wakefield cycle). Having
been raped once, Margy is condemned forever in George's eyes as a whore.

The viciousness of George's attack energizes the sympathy that the
audience is asked to feel for her when she reveals her vindictiveness: "You bet
your ass I'm gonna get even! Yuh, George, yessireebob! I'm gonna get even. I
am! Wicked awful even! I'm gonna get sooo even with you, George, I can taste
it! Taste . . . it!" (100). At her most powerful, she reduces the men to
figurative women by slapping Archie and reproaching George for his
"feminine, childlike" giggle. Her longest outburst in the play is her satiric
attack on the two men for their obsession with her breasts: "Thinking it over,
Archie and George, I will gladly give my breasts over to you, for whatever
purpose you choose. George, you could wear them on the odd days; Archie, on
the evens. And I'll be free to get back to work . . . to get back to sleep at night
. . . to end the constant and unrelenting fondling" (78). She jeers at them for
their reduction of her to her chest and figuratively unmans them by suggesting
that what they truly desire is to wear her breasts. Their fetishization of her
breasts depends upon reducing women to physical objects. By revealing the
stupidity and arbitrariness of this obsession, Margy reveals the unthinking
sexism and implicit violence in the men's treatment of her.

Far from being a compliant Indian like Gupta, she seems to enact the
revenge of the empowered women, a victim striking back at her oppressors.
Horovitz counts on the horror and frustration with which rape is surrounded by
a liberal discourse in late-twentieth-century America. In the theater, it would
be difficult not to sympathize with Margy for getting even with her attackers,
no matter what means she uses, particularly when the rapists are as unattractive
as Archie and George. After so many centuries of female compliance, the
fantasy of female revenge is refreshing.

Yet the effects of Margy's actions are as disturbing as their causes.
Profoundly sympathetic though she is as a victim of a violent gang rape, she is
also a distinctly efficient enforcer of heterosexual norms. Her behavior neatly
eliminates the messy friendship between George and Archie, replacing a close
male-male relationship with a teasing hint of a continued heterosexual
relationship between her and Archie. Her final speech notes threateningly and
tantalizingly, "I'll be back, Archie" (107). In this capacity, she is far more
effective than Gupta in *Indian*. At the end of that play, the rapport of Joey and
Murph, threatened by the possibility of sexual betrayal that Gupta represents, is
reestablished when they exorcise their tensions on his body, or so the final duet
suggests. The homosexual charge in the relationship between Archie and
George is recuperated only to the extent that Archie's grief at his murder of
George seems more passionate than any of the language he directs at Margy.

From the play's opening, Archie and George cannot keep their hands off each other, literally or figuratively. In the 1981 version, George, for example, taunts Archie about his lack of sexual success in crudely suggestive language:

George: Meaning something in the neighborhod of "The rich bitches from the Park section of Wakefield, over the years, have fucked you over"?
Archie: Approximately.
George: Given you the shaft?
Archie: You might say that . . .
George: Screwed you royally?
Archie: Not *so* bad, really . . .
George: Really shoved it right up your old keester! (1981, 15)

Imagining the "rich bitches" as having "shoved it up" Archie's "keester" is to masculinize them and place Archie in the position of a passive partner. Whether this impression of the "bitches" is correct, the passage links George's taunting of Archie with homosexual relations, for he, far more than the "rich bitches," enjoys "screwing" Archie by stealing his girlfriends. The effect of his actions is to keep their "screwing" mostly figurative; no woman interrupts their relationship for long.

This passage reveals the extent to which their friendship is predicated on verbal and physical violence, the first usually teetering on the brink of the second. The more graphic such violence becomes during the action of the play, the more orgasmic it seems. The most disturbingly erotic moment in the 1989 version has nothing to do with Margy, but with Archie's description of having attacked a fellow-worker at the plant, Lum, when he was eleven years old: "I ran myself forward as fast as I could, whipping him around backwards . . . and he flew! He *flew*! He hit the front of the baler so hard, it was like his face exploded. He landed on the stack and just lay there, blood oozing out of him, staining the papers"(66). Archie labels this attack "a big day in the life of this little Arnold 'Billy-Goat' Crisp" because it taught him that "gaining respect is what life is all about" (67).   Although ostensibly a gesture of adolescent self-assertion against an older bully (Lum is forty), Archie's vocabulary associates conquering Lum with a sexual awakening, a homosexual rape that is far more vivid to him than the lackluster heterosexual encounters that he and George discuss. While the prospect of sexual relations with women entirely "unmans" Archie, he associates sexualized violence against men with "respect." The entire action of the play drives toward the moment when Archie reasserts his need for respect by murdering George. He does so by reenacting his assault on Lum, and Horovitz's stage directions recall Archie's orgasmic description when they note that George's face "*'explodes,' blood suddenly erupting, staining front door of baler*" (106).

This violence arises from Margy's ability to destabilize the sexual element in the always-tense relationship between the men. George and Archie recognize that Margy uses sexual paranoia to turn them against each other:

George: You're really tryin' ta start trouble here . . .
Archie: Between me and George . . .
George: Me and Archie . . .
Archie: Split us up . . .
George: Yuh. That's it. (81)

George's summary of her motivation is ultimately more revealing than anything she says: "I'd like to point out to you, Archie, that this Margy Palumbo is tryin' . . . and succeedin' . . . in making God damn fools . . . idiots! . . . outta the rotten two of us" (88). The replacement of male-male bonds with heterosexual ones involves not merely a shift in gender categories but also in power relations. Archie and George are roughly equal in their friendship. If George continually takes over Archie's women, Archie seems more capable than George of getting women in the first place; moreover, Archie has a higher position at the baling plant than George does. The relationship between Margy and the men, however, is characterized by none of the same aggressive mutuality. By the end of the play, she has become the misogynist's nightmare of the woman who renders men powerless. She reduces Archie to a weeping murderer and George to a corpse but exits the play speaking "simply, clearly" (107).

Throughout the play, Horovitz links the characters' sexual conflicts to conflicts about class. The paper baler that dominates the stage set is an ever-present emblem of the class differences between the men and Margy. The physical violence to which she incites Archie displaces the more subtle forms of social violence implicit in her Boston accent and finicky grammar. Archie and George are stuck in a mind-numbing routine as workers; as Archie says, "I never figured when I was twelve and doin' this, that twenty/twenty-five years later I'd still be here, you know . . . doing this" (15). At the end of the play, when he beats up George, Archie talks not about their sexual rivalry over Margy but about the perceived pointlessness of his job:

(*Archie goes to George and kicks him in the stomach. He then chases George behind baler and kicks George with a terrible blow . . .*) They buy our paper and they process it, see? And they make it into paper. Use ta bother me that I was workin' so hard takin' paper to people who were makin' paper. . . . I mean, it never seemed like too much of a life bringin' paper all's the way up ta Fitchburg, just so's they could make more paper. I mean, what's the world gonna' *do* with so much paper, anyhow? (106)

Companies like the West Side Waste Paper Company are grinding down men like Archie and George so effectively that Margy's intervention seems almost superfluous. The newspapers that George and Archie bale are reminders of Margy's class domination: She appears in them, but they do not. When she indulges in a bit of "slumming" by offering to help them bale the newspapers, they insist vehemently on the gendered nature of their work. Archie insists that "this is *man*'s work" (45), allowing himself to disguise his class position as a mark of masculine superiority. Ultimately the play itself is one more piece of language that marks the classed nature of Margy's victory: The play's actors, directors, and audiences speak her language, not Archie and George's.

Horovitz's plays depend for their effectiveness upon promoting sympathy with victims of violence, who are characterized, at least on first appearance, by their ethnic or gender difference. Yet in all cases, this sympathy is a highly suspect emotion because under the guise of promoting a liberal concern for the plight of the oppressed, it reinforces more subtle, less visible forms of hegemonic domination. The point is not to argue that Joey and Murph, or Archie and George, truly deserve the audience's sympathy and that Gupta and Margy do not. Rather, it is to emphasize that sympathy is never innocent in these plays. In both cases, it is complicit with a gesture that locates the origin of violence in the unresolved homoeroticism of relations between men.

NOTES

1. Quotations from *Indian* from *First Season* (New York: Random House, 1968), 127. All subsequent citations to the play will appear parentheically in the text.

2. It was an overdetermined coincidence that the "unfortunate East Indian who couldn't act a credible East Indian" (*First Season*, xv) was replaced in the original cast by John Cazale, an Italian from Massachusetts.

3. See the review of *Indian* in *Women's Wear Daily*, 18 January 1968.

4. See Oliver's discussion of *Indian* in "The Second Coming of *Twelfth Night*," *New Yorker*, 27 January 1968, 86–87.

5. See her *Between Men: English Literature and Male Homosocial Desire* (New York: Columbia University Press, 1985).

6. Walter Kerr, in a review of *Indian* in *New York Times*, 30 June 1988, 11.

7. Quotations are from *The Widow's Blind Date* (Garden City, N.Y.: Fireside, 1989), unless specifically noted as from the 1981 version, in which case they are from *The Widow's Blind Date* (New York: Theatre Communications Group, 1981).

8. *An Israel Horovitz Trilogy* (Garden City, N.Y.: Fireside, 1987), 272.

9. *Our Father's Failing* in *The Wakefield Plays* (New York: Avon, 1979), 169.

The Influence of Samuel Beckett on Israel Horovitz

Robert Scanlan

It is hard to imagine two personalities more widely disparate than those of Israel Horovitz and Samuel Beckett. There is almost no characteristic one could attribute to the one that would accurately describe the other, in their personal habits and demeanor, their worldly appetites, their literary and theatrical accomplishments, their characters, appearances, manners, or their apparent goals in life. But such pronounced disparities between human beings have often enough been the basis of inexplicable friendships, especially, perhaps, among creative writers. It is certainly plausible, for instance, that Samuel Beckett and Israel Horovitz might have been mutually fascinated by the complete and utter otherness each of them presented to the other. However, this may have sorted itself out in their personal lives, and there is, not surprisingly, contradictory evidence of the nature and extent of their friendship. It has led to very little tendency among literary and dramatic critics attracted to the study of either one of them to treat comfortably of the other.

It is tempting to conclude, after due consideration of the works of both men, that there is no significant literary influence of Beckett on the works of Israel Horovitz. But it is probably more accurate to say that the influence has been intensely personal, that for a very brief time—when the friendship between them was new, and their contact was frequent—the influence was overwhelming. When their friendship cooled, following an embarrassing scandal in Horovitz's life, the open mimicry of Beckett ceased in Horovitz's work, and any lasting influence—as Horovitz has said himself—was to manifest itself not in content or form or style but in the inspiration of Beckett's example and the emulation of his daily work habits.[1]

Since he first got to know Beckett in the early 1970s, Horovitz has been consistently industrious as a writer–in fact, few other American playwrights of his generation have been as prolific. But the Beckett phase in his development as a writer is long since behind him, and it was confined distinctly to the years

1972 to 1976.   During this brief time, Horovitz imitated Beckett with
breathtaking ingenuousness, producing most notably two "copycat" prose texts
(the novel *Cappella* and the novella *Nobody Loves Me*) and two especially
Beckett-like one-act plays (*Stage Directions* and *Spared*), which verge on
parody.   Yet it is clear that these exercises in imitation were a form of open
admiration on Horovitz's part.   He remains free to this day of any apprehension
that such flagrant mimicry might have been construed as presumptuous or
invasive by a fellow writer.   As a result, Horovitz, ever the autodidact, indulged
in a total-immersion practical exploration of the master's style.   The works of
Horovitz's Beckett phase are really his own improvised and uninhibited
experimentation with Beckett's creative tools.

It would be foolish to underestimate how much a serious writer might learn
while seeing several such exercises through to completion, and Horovitz clearly
enjoyed Beckett's benign indulgence during this experimental phase. Horovitz
himself reports an admonition he received from Beckett at the time: "There will
come a time," Beckett is supposed to have said, "when you will have to break
away from the influence of my style." That, with its understated irony, rings
true to Beckett. What does not ring as true is the tag on that quotation supplied
by Horovitz: " ... just as I had to break away from Joyce."[2]   That smacks more
of Horovitz's remembering what he read in Deirdre Bair's biography of Beckett,
in which the Joyce influence is a running motif,[3] than it does of Beckett
himself, who was horrified by glib talk of Joyce's influence on him.   Beckett
would have been the last person to bring it up. But if the Horovitz quotation
does not sound like Beckett, it is just another instance of the fundamental
divergence of two irreconcilable temperaments.   The time for breaking away
from each other came all too swiftly, and the "influence" of Beckett on Israel
Horovitz turned out to be a merely temporary possession   by the magisterial
voice of Beckett's mature prose.

As Enoch Brater (among others) has pointed out in his 1987 study, *Beyond
Minimalism*, this great voice of Beckett, the voice of the postwar fictions, was
making its way, now that Beckett's seminal full-length plays of the 1950s were
firmly established, into the innovative series of short plays that began with *Not
I* (1972) and *That Time* (1974–75).[4]   These and subsequent works would
become the plays critics and commentators now refer to as the late plays of
Samuel Beckett. Horovitz was in his early thirties when he first encountered a
Beckett who was just beginning this phase of his long career. Horovitz's two
plays, *Spared* (1973–76) and *Stage Directions* (1975–76), are steeped in the
voice of *Not I* and *That Time*. During the same period, Horovitz wrote the
Beckett-like novel *Cappella* (published in 1973) and fourteen pages of
experimental prose fragments put forth as the novella *Nobody Loves Me*.
Beckett arranged for his French publisher (Les Editions de Minuit) to issue a
Paris edition of *Nobody Loves Me* in 1974.

Spared is the most obviously imitative of Horovitz's Beckett plays. Its central set-up, of a lone old man perched high over the stage, surrounded by impenetrable dark, is copied from *That Time*. The text's initial rhythms are echoes of *Not I*, as is the "birthing" sequence, and the basic structure of recapitulating a life in muttered monologue. The punctuating screams are also taken out of *Not I*, and the repeated attempts at suicide are glib farcical variants on the cyclical urges to end life in *That Time*. Phrases like "life to play" echo the text of *Endgame*; [5] the protagonist's stumbling over the word love is taken from *Krapp's Last Tape*; Beckett's tiny "dramaticule" *Come and Go* is evoked in the line, "Girls all blab. Heard them come, watched them go"(31); some comic business with a sneaker tossed out of reach evokes stage business in *Happy Days*, while the recorded voices emanating from carefully placed speakers is a central device in *That Time*. And to cap it all, as if the density of borrowed allusions were not thick enough (the play is only seventeen pages long), a crowning allusion, not to Beckett but to Eugène Ionesco, is thrown in for good measure in the form of a bald soprano: "His wife. Erica. Stone bald. . . . She sang an awful aria in that horrid coloratura soprano voice of hers" (43). No Monty Python sketch could do more by way of parody or ridicule of a style, yet *Spared* remains apparently sincere in its attempted imitation.

There are many ways in which *Spared* fails to sustain the expectation it provokes by so blatantly declaring itself to be an attempt in the Beckett mode. The use of the monologue is not constitutive of an action, as it invariably is in Beckett. Here the monologuing old man is simply delivering expository information, and there is no basis for this activity. It is a surface mimesis of a style, not an anchored organic impulse on the part of a character. And the device breaks down purely stylistically in Horovitz's case through a rapid deterioration of the tone and imaginative integrity of the narration. It is as if Horovitz repeatedly lost the thread of his own work, grew bored with it, and resorted to having his actor say any old thing to get to the end of his appointed time on the stage.

Many of Horovitz's works give this impression of petering out after an initial inspiration. Play after play seems born in a clever, sometimes brilliant flash of initial inspiration. In fact, Horovitz is extremely fertile in ideas for plays. But he seems consistently to flag in the act of fleshing these concepts out; few develop into fully realized works of art. The characteristic Horovitz progression in a script, regardless of the style, is one of desultory improvisation, a fitful, often whimsical ongoing that gives the impression that the author himself at some point stops caring much about where the play is going, or what the characters are saying, so long as the play eventually reaches an end. Script after script reads like a pensum impatiently and distractedly brought to completion.

It will not be lost on anyone familiar with Beckett that this image of a coerced, reluctant creator laboriously bringing stories to birth, and having to tolerate their embarrassing imperfections, is a central motif throughout Beckett's fiction. But Beckett created this figure of perpetual failure in works of increasing formal perfection.

Stage Directions is a short one-act play that follows the basic pattern just described. Born in an original and intriguing idea—the actors do not speak any conventional dialogue, but instead they speak their own third-person stage directions as they perform them—the script does not deliver on its own premise. The ground situation of the play is three siblings who have just returned from the funeral of their parents. It is a completely Beckett-inspired idea to take a situation of extreme grief and suffering and to devise a masking formal construct to evade the sentimental portrayal of the deep emotions involved. In Beckett's works, these formal devices perfectly imitate the internal actions of grieving souls holding themselves together by mental strategies of displacement, distraction, and consolation. But in Horovitz's script, the three siblings do not so much displace their grieving as lose track of it.

The stage-directions device, which is reminiscent of Beckett's two *Act without Words* pantomimes, creates formal problems that Horovitz does not solve. It prevents the three characters from ever speaking to each other, and it becomes an end in itself to sustain the comic pantomime of three people in a single room, united by a central tragedy, yet separated by a rule of stage behavior. What they do in the room starts out with some semblance of psychological complexity, but it rapidly devolves into a sort of theatre game governed not by an interest in the difficult emotions implied by the situation but by Horovitz's ground rules for the improvisation. We see, in fifteen pages of text, his initial stage idea worked out to completion, but at the expense of any potential insights into his characters. Such a procedure—one in which the absurd mechanics of performance outweigh the supposed seriousness of the situation—owes perhaps more to Ionesco than it does to Beckett, but the funereal circumstances are more clearly taken from the Beckett ground. And the telegraphic terseness of the stage directions themselves is an example of what I have called possession by the Beckett voice and syntax: "He inspects stain on palm, lowers hand to side, pauses, returns to chair, sobs once, sits, bows head, notices shoe, removes same" (8). [6]

Cappella is surely the centerpiece of Horovitz's Beckett phase. It most closely resembles Beckett's *Malone Dies*, borrowing its basically static,bedridden setting and reproducing its prose rhythms along with innumerable reference expressions about going on against the odds. Closely following Beckett, Horovitz created nested narrative voices, or points of view, each of which freely invents characters and anecdotes as it goes. The novel proceeds along a rambling, improvised narrative line that is centered on a character the narrator calls Byron. Byron is placed in a hospital room where he endures repeated abdominal operations and the drugged recoveries that follow. In an adjoining hospital bed, an ailing old Jew named Cappella shares Byron's fate and provides narrative grist of his own for the novel's mill. The first-person narrator identifies himself as "the copyist" and claims responsibility for all the text we read. He frequently addresses the reader in his own voice, outside of the tale.

There is a telltale passage midway through *Cappella* and it bears quoting in full:

Copying is more of an art than a science. The world would laugh at copyists. Really. But you must consider what you've been reading. I am blind, totally blind, yet I have guided you through eighty-six pages of this tedium and it appears that you have gone on to page eighty-seven. Art is undeniably artful.[7]

This text makes up the entire forty-first section of the novel, and it is a typical example of the airy metafictional prose that interrupts the more conventional short passages of narrative. The voice is that of the blind copyist, who is a stand-in for the author. In many unintended ways, the copyist passage just quoted tells the whole story about Israel Horovitz at the time of the writing, and it especially epitomizes his ambiguous relationship to Samuel Beckett.

In the midst of such a naive imitation of Beckett as *Cappella* represents, the copyist's anxiety expressed in section forty-one is more than understandable. But the passage expresses the author's diffidence and his shrewdness at the same time; it reveals an instinct for the con and a simultaneous urge to confess and be forgiven. It rips the mask off itself but goes on to insult the reader as it attempts to seduce him or her with cleverness.

None of these procedures is remotely connected to Beckett. Samuel Beckett's fiction is based fundamentally on the evanescence of character, on the insubstantiality of the thing we call a self, and the pain and terror of retaining full consciousness past the tidy boundaries of conventional identity. The tortuous inroads Beckett made, in the late 1940s, into what we now call metafictional areas of discourse, were pioneering forays into hitherto inarticulate consciousness. This is not the place to trace Beckett's precursors (Joyce, Proust, Virginia Woolf), but suffice it to say that Beckett's prose transcriptions of "things heard" (his fictions—novels, shorts, and fizzles) as well as his meticulously recorded "things seen" (among them the late plays), he was not playing games with his audience.

The quoted passage from *Cappella*, however, openly acknowledges that the copyist is imitating another voice—not just Byron (which is the premise of the novel) but a voice outside the novel. Horovitz so openly and deliberately mimics the published prose of Samuel Beckett that he forces his reader to confront a different reality from that discovered and evoked in Beckett. What seems foremost on Horovitz's mind is the authority he acquires through imitating Beckett. The passage quoted emanates from a voice conscious above all of the power inherent in authorship and the capacity of this power to impose on its audience and, if need be, counterbalance any lack of content. It may be laughably ridiculous to "copy" as Horovitz does, but he rubs the reader's nose in the humiliating recognition that wherever he, the author, chooses to lead, we his readers have no recourse but to follow.

If Horovitz's passage is a taunting putdown of the reader, it is also an attempt to be honest about what is going on in his novel. This book takes place between author and reader; everything else is gimmick and pretext. The principal characters, Byron and Cappella, the hospital where both are ailing and recuperating, the variously grotesque nurses and attendants—all are currency pilfered from Beckett, and defiantly so, for Horovitz's own confrontation with a public of his own. The novel reads like an aggressive attempt to appropriate not Beckett's material but Beckett's function as an artist, to attain at one swipe a relation like Beckett's to his public, perhaps even his success, his fame.

A decade later, this same urge, so foreign to Beckett, produced the aptly titled Horovitz film, *Author! Author!* a transparently autobiographical fantasy in which Horovitz portrays himself (played by Al Pacino) as a universally loved, sexually irresistible, invariably successful Broadway playwright who can have directors hired and fired at will. As a medium for this power fantasy, film proved much more congenial than did avant-garde fiction. But *Author! Author!* clarifies the authorial power fantasies at the core of *Cappella*.

By an odd and embarrassing concatenation of events, the publication of *Cappella* in 1973 was fated to cool (if not end) Horovitz's close relationship with Beckett and to sour Horovitz's reputation in America. It is known among Beckett circles that Beckett could never reconcile himself to the dishonesty incidentally uncovered by the publication of the novel. An undergraduate journalist at Harvard was the first to break the story that the biographical blurb in the back of Horovitz's published novel reproduced a lie, originated by Horovitz, that he had attended Harvard as an undergraduate in the class of 1961. Horovitz never attended Harvard, but he claimed that he had in his application for a teaching position he obtained at the City College of New York. An editorial assistant at Harper & Row had retrieved Horovitz's academic credentials while preparing the book for publication, and when the story broke in the national press, Horovitz was fired. [8]

With dreadful echoing irony, the first-person narrator of *Nobody Loves Me* (written roughly at the same time as these events) confesses to having lied to his employer ("a great scholar who wishes to remain nameless"), adding the pitiful observation: *"A small lie told with discretion has never killed a golden goose. Of course I've had to cover the lie often."* [9]

Horovitz has paid again and again for his lapse in judgment over the City College of New York application. He has tried every way possible to leave it behind him, owning up to his error, shouldering its consequences, speaking frankly and unevasively about it to one interviewer after another. But it has dogged him almost brutally, for reasons curiously linked to his imaginative writing.

The City College incident would not be worth retelling were it not that it bears on the central topic of Beckett's influence on the work of Horovitz. Horovitz's impulse to embellish his credentials suggests a fierce desire to achieve an identity that continually eluded him. As he describes it himself, the circumstances of the academic application seemed to demand the identity he invented for the occasion.[10] The gesture was the reflex action of a habitual fictionalizer. It was the work of a man inventing a character.

Born and raised Jewish in New England—a circumstance Horovitz was to explore seriously in a trilogy of "growing-up Jewish" plays he completed in the mid-1980s—Horovitz had made his way from working-class Wakefield, Massachusetts, without a proper education, and he had managed by sheer native wit, ambition, and imaginative energy to make quite a success of himself by the end of the sixties. At the time of his initial meeting with Beckett, the much younger Horovitz was flush with the enormous initial success that launched his theatrical career (two Obies in 1968 and 1969, a Vernon Rice-Drama Desk Award, two Rockefeller fellowships, a Prix du Jury at the Cannes Film Festival in 1970). Beckett, on the other hand, was in his sixties when they met, and he had endured years of painful obscurity in his early writing life. Beckett's laborious journey toward critical acceptance had only recently reached the climax of a Nobel Prize, something that at first horrified Beckett when it descended upon him in 1969.

Before they met, there was no hint of a Beckett influence in Horovitz's writing. But Horovitz soon familiarized himself with the basic works of the Beckett canon: *Waiting for Godot, Krapp's Last Tape, Endgame,* and *Happy Days.* And he reports that, far more than the plays, Beckett's prose from *Molloy, Malone Dies,* and *The Unnamable* (in their English translations), *How It Is,* and *Texts for Nothing* impelled him to the composition of *Cappella.*[11] Throughout this apprenticeship, Horovitz was strenuously at work inventing the next phase of his career. The struggle with identity, self-definition, the strenuous need to emerge from obscurity, and the anguish of feeling alternately like a god (when he won prestigious prizes) and like a nobody (when his critics lambasted him): these issues were cognate to the material he found in Beckett. The constant necessity to invent a self, coupled with the constant elusiveness of such an object, is, indeed, a central motif in Beckett's fiction. But it is only the surface of the much deeper ontological problem that Beckett has made accessible to literature.

Cappella is not very interesting as an imitation of Beckett, but it acquires irresistible fascination as a free-form portrait of the unrestrained thoughts of the young Horovitz. In section thirty-six, for instance, Horovitz's fictional amanuensis delivers an achingly portentous passage, considering the public humiliation in store for the author: *"I've almost lost my facility to differentiate between the memory of an event and the memory of a memory. I can't worry long though. Finally, I am certain event-memories are as fictionalized as memory-memories. So what does it matter what is? What will be will be made in the mind"*(72).[12] This flawed conclusion, based on a profound misprision of the central problem of consciousness presented in Beckett's fictions, reappears in the play *Spared*. There, the protagonist, closely modeled on several Beckett sources, delivers the following observation: *"Over the years, I lost track of what was real and what was imagined. The distinctions between the two became . . . unimportant"*(43).[13] *Spared* was completed well after such distinctions had proved themselves to be important indeed in Horovitz's life. Yet the inherent frustrations of a literary career, the inevitable dependence on the approval of critics, and the seeming blockade of his access to unambiguous success seemed to preoccupy Horovitz and divert his attention from a deeper reading of Beckett's explorations of the self in fiction.

The Beckett phase was a distinct part of Horovitz's writing life, but it was never all-absorbing, and he kept up other writing, which was not deeply affected by his fascination with the Beckett-inspired "voice" dramas. It is important to note that Horovitz wrote *Dr. Hero*, as well as two of the three principal full-length plays of his Wakefield cycle (*Alfred the Great* and *Our Father's Failing*), during the same period as the Beckett derivatives I have discussed here. The Alfred plays are explorations more in the direction of Edward Albee (there are striking resemblances to *Who's Afraid of Virginia Woolf*) and Harold Pinter. Although a few passages of *Dr. Hero* sound Beckett-like (Hero's narrative monologues, for instance), the bulk of the play returns to a snappy, loose-tongued repartee rooted in American vernacular realism, a voice that the passage of time has revealed to be Horovitz's best vein. However Beckett-like *Spared* might be, its central character is the protagonist of a larger fictional cycle that leaves the Beckett baggage behind.

Literary evidence of any lasting or significant influence of Samuel Beckett is scarce in the work of Israel Horovitz. It is hard to think of Beckett at all (or even the freewheeling absurdism and panache of the off-Broadway scene of the late 1960s) while watching recent work of Horovitz like *North Shore Fish*, *Park Your Car in Harvard Yard*, or *Fighting over Beverley*. The journey Horovitz has taken is an unusual one, but he seems to be mining a promising vein in the locally realistic regional genre pieces he has been writing since *North Shore Fish*.

The desperate disintegration, of both the subject and the formal frame in the Beckett oeuvre, was never taken seriously, never sensed as a true catastrophe (as it was for Beckett) in any work by Horovitz. For a brief time, Horovitz seemed drawn to the tone in Beckett as a promising path to his own writerly development. But it was abandoned without having yielded any real successes, and it was replaced by new styles and tones unrelated to anything to be found in Beckett.

Because the very act of imitating Beckett smacks of an attempt to put one over on a gullible public, the suspicion lurks that Horovitz might simply have been taking high-handed liberties when he raided on Beckett's turf. But there are countervailing signs at every turn that the governing characteristic was not chutzpah but devastating diffidence, self-doubt, and crippled dignity. And here the topic becomes circular, for these dreadful symptoms are deeply Beckettian and likely to have elicited considerable sympathy from Beckett.

Brater quotes a particularly apt fragment of *The Unnamable* while illustrating (in the study already mentioned) the deeper nature of the voice Beckett was transposing into *Not I* at the time Horovitz made his acquaintance:

Oh I know, I know, attention please, this may mean something, I know, there's nothing new here, it's all part of the same old irresistible boloney, namely, But my dear man, come, be reasonable, look, this is you, look at this photograph, and here's your file, no convictions, I assure you, come now, make an effort, at your age, to have no identity, it's a scandal.

The Unnamable (377) [14]

It is a passage typical of those Horovitz must have been reading when he launched into this strenuous emulation in of his Beckett phase in *Capella*:

When it finally seemed, became, was impossible to continue reading, I began. I am clever enough to lend you a name straight off . . . Better hurry. I am . . . make it good . . . make it not pretentious, not scholarly . . . oh what, what? . . . just a name for him . . . me (1).[15]

Who can fail to see Beckett's great metaphysical whirlpool tugging a young, ambitious writer into strenuous efforts to make a name for himself. This is "influence," in the end, and significant in that it altered and shaped Horovitz's life, but the personal intensity of Beckett's influence is not matched by the literary consequences in Horovitz's creative output.

NOTES

1.   In an interview between this author and Israel Horovitz in Gloucester, Massachusetts, 29 August 1992.

2.   Ibid.

3.   Deirdre Bair, *Samuel Beckett: A Biography* (New York: Harcourt Brace Jovanovich, 1978).

4.   Enoch Brater, *Beyond Minimalism: Beckett's Late Style in the Theater* (New York: Oxford University Press, 1987).

5.   Israel Horovitz, *Spared,* in *Stage Directions and Spared*   (New York: Dramatists Play Service, 1975, 1977), 30.

6.   Samuel Beckett, *The Collected Shorter Plays: Act Without Words I & II* (1956), *Krapp's Last Tape* (1958), *Film* (1963), *Come and Go* (1966), *Not I* (1972), and *That Time* (1976) (New York: Grove Press, 1984). Note similar passages in Beckett's *Film,* for instance: "He tears print from wall, tears it in four, throws down the pieces and grinds them underfoot. He turns back to chair, image again of its curious headrest, sits down, takes case on his knees" (167).

7.   Israel Horovitz, *Capella*   (New York: Harper & Row, 1973), 87.   All subsequent citations from this edition will appear parenthetically in the text.

8.   The City College story was retold to me in the 29 August 1992 interview. It also appears in print in a Ross Wetzsteon interview: "Author! Author!—It's Horovitz," *New York Magazine* (2 August 1982), 28–35 and in a Peter Sagal profile: "The Mellowing of Israel Horovitz," *Boston Magazine,* October 1986, 172, 239–48.

9.   Israel Horovitz, *Nobody Loves Me* in *Statements: New Fiction from the Fiction Collective* (New York: Braziller, 1975), 101. Italics mine.

10. Interview of 29 August 1992.

11. Ibid.

12. Italics mine.

13. Italics mine.

14. Samuel Beckett, *The Unnamable* in *Three Novels: Molloy, Malone Dies, The Unnamable* (New York: Grove Press, 1965), 377. Italics mine.

10

The Place, the Thing: Israel Horovitz's Gloucester Milieu

Thomas F. Connolly

Gloucester, situated on Cape Ann, is a rocky outcrop on the crest of Essex County on Massachusetts' North Shore. Predominantly a fishing community, Gloucester is both a real place famous for its Fisherman's Monument and annual Blessing of the Fishing Fleet, and an enchanted setting whose landscape has inspired William Vaughan Moody, Rudyard Kipling, T. S. Eliot, and has a romantic place in the American consciousness. Cape Ann is the haunt of captains courageous and the location of the "Dry Salvages," that inspired Eliot's poem of the same title. And in the most recent plays of Israel Horovitz, Gloucester is a place of grim reality and fanciful imagining.

An analysis of Horovitz's Gloucester plays reveals that they constitute the portion of his work that is not only the most successful, but that these are plays where his voice has managed to find its own sound. Horovitz identifies eight Gloucester plays: *Park Your Car in Harvard Yard, Henry Lumper, North Shore Fish, Strong-Man's Weak Child, Firebird at Dogtown, Sunday Runners in the Rain, Mackerel, and Fighting over Beverley.*[1] The success of these plays lies in their ability to capture the concerns of a community and its people with compassion and intensity. Horovitz is concerned with the human reality of Gloucester, but he shows us his Gloucester, a town whose reality is vividly theatrical.

Horovitz is quick to point out the working nature of the community where he functions as a dramatist. He is by no means any sort of distinguished playwright in residence; he genuinely identifies with the city and revels in its working-class pulse. He has said, "Gloucester is a real place, not just for tourists. I identify with [its] laborers. My father was a truck driver until he was fifty."[2] Horovitz respects proletarian virtues, but he is no socialist realist, and his plays do not glorify the masses. He writes about individuals working their way through life. The Gloucester plays are not overtly political; there is no speechifying or direct reference to any political program or philosophy.

Horovitz's characters live from day to day. Only occasionally, when they voice misgivings about what is happening, are they able to articulate why something is happening to them. Even then they are usually resigned to the inevitability of their situations. Possessed by long memories, the stunted lives of Horovitz's characters are punctuated by recollections of events from high school and even grammar school. Florence Rizzo, the most important female character in *North Shore Fish* was "once a high school bombshell." In *Henry Lumper*, the hero, Hal Boley, attempts to seduce his old flame, Patty Percy, now married to his old high school rival, Harry Percy, by recalling his days as team captain and her days as head cheerleader. We learn of intramural school squabbles that have been carried on through generations. This is not the stuff of Jungian racial consciousness, nor is it of any great historical impact, but it underscores the strength of the community ties that Horovitz seeks to depict. There are almost no references to the world beyond Cape Ann. Hal Boley has spent time away at college and lived in New York City, but the townspeople use this against him, believing he has forgotten where he came from. The people of these Gloucester plays are proudly parochial and fiercely territorial.

There are recurring references to real estate speculation in *Henry Lumper*. These references explicitly convey the attitude that people taking part in the sale of waterfront property are selling out—themselves and their community. *North Shore Fish* consecrates the lives of Gloucester people to the sea; "the water gets in yo'r blood" says one of the women. Horovitz's characters mourn the transformation of Gloucester from a working harbor to a seaside residential area. Gloucester has been a summer retreat for well over a century, but the more recent, gradual decline of the local fishing industry is critical to Horovitz's vision of a society that is falling apart.[3]

Along with the spiritual and economic decay that Horovitz chronicles, there is also in his Gloucester plays a curious, grudging affirmation of life in spite of its bleakness, bitterness, and hopelessness.   In these plays, one discovers a peculiar work ethic—not the so-called Protestant work ethic but one that reveres hard physical labor in trades passed on from generation to generation as an end in itself. Labor is its own result, yet its only reward is exhaustion. Prosperity is neither guaranteed nor expected. All that one can anticipate is marginal survival.   And the working men and women of Gloucester have but one ideal: continuity in a craft or trade, which is all the affirmation one can hope for in life. Without this respect for and passing on of tradition, there is nothing—no personal identity, no familial loyalty, no values or ideals worthy of the name at all. In the final moments of *North Shore Fish* as the employees leave the processing plant after it has been closed for good, Florence "looking around the empty plant," says:

This is all I know how ta do, Porker. Me, my mother, my grandmother, all of us ... we knew the fish business. (*Pauses*) I've got nothing left to teach my children, Porker.

They're gonna look at me and that's what I'm gonna think. . . . (She sobs, chokes back tears, continues) I've got nothin' left to teach my children. (*Three Gloucester Plays*, 277)

It is significant that the cloddish Porker Martino, hopelessly in love with Florence, tries to cheer her by telling her that "it's only work, it ain't life!" Florence's profound identification with her work sets her apart from Martino. He amounts to nothing; she embodies the play's dramatic theme. Horovitz does allow Martino to do the one thing he could do to earn Florence's respect. Before he leaves, he "mops and tidies the work area" until it "sparkles" (*Three Gloucester Plays,* 276). The protagonists of Horovitz's Gloucester plays are those who bond with their labor. When these elements of hard work and identification with one's job vanish from the scene, whether in the thinly veiled "Glossop" of *Henry Lumper* or the overt Gloucester location of *North Shore Fish*, life loses its meaning. Even the most inarticulate of Horovitz's characters sense this, and with this element Horovitz assumes the mantle of the playwright of the inarticulate. He has said that he admires inarticulate people.[4] Taken as a stray comment, this association would not seem to be the most fruitful one for a playwright to make, but in his plays for and about Gloucester, he transcribes the dirges and paeans of the voiceless. He reveals the thoughts of the intellectually diffident. The people in Horovitz's Gloucester plays are not philosophical, but the playwright is. Gloucester people are frustrated and filled with rage because their livelihood and their way of life are vanishing. It would seem that only the sea itself is permanent. The characters who can survive must have a respect for the old ways of Gloucester, even if this respect is only obtusely understood. This is Horovitz's conception of a proletarian code of honor; it complements the work ethic he has created for his characters. It is a harsh code that exists only to be adhered to, bringing neither solace nor salvation. Horovitz will overlook blasphemy, adultery, and a host of other conventional sins, but any threat to the Gloucestrian birthright of hard work for anyone who wants it must be forcefully condemned.

In *Henry Lumper's* epilogue, Hal Boley delivers a rousing speech to the townspeople of Glossop. Boley's bully pulpiteering is contrapuntally underscored by Lissa, the play's chorus:

Hal: My father believed that any man, woman and child who wanted to live in Glossop and work hard for a living should and would have that chance . . . [ellipsis added]
Lissa: Glossop is gone, but for the odd scrap, the odd vestige, a blade of an ice skate, a handle from a glazed ceramic coffee mug. Otherwise Glossop is gone . . .
Hal: There are plenty of fish in the sea for everybody! My father believed that and I believe that. And I am ready to defend that ideal against anyone and anything . . .
Lissa: Ideal, like honor, is just another word. A holy war is finally nothing but a war. And murder, in the name of goodness, is nonetheless murder. And fishermen who sink

their boats or sell their piers in the name of money can never again call themselves fishermen. They are simply, ordinary men with their pockets full of paper money . . .

Hal: I swear upon the memory of my father to run this waterfront in my father's way. Glossop will be great again! . . . [ellipsis added]

Lissa: . . . Where Glossop was now stands a thousand towers: condominiums staring over a filthy, fishless sea . . .

Hal: I am my father's son. Whatever my father began, I will . . . continue . . . I promise, with my blood, Glossop will be great again . . .

Lissa: For we the living now, there's still time to take down our "For Sale" signs . . . and to live. (*Three Gloucester Plays,* 167–168)

The play ends as it began, with Lissa and the assembled townspeople hiding their faces behind newspapers. Horovitz has nothing but contempt for those who would retreat from the values of the past by taking refuge in the present's passing show. The code of honor and the work ethic that he presents are Calvinistically grim—no respite proffered, no rewards to be reaped. Horovitz's characters must outdo their Puritan predecessors in stoic forbearance; there are not even any allusions to God or God's elect. One must endure because one must endure. Hal Boley makes no promises to the individual lumpers except that they may have the privilege of hard work; it is "Glossop" that will be great again. It is only the ideal that matters.

What is Horovitz trying to say with these voiceless characters? Their language debased by profanity, their opportunities in the control of forces far beyond their own dominion, these people are not the stuff of tragedy, surely not of comedy or even of melodrama. Horovitz himself makes no generic claims for what these plays are, and one must acknowledge his wisdom in consistently rejecting labels for his plays. In this way, they are better able to stand simply as what they are: dramas of a Cape Ann consciousness for the world to share.

The Cape Ann consciousness that Horovitz explores in these dramas is neither sentimental nor noble. He dignifies his people without glorifying them; there is much to admire in these people but much that one must forgive as well. We may cringe at his characters' relentlessly foul language as their linguistic poverty so graphically reflects their economic straits. He makes no effort to create a functioning Gloucester idiom, because these are not dialect plays. In this age of telegenics and homogenized voice-overs, we hardly seem to have dialects anymore. Besides, Horovitz is not simply out to preserve a dialect or a language; if anything, he is a reporter of the spoken word.

What Horovitz manages to create in the best of his Gloucester plays is the lives of people whose dreams are not merely deferred but entirely dashed and who nonetheless go on. The hopeless hope that certain of O'Neill's characters venerate is a subtextual given for the people of these plays. The women toiling on the line for the North Shore Fish Company do not analyze their situation, nor does Horovitz; it is thrust before us. Even *Henry Lumper,* his large drama of a union struggling with the sinister specter of narcotics, does not deal with models of behavior; indeed, no socialist realism on Horovitz's part is implied here. The authenticity in the best of his Gloucester plays comes from Horovitz's dramatic representation, not any imposed ideology. Although his characters are rarely intellectual, his dramas are not as anti-intellectual as Horovitz's interviewers and critics would have us believe.[5] Horovitz may be partly to blame for this perception; he occasionally appears overly fond of the false humility trope: "I am an untalented painter, frustrated by my lack of talent. It would appear that I sometimes paint in my writing. Yes, I am also an untalented, frustrated musician. I'm sure that this explains other qualities in my work. I don't know which."[6]

Thus, we see that Horovitz is more than a playwright of local color; the setting of the Gloucester plays is crucial to their significance, particularly if we consider the Gloucester plays in relation to Horovitz's earlier absurdistly tinged dramas such as *The Indian Wants the Bronx, Line, and The Primary English Class*. In these plays, physical violence and gross carnality are shown as abstracts of the human condition. Conversely, the Gloucester plays specify how human beings may be overwhelmed by psychological factors and socioeconomic circumstances by showing us where these things happen.

The notion of theatrical local color, or rather theatricalized location is essential for the understanding of the Gloucester plays, even for a work such as *Henry Lumper* with its obvious Shakespearean analogue (*Henry IV, Part One*), located in the pseudonymous Glossop. More than any other of his plays, *Henry Lumper* successfully reflects the Gloucester dramaturgical shading of the playwright and his desire to show Gloucester to the world. *North Shore Fish* is equally effective as a Gloucester drama, but because its impact is achieved through its characterizations rather than through any significant action, it is Gloucester to scale, Gloucester life-sized. *Henry Lumper* is Gloucester as the great theatre of the world. It is almost pageantlike in its presentation of Gloucester life and times in the final decades of the twentieth century.

The central question raised by this issue of site-specific drama is not in fact whether the drama has only local interest; a good play transcends all boundaries. Rather the question is: Does localization create in and of itself a situation whereby the drama is reduced in scope? We may consider this question in two ways: (1) if the drama is composed of locating elements that are sufficiently interesting in and of themselves, then they may in fact augment or even amplify the dramatic situation, and (2) if the situation of the drama—the action, if you will—offers sufficient interest, then we may overlook the location.

For these last points it is a question of relevance as well as resonance—relevance because of what Horovitz is trying to do and resonance because of how he does it. Nonetheless, both *Henry Lumper* and *North Shore Fish* were written for his own theatre, the Gloucester Stage Company. These

two plays premiered in Gloucester and went on to have successful stagings in
New York City. They are written about a particular town, to be performed by a
particular theatre company. In these two plays he shows us the economic plight
and spiritual crisis confronting Gloucester and its people. It is worth noting
that Horovitz provides his most effective Gloucester drama in the only two
plays (to date) that have received their first productions there. Horovitz's
service as artistic director of the Gloucester Stage Company is, among other
things, his self-proclaimed community service to Gloucester (to which the city
has responded favorably).[7] He started it in 1979, using almost any spare room
he could find. Today the theatre is housed most appropriately in what was once
a fish company warehouse and has a quarter-million-dollar budget. Horovitz
says the "passion of the Gloucester Stage is creating or attracting plays that
reflect life in our tiny dot of the planet Earth."[8] And what Horovitz has to say
about the first production of *North Shore Fish* sums up his concern for his
theatre and his thematic concerns as a playwright:

I think it's about men and women and who controls who [*sic*]. Wherever people do
labor, that play will touch them. The thing that's extraordinary about *North Shore Fish*
is to see it in Gloucester . . . They are testing it for verisimilitude. They're not looking
at it as a play about love and courage. They're looking at it as a play about people who
cut fish.[9]

The site-specific plays *Henry Lumper* and *North Shore Fish* have greater
resonance as plays about Gloucester life than *Mackerel, Year of the Duck, and
Strong-Man's Weak Child*. These three plays nominally occur in Gloucester
and are full of local locutions but do not have the urgency, power, and depth of
the two plays that actually have Gloucester concerns in them. *Park Your Car in
Harvard Yard* stands somewhere in between these two groups. In some ways, it
is an effective Gloucester play, but its sentimental tone overwhelms any
seriousness that its characters dally with. Kathleen Hogan and Jacob Brackish
may articulate Gloucestrian concerns better than any of the figures in *Henry
Lumper* and *North Shore Fish*, but the play has little more to offer than their
wistful and winsome dialogue. *Park Your Car in Harvard Yard* may not be of
the same caliber as *Henry Lumper* and *North Shore Fish*; nonetheless, its
unpretentious and straightforward characterizations allow us to hear and
understand what it is like to live in Gloucester. Horovitz has said of this play:

I would never have written Kathleen's speech if I hadn't lived here, the speech where she
says it's wicked lonely and bleak in the wintertime, and she talks about the boats going
and the people not coming back. You get that from people. You hear people say that.
They break down and they say, "The winter is tough here. We have friends that go out
on the boats and some of them don't come back, and it's tough and it's full of snow and

it's tough." And finally it hits you that it is tough. It isn't just beautiful little fishing boats and beautiful painted houses.[10]

In his prefaces and introductions in print and before the curtain of the Gloucester Stage Company, Horovitz presents himself as a dramatist engagé. Horovitz the playwright is the man of Gloucester, not going down to sea in a ship but treading across the boards of a stage. The actuality of antidrug crusading that Horovitz imputes to *Henry Lumper* in the preface to *Three Gloucester Plays*—

The then-mayor of Gloucester told me he learned of his city's drug problem from my play. Ultimately so did the *Boston Globe*. Gloucester's drug problem was out in the open, ready finally for a cure. It was a thrilling time in my life. To be a playwright and to actually have impact on a community! To be . . . timely!—

is belied by the chorus figure who intones at play's end that "'Glossop' is no more."[11] The timeliness Horovitz is so proud of is no doubt explicable within the context of the play's original production, but the play has greater resonance as a drama than as some sort of call to social action. And it is strange indeed that a play that ostensibly takes place in the present could be about a place that no longer exists. Unless one is a partisan of kitchen-sink realism, there can be no doubt that this paradoxical chronological twist instantly renders the play more theatrical and makes it a better drama—more timeless, if you will. Otherwise we would have the case of a play such as John Galsworthy's *Justice*, now little more than a footnote to a development in the annals of English crime and punishment.[12]

Henry Lumper is much more than a problem play. The dynastic labor conflict in it creates a clear dramatic focus that, coupled with the scandal of drug smuggling, gives us a play that transcends topicality. The themes of integrity and loyalty that drive the drama are eternal issues. *Henry Lumper* is not a play about drug-running. It does not preach; it dramatizes what happens when a community loses its sense of itself. Horovitz achieves theatrical distancing without sacrificing any Gloucestrian resonance. In terms of the Gloucester cycle as a whole, though, because *Henry Lumper* is a reflection of an actual problem, it gives us a more satisfying and significant dramatic situation than the enormous fish of *Mackerel*.

Let us consider briefly this first of the Gloucester plays, if only to contrast its lack of genuine Gloucester ambience with Horovitz's more recent efforts. Alternately surrealistic and naturalistic, *Mackerel* is about a 250,000-pound fish tossed by a hurricane into the living room of a Gloucester family. We witness the killing of the creature by the entire Lemon family. Its slaughter follows, and the Lemons attempt to make a killing off the sale of the fish's carcass. As the fish rots away in their living room, the family systematically downgrades the marketing of the product from filets to cat food to fish meal. Bizarre complications ensue, the upshot being that the world is destroyed. It is interesting that in the "place" description that Horovitz provides in the published text of *Mackerel*, he does not say that the play takes place in Gloucester; it is simply described as occurring in "the dining room of the Lemon's seaside home" (*Mackerel*, 8). He does identify it, though, as a Gloucester play in the preface to *Three Gloucester Plays*. *Mackerel*, despite its absurdist theatricality, actually shows the existence obtained from fishing in a way that his other Gloucester plays do not. We actually see the family carving up the monster mackerel on stage; there is a primal intensity to this action that makes this the play's high point. Even so, the obviousness of the play's absurdism and its relentlessly conspicuous symbolism give us a play that wants to mean something more than it is.

Mackerel is alone among the Gloucester plays in its heavy-handed symbolism. Even a lesser effort, *Year of the Duck*, manages to dramatize the putting on of a play without any attitudinizing (no small feat given Horovitz's obsessive concern with the production of his plays and film scripts). In this play about a community theatre whose members' lives are unduly affected by their production of Ibsen's *The Wild Duck*, Horovitz spares us any disquisitions on the art of the theatre. The Wingaersheek Players are interested in learning their lines and not bumping into the furniture. The difficulty in this play comes from Horovitz's attempt to impose Ibsenism onto Gloucester. What is lacking in it is a tradition of some sort that is endemic to Gloucester; a dozen or so seasons of a community theatre troupe do not provide an adequate context for a site-specific Gloucester drama. There is also something unsatisfying about *Year of the Duck*'s happy ending. Horovitz theatricalizes the play's finale and renders it doubly happy: not only does Sophie, the Hedvig character, manage to kill the duck, thereby avoiding suicide, but Horovitz also instructs us that the duck is to be brought on for the curtain call "to 'prove' to the audience that the bird is still alive" (*Year of the Duck*, 87).

It is a telling commentary on Horovitz's Gloucestrian milieu that it is successfully encompassed by Shakespearean themes but is unable to accommodate an Ibsenite formula. Thornton Wilder once told Horovitz that there wasn't much "Wakefield" in his Wakefield plays;[13] nevertheless, the family names and geographic references that recur in the Gloucester plays are more than Horovitz's remedial work. Certainly few audience members outside Gloucester pick up on the frequent references to Good Harbor Beach and the various coves of Cape Ann, not to mention the references to other points on the Massachusetts map that resonate in these plays. But taken as a whole, this is indeed a dramatic realm, a place as clearly configured as Eugene O'Neill's New London or Tennessee Williams's Mississippi Delta. Moreover, the recurring names of Horovitz's characters are not the old-line founders' surnames but the names of immigrants. There are almost no references to the old Yankees, although in *Park Your Car in Harvard Yard* Horovitz respectively describes Brackish and Hogan as a "Jewish Yankee" and an "Irish Yankee." The descendants of the original settlers are allotted allusive respect, but it is not history of the Samuel Eliot Morison sort that Horovitz presents for us.[14] He is interested in creating a dramatic location that serves him well.

Horovitz is presenting neither factual history nor his own story (as has been suggested in the Wakefield plays), nor Gloucester's story, despite his assertions to the contrary. The Gloucester plays constitute a dramaturgical landscape, not a mirror reflecting Bass Rocks, Ten Pound Island, or Rocky Neck. What is more, there is not really much dialect in the plays.[15] Though in each of these plays Horovitz gives instructions for the "typical North Shore Massachusetts accent," save for the frequent inclusion of *wicked* as an adjectival-adverbial intensifier, there are few words that any native English speaker from Glasgow to Sydney could not grasp. Even if one does not know that a lumper is one who loads and unloads ships, the word's meaning becomes quite clear as the play unfolds. Rather than attempting to discern any quaint Gloucesterisms in these plays, it is more to the point to recognize that Horovitz theatrically recreates Gloucester on the stage. There are no brave and reckless mariners hauling in the sacred cod here. Horovitz's toilers of the sea are more likely to be drug runners than fishermen.

The recurring complaints in the Gloucester plays about tourists are interesting because in the goldfish bowl economy of Cape Ann, the tourists and "artist" colonies now account for the lifeblood of the local economy more than the fishing fleet. Thus, the carping by Horovitz's characters shows us their love-hate relationship with the city's own self. The characters who make their living from manual labor seem to hate themselves for not actually working the sea. The women of *North Shore Fish* who pack frozen fish product and the men of *Henry Lumper* who haul crates of processed fish meal all feel an overwhelming sense of inadequacy. They perceive that in some way they have betrayed their heritage, if not lost it entirely, and are denying their children any legitimate legacy of identity. Yet at the same time, they recognize that these things are completely out of their control. The expository scenes in *Henry Lumper* and *North Shore Fish* are in some ways the best proof we have of Horovitz's skill as a dramatist. Here he is totally at ease, presenting a vanishing way of life, his confidence resulting, no doubt, because of his desire to preserve this way of life by dramatizing it. He seems most confident when showing us these people's lives than when he is symbolically interpreting them for us as in *Mackerel* or *Year of the Duck*. Horovitz seems to draw dramatic strength from his characters' frailty. They cannot preserve their heritage, but he can.

Thus, despite his attempt at renaming Gloucester as "Glossop," the site-specific plays *Henry Lumper* and *North Shore Fish* have greater resonance as dramas than the plays such as *Mackerel* and *Year of the Duck* or *Strong-Man's*

Weak Child that nominally occur in Gloucester and are just as full of local references but do not have the urgency, power, and depth of the two plays that actually have Gloucester concerns in them.   One could argue that Horovitz is in many ways at his most successful when he writes a Gloucester play that is of Gloucester.   The physical violence associated with Horovitz's early plays is not so pronounced in his Gloucester plays.   Rather, in these, there are inner struggles of souls pitted against immutable, incredibly powerful forces.   The women of *North Shore Fish* are sexually and economically enslaved by men who could not care less about their well-being.   Even Porker Martino, the dim-witted janitor who pitifully attempts to stand up for his female co-workers against the sexually rapacious manager, Salvatore Morella, is himself really only interested in an affair with Florence Rizzo.

As far as his Gloucester cycle is concerned, the less symbolic, the better the play.   He takes on personal and humane issues, but to be most successful, Horovitz must also include the work ethic and code of honor in his Gloucester plays.   In this respect, he is not dramatically infallible.   *Strong-Man's Weak Child* offers a cogent metaphor with its bodybuilder's literally physical sacrifice for his cancer-stricken child, but this play has nothing of the lost seafaring tradition in it.   Its characters have only personal issues to deal with; it could take place anywhere.   *Strong-Man's Weak Child* has abundant local references, but it does not seem to be of Gloucester. The play has an immediacy about it, but it is even less of a Gloucester play than *Park Your Car in Harvard Yard*. Unlike *Henry Lumper* and *North Shore Fish*, it does not adequately serve as a means by which Horovitz's proletarian code of honor and his work ethic can be dramatized.

Geography aside, the only thing that *Henry Lumper* and *North Shore Fish* have in common with the other plays is sexual betrayal.   Infidelity runs rampant through all of these plays.   In *Henry Lumper*, Hal Boley's degeneration is most graphically depicted when he disports in bed with the Fusco sisters and cannot recall the name of either one of them—not that either seems to care. This is the only instance, though, in the Gloucester plays, when sexual behavior is used to make a point beyond its impact on a marriage.   Hal is unmarried, and the Fusco sisters are consenting adults, so it is only Hal's individual moral consciousness that matters at that moment.   Elsewhere, the extent to which Horovitz's characters give in to lust is not so important as their loyalty to Horovitz's Gloucestrian ideals.   In *North Shore Fish*, Salvatore Morella's sexual depredation of the women he supervises is not presented as his major flaw; it is his inability to stave off the plant's closing that makes him a worthless character.   Horovitz emasculates Morella by having him break down in front of "his" women—"he sobs and moans, openly, like a hurt child" (*Three Gloucester Plays,* 268)—when North Shore Fish is closed.   The stunning hypocrisy, not to mention clumsy sexual innuendo and virtual blasphemy, of Morella's tearful speech reveals his impotence: "I loved every woman whoever worked for me. I did. I'm not ashamed of it, either. I'm a natural leader . . . you watch me: before Labor Day. You watch me. I'll have ya's all workin' back under me in some local fish situation, before Easter" (*Three Gloucester Plays,* 268). He has used these women's bodies but failed to preserve their jobs.

The dramatic truth of Horovitz's Gloucester cycle is revealed by his depictions of life as it is lived in Gloucester. Nonetheless, there is more to the Gloucester cycle than theatrical reportage, particularly in *Henry Lumper* and *North Shore Fish.* Horovitz's stern work ethic and proletarian code of honor give these plays a historical continuity and a dramaturgical unity. The more precisely Gloucestrian the plays in this cycle are, the more universal they are as dramas.

NOTES

1. Israel Horovitz, *Three Gloucester Plays* (Garden City, N.Y.: Fireside Theatre, 1992), vi, vii. All quotations from *Park Your Car in Harvard Yard, Henry Lumper,* and *North Shore Fish* are from this edition. The quotations from *Mackerel* are from the text published by Talonbooks (Vancouver, 1979). The quotations from *Year of the Duck* are from the script published by Dramatists Play Service (New York, 1988).

2. Quoted in Iris Fanger, "Israel in Gloucester," *Boston Herald Sunday Magazine,* 5 October 1986, 10.

3. *The Standard Atlas and Gazetteer of the World* (Chicago: Standard Publishing Co., 1887), 306.

4. Tom Connolly, "Hard Bodies, Soft Soap," *Boston Journal,* 30 August 1990, 10.

5. Quoted in Kay Lazar, "Center Stage," *Runner's World* (November 1992): 40-43.

6. Quoted in *Contemporary Dramatists,* ed. James Vinson (London: St. James Press, 1973), 391.

7. Editorial, *Gloucester Daily Times,* 17 June 1992, A10.

8. Quoted in *The Source: The Greater Boston Theatre Resource Guide,* ed. Marjorie O'Neill-Butler and Ingrid Sonnichsen (Boston: StageSource, 1989), 115.

9. Quoted in Fanger, "Israel in Gloucester," 20.

10. Quoted in Ronald Jenkins, "Theater on the Run," *Boston Sunday Globe Magazine,* 18 July 1982, 30.

11. *Three Gloucester Plays,* vii.

12. The 1916 New York production also provided John Barrymore with his first serious role.

13. *Three Gloucester Plays,* viii.

14. Samuel Eliot Morison, *The Maritime History of Massachusetts* (Boston: Houghton Mifflin, 1949), 308-12.

15. There is considerable scholarly literature on the linguistic traits of New England. Among the sources that are useful for further study of this topic are Hans

Kurath, *Handbook of the Linguistic Geography of New England* (Providence: Brown University Press, 1939) and his *Linguistic Atlas of New England* (Providence: Brown University Press. 1943); Hans Kurath and Raven I. McDavid, *The Pronunciation of English in the Atlantic States* (Ann Arbor: University of Michigan Press, 1961); and Carroll E. Reed, *Dialects of American English* (Amherst: University of Massachusetts Press, 1977).

11

Portraits of Wo(Men) in Israel Horovitz's *North Shore Fish* and *Park Your Car in Harvard Yard*

Susan C. Haedicke

During the opening tableau of Caryl Churchill's *Cloud Nine*, Clive, the patriarch of a British colonial family in the 1880s, introduces his ideal wife: "My wife is all I dreamt a wife should be. And everything she is she owes to me."[1] His lovely wife, Betty, is obviously played by a man who, rather than trying to hide his gender, actually draws attention to it by responding in pointedly gestural language:

I live for Clive. The whole aim of my life
Is to be what he looks for in a wife.
I am a man's creation as you see,
And what men want is what I want to be. (251)

Churchill's cross-dressing of Betty, while very funny, can also disturb the spectator because it theatrically highlights the image of a woman so alienated from her female self that she must be played by a man since all that is left of the woman is the male construct. Throughout act 1, Clive remains the clear orchestrator of Betty's life. Her story is merely an extension of Clive's, a representation of Clive's fantasies. The "woman" Betty clearly lacks a voice or identity of her own, separate from her husband's. Through this hilarious concrete representation of "woman" created in a man's image, Churchill subversively and effectively demonstrates the power of patriarchal discourse and forces the audience to reevaluate its assumptions about voice and individual freedom.

While Churchill's character of Betty draws attention to the possibility of woman as a fiction constructed by men, the portraits of women in many of the plays of Israel Horovitz, particularly *North Shore Fish* and *Park Your Car in Harvard Yard*, often elide the fact that the female character's perspective is actually written from and expresses a male point of view. Writing about a woman and foregrounding her life does not give her a voice if she is living out a male-derived narrative, a narrative that has appropriated her voice as it follows the prescribed story of a woman's life dictated by the dominant patriarchal culture. Thus, instead of drawing attention, as does Churchill, to the primacy of patriarchal discourse as it silences the female voice, Horovitz masks, often unconsciously, the lack of an independent female voice. So assimilated into the dominant culture does his position in these two plays appear to be that he does not hear another voice and cannot even imagine another ending to the story. I do not wish to imply that Horovitz is unique in this duplicity in the presentation of the female character; in fact, he follows a long and revered dramatic tradition from the Greeks on. Other disciplines as well echo this "ventriloquism"; Shoshana Felman, for example, has pointed out that Freud really meant, "What is femininity—for men?" when he asked his famous question seeking the definition of a woman.[2]

In a provocative account of metaphoric cross-dressing, Mary Jacobus writes that when a male playwright, critic, or character speaks "for" a woman, he effectively displaces her and thus silences or marginalizes her voice.[3] To rectify this situation, J. P. Cholakian defines one crucial task of the critic as to "identify and unmask the 'imposter,' the male author masquerading as a woman,"[4] as he ostensibly tells the woman's story. The critic must distinguish between the woman's story and the male version of the woman's story, between the true female characters and those who are men disguised as female characters, and are, therefore, responding and reacting in a way that a man assumes women would respond or wants them to respond. The importance of this task of the critic cannot be underestimated if art is awarded any significant cultural role at all whether it reproduces existing gender identities or, more substantially, whether it helps to construct them.

The women in the *North Shore Fish* and *Park Your Car in Harvard Yard* exemplify metaphoric cross-dressed characters following a script defined by the dominant patriarchal culture, a script that locates female fulfillment in the home. There is no question that Horovitz portrays the women in these plays sympathetically, often exposing the forces that exploit them. His female characters are strong, complex, and interesting, but his honorable intentions do not displace the fact that he speaks in his own voice that he projects into these characters. What is at issue is that the women do not have an alternate voice; they speak the patriarchal language, not their own, and without an independent voice, they are effectively silenced. Thus, rather than furthering the cause of women, Horovitz reinforces the status quo.

Horovitz's camouflage of the male perspective in female clothing becomes especially clear from an examination of two aspects of *North Shore Fish* and *Park Your Car in Harvard Yard:* the enforced aphasia of the female voice in a male-derived narrative and the way the female characters are presented to the audience as objects for viewing. These characteristics of Horovitz's dramaturgy reveal ideological assumptions reaffirming gender roles dictated by the dominant culture that underlie these plays, and it is to his ideology that I will first turn.

The source of Horovitz's blindness to the possibility of a separate story for women comes from an ingrained ideological position, from assumptions so assimilated that they appear to be a priori truths or universals instead of being recognized for what they are: the dominant patriarchal position. The task of uncovering the assumed ideology of *North Shore Fish* and *Park Your Car in Harvard Yard* thus becomes to discern culturally constructed beliefs that are accepted as truths and to expose the source of those constructed "truths." That process is particularly difficult when dealing with gender identity and representation as Simone de Beauvoir, in *The Second Sex*, explains:

Humanity is male and man defines woman not in herself but as relative to him; she is not regarded as an autonomous being . . . She is defined and differentiated with reference to man and not he with reference to her; she is the incidental, the inessential as opposed to the essential. He is the Subject, he is the Absolute—she is the Other.[5]

This otherness, de Beauvoir insists later in the book, is learned, enforced, and becomes so ingrained that it seems to be natural or essential: "One is not born, but rather becomes, a woman. No biological, psychological, or economic fate determines the figure that the human female presents in society; it is civilization as a whole that produces this creature, intermediate between male and eunuch, which is described as feminine. Only the intervention of someone else can establish an individual as an *Other*."[6] Yet de Beauvoir does not lay all the blame for otherness of women on men and points out how women become agents of their own subordination for protection, security, simplicity, and comfort. The combination of men seeing themselves as the subjects and women having a penchant for complicity results in a culturally constructed state of affairs that reproduces itself generation to generation and thus acquires an appearance of truth. "When an individual (or group of individuals) is kept in a situation of inferiority, the fact is that he *is* inferior," admits de Beauvoir as she highlights the blurred boundaries between constructed and a priori truths.[7]

De Beauvoir's insights do not justify men masquerading as female characters and putting words into their mouths, but they do reveal the inherent difficulty in trying to discover the camouflage. The recognition that Horovitz's gender assumptions are based on the dominant patriarchal ideology and appear to be self-evident truths is more easily understood by drawing on Mikhail Bakhtin's distinction between heteroglossia and monoglossia or unitary language on which, I will argue, Horovitz relies. Although Bakhtin had little to say about drama as a literary form and nothing to say about the theatrical experience, his insights into ideological discourse help clarify the problems I see with Horovitz's portrayal of women.

Bakhtin establishes monoglossic discourse as that which admits only one voice supposedly endowed with the ultimate truth as opposed to heteroglossic discourse, which challenges and parodies a unitary language by its validation of multiple, often opposing, languages/voices in dialogue with each other, renewing and clarifying each other. Unlike heteroglossic discourse (the dialogic language of "both/and"), monoglossic discourse, the voice of "privilege," reflects the dominance of one specific group that shapes the evolution of the language so that its concepts, ideas, and images take on the aura of truth or universality. Churchill, in act 1 of *Cloud Nine*, theatrically exposes (and subverts) the potential power of the unitary language, represented by Clive's discourse, to overcome all other languages, not only through the theatrical convention of having Betty played by a man but with the African servant played by a white, the dominated son played by a woman, and the young, obedient daughter who is "seen, but not heard" portrayed by a doll. She thus draws attention to the silencing of all other voices. Horovitz, on the other hand, assumes universal agreement with his sympathetic portrayal of exploited women in *North Shore Fish* and *Park Your Car in Harvard Yard*, but he rarely lets them speak for themselves from their own experiences rather than those projected on them.

For Bakhtin, monoglossia represents "the forces that serve to unify and centralize the verbal-ideological world" and discourage, even repress, diversity and alterity. He assures his readers that this unitary language is not a given but something constructed by those in power, and it represents "the victory of one reigning language (dialect) over others, the supplanting of languages, their enslavement, the process of illuminating them with the True Word."[8] Monoglossic discourse does not lack nuance, complexity, and ambiguity in spite of the dominance of one voice; instead, it reassures with its familiarity and apparent truth.

The power of a unitary language does not just come from its suppression of other voices within a literary work, however. Language, for Bakhtin, whether it is monoglossic or heteroglossic, is "ideologically saturated" and thus represents "a world view, even as a concrete opinion, insuring a *maximum* of mutual understanding in all spheres of ideological life."[9] Thus, a unitary language base offers a single ideological position, a single way of looking at the world, and this dominant worldview seeps out of the literary work into all phases of social life. Bakhtin begins "Discourse in the Novel" with the statement that "form and content in discourse are one, . . . verbal discourse is a social phenomenon—social throughout its entire range and in each and every of its factors, from the sound images to the furthest reaches of abstract meaning."[10] An examination of a play's discourse, which includes not only the written text but also the "language" of the stage, thus reveals the verbal-ideological stance. In fact, according to Patrice Pavis, what is unique about theatre (a play in production) is its ability to put ideology into actual space—to

give it "body" or to actualize it.[11]   Thus, a stage presentation becomes a
(re)presentation of an ideology.   For Horovitz, the worldview is single-voiced
(monoglossic), and Bakhtin insists that when an author "comes forward with
his own unitary and fully affirming language" that privileges one point of view,
the author's choice to make meaning appear unified, whether conscious or
unconscious, represents a profound ideological position located in the dominant
authorial and cultural voice. [12]

Horovitz insists that he tells the stories of the women of Gloucester, and in
fact, he wrote *North Shore Fish* as a companion piece to *Henry Lumper,* which
concentrates on the lives of Gloucester men.   Horovitz is proud that several of
his plays grow out of the lives of the inhabitants of Gloucester and that in some
cases, for example, Florence Rizzo in *North Shore Fish*, the female characters
are based on actual women living in the town.   But his modeling of the female
characters on real women does not guarantee the sound of their voices since the
lives of "women" as historical beings and the stories of the fictional constructs
do not necessarily coincide.   The problem becomes apparent when the actual
Gloucester women are transformed into dramatic icons who "speak" only part
of their stories, the part chosen by Horovitz to satisfy his dramaturgical needs.
De Lauretis warns about the ideological dangers of the blurring of "women"
(historical people) and "woman" (fictional constructs):

The relation between women as historical subjects and the notion of woman as it is
produced by hegemonic discourses is neither a direct relation of identity, a one-to-one
correspondence, nor a relation of simple implication. Like all other relations expressed
in language, it is an arbitrary and symbolic one, that is to say, *culturally set up* [italics
mine].[13]

The task of the critic, therefore, is to discover the ways in which this
relationship is culturally set up in order to understand the ideology that informs
the playwright's work.   The ideological position that informs in *North Shore
Fish* and *Park Your Car in Harvard Yard* is that of the dominant patriarchal
culture and thus is culturally set up by the norms and values of patriarchy that
define women in relation to men and locate female fulfillment in the domestic
sphere.   Thus, these women are confined to stories dictated by the male voice.
The result is, of course, that their words are not their own.

In *Feminine Sentences*, Janet Wolff traces the cultural and institutional
"separation of the spheres" into male and female, public and private, from the
time of the Industrial Revolution and shows how the cult of domesticity
persuaded men and women alike not only that a woman's place is in the home
but also that the family is the source of feminine happiness in spite of realities
to the contrary.[14]   The "dominant modes of cultural representation," for
example, the arts, she argues, from the beginning, helped to establish and now
continue to reinforce a domestic ideology that firmly restricts a woman to her

domestic—and subservient—role of caretaker while simultaneously elevating that role in popular mythology to the primary source of feminine satisfaction.[15] Carolyn Heilbrun underscores the power of that constructed prototype when she writes that for real people in everyday life, "what matters is that [actual] lives do not serve as models [for social behavior]; only stories do that."[16]

The cult of domesticity clearly dominates the ideological substructure that informs *North Shore Fish*. The play takes place in a frozen-fish-processing company in the 1980s in Gloucester, Massachusetts. For the women on the fish packaging line (Flo, Josie, Maureen, Marlena, Ruthie, and her mother, Arlyne), their jobs, often in the family for generations, are more than a livelihood; they represent a way of life. Nevertheless, these working women, most of whom are raising their children alone, do not regard themselves as independent individuals but see themselves in relation to the men in their lives. Although they narrate experiences of domestic unhappiness, even violence, each clings to the myth of domestic fulfillment as love relationships blossom and a baby is born during the play. In fact, this birth of a little girl at the factory, as opposed to home or hospital, is a source of great joy, even awe: "Wonderful thing, isn't it, bein' born right here, right in the middle of it . . . Gawdd! I wish my mother coulda' been alive ta see it. Gawdd!"[17] says Arlyne, the baby's grandmother. The highest commendation for the workplace is not job satisfaction or sense of self but one of the most domestic of activities, the birth of a baby. The roles of home and work merge.

The closure of the plant at the end of the play does raise some work-related anxieties, however, as Flo sobs, "This is all I know how ta do, Porker. Me, my mother, my grandmother, all of us . . . We know the fish business. (Pauses) I've got nothing left to teach my children," to which Porker, the male assistant foreman, answers, "Don't cry, Flo, huh? It's only work. . . . It ain't life!" (277). One is tempted to add "for a woman," for the plant closure brings Flo's love relationships to a climax. She and Sal Morella, the father of her unborn child, break off their relationship, and then a few moments later, he promises to leave his wife and children for her. Flo refuses this questionable offer, however; she has heard it before. But when Porker proposes marriage to provide a father for the baby she is carrying, her story is over, and the curtain falls. As Heilbrun persuasively argues, "Women's stories always end with marriage, with wifedom and motherhood."[18] Now that Flo has achieved a "place," theatrically signified by the closing embrace between her and Porker, there is nothing more to say. No questions are asked as to whether she could actually be happy with this man she has mocked throughout the play or whether Porker will refrain from reminding her of the reason they married. The final image glosses over real-life problems and suggests the fairytale ending of "they lived happily ever after." And, in fact, Porker does appear or is mentioned in some of the other Gloucester plays, for example, *Sunday Runners in the Rain*, but Flo is rarely mentioned.

Gayle Rubin explains how the domestic ideology results in female aphasia. Starting from Levi-Strauss's premise that one organizing principle of society is gift giving and the most precious "gift" is a woman, Rubin, in "The Traffic of Women: Notes on the 'Political Economy' of Sex," postulates that the domestication of women whereby women are relegated to the role of gifts exchanged by men for their own gain and lose control over their own destinies, subordinates females to the position of "conduit of a relationship [between men] rather than a partner to it."[19] Luce Irigaray, in *This Sex Which Is Not One*, concurs, stating that "woman has functioned most often by far as what is at stake in a transaction, usually rivalrous, between two men, her passage from father to husband included. She has functioned as merchandise, a commodity passing from one owner to another, from one consumer to another, a possible currency of exchange between one and the other," most often between father and husband, from one domestic sphere to another.[20] As a commodity, the woman is silenced since goods do not speak, do not have anyting to say in their exchange. Thus, an essential aspect of being feminine is aphasia, and in order to become a valuable gift, the woman must become feminine, and therefore silent. This aphasia does not signify the inability to form the actual words; it connotes the loss of a voice distinct from the dominant patriarchal one.

In *Park Your Car in Harvard Yard*, Kathleen Hogan, now a widow, seeks out the domestic role by becoming the housekeeper to the dying Jacob Brackish, her former high school teacher who destroyed her chances for higher education twenty years earlier by giving her very low grades. Not only had he prevented Kathleen's advancement; he had also failed her husband and, twenty years before that, her mother and father. The play opens as she begins her first day of work. Brackish does not recognize her or remember her husband: "My memory system has set up a kind of magical defense against remembering the failures: they fail, I forget," he arrogantly confides.[21] Determined to make his final months unpleasant and to force him to apologize, Kathleen timidly enters his private life and begins to take control. She challenges his obsessive order by hanging freshly ironed shirts all over the living room so that it looks like a "regatta"; she neglects to clean up the rusty water from the leaky iron and "accidentally" drops several shirts in it; she changes the radio station each chance she gets, and, as her confidence builds, she mocks and even verbally abuses him whenever he takes out his hearing aid. When Brackish finally takes the time to learn Kathleen's real identity, he is quite angry and feels betrayed. His discovery that she is the daughter of the one woman he loved and with whom he had a long-standing affair encourages him to view her more as a person than just a housekeeper to meet his needs, but she has not acquired a separate identity for either Brackish or for the audience. She is still defined in relation to him. She now has a face in addition to a pair of hands, but she still has no voice. When Brackish asks her what she wants by way of an apology, she chooses to retake the final music exam to prove to her "teacher" that she can succeed. She gets a perfect score on the identifications of pieces of music, which he does admit is better than he did as a freshman at Harvard, but for her, that is only half of the test:

Brackish: The other fifty per cent is all on Section Two, which I have decided to make oral: one question. You ready?
Kathleen: I am. Yuh.
Brackish: Here goes then. Final question . . . worth fifty per cent. This is probably the most important question you'll ever have ta answer in your entire life about classical music! . . . Ready?
Kathleen: Yes. I'm ready.
Brackish: Did you enjoy the music, Kathleen?
Kathleen: I did. Very much, Mr. Brackish. I did.
Brackish (pause): Congratulations. A perfect score. (54–55)

Brackish has reasserted his dominance over her by making her passing grade depend not on knowledge that she can control but on holding the same position as he holds—a position based on *his* personal taste. To succeed, she must agree with him, so her voice is effectively silenced. Once she gets the "right" answer, Kathleen and Jacob settle into domestic harmony preparing cookies and decorating for Christmas, and when he dies, she gives him her mother's locket to ease his journey into death and whispers, "Thanks, Mr. Brackish . . . Jacob. I'll always be grateful." The question is, of course, Grateful for what? For being allowed to share the last months of his life? For being allowed to retake her exam? For being allowed to learn how truly wonderful he really was? Is this really Kathleen's story or a male fantasy of the loyal and loving woman—the male voice put into the woman's mouth? The play ends with Jacob's death; in fact, Kathleen's final words are, "I wanna report a death" (62). These final moments highlight that her identity exists in relation to him: The story ends with his death; she has no further story. Kathleen represents a clear example of a male construct, of a character like Betty in *Cloud Nine* (but not so obviously played by a man) who lacks a voice of her own. Instead of decentering the ideological world by presenting female characters with opposing social visions, Horovitz rejuvenates the cult of domesticity.

Another way in which to discover the author's worldview is to examine the way in which she or he presents the female characters to the audience. Not only are the women's voices taken away in Horovitz's plays, but the female characters become objects for viewing. In *North Shore Fish*, the women are clearly erotic icons. The play opens early in the morning as Porker, described in the cast list as "small, sadly comic" (179), readies the plant for the day's work. As he mops, he tries to sing a love song, "Strangers in the Night," but he forgets the lyrics so he makes up lewd verses, thus preparing the audience to look at the characters sexually. During the finale of the song, Florence Rizzo, the female lead described as "once a high-school bombshell," arrives dressed in "shorts, bright blouse, sunglasses, carrying two largish pocketbooks, cigarette in her lips" (179). In the production at the Studio Theatre in Washington, D.C., she enters on a walkway, approximately eight feet above the stage floor that extends from the upstage left entrance halfway across the stage. Thus, Flo is immediately privileged visually—almost on a stage on the stage. After announcing her arrival by using foul language to disparage Porker's singing, she immediately takes off her shorts and her blouse to reveal sexy underwear, of course, announcing that she is changing and ordering Porker to "turn your head around!" which he does reluctantly only after he has watched the display meant for him. Guided by Porker, the spectator, in the role of voyeur, watches the disrobing. This is not the only time Flo is placed on display. At various times during the play, she mounts the stairs to the office of Sal Morella, the plant manager, with whom she is having an affair. The interior of the office is visible to the characters on stage and to the audience through a large glass window. Twice during the play, Flo is framed by the window, almost as though on a screen, in "a passionate embrace" with Sal, and again the onstage characters draw attention to the "viewing" of Flo. Horovitz clearly displays Flo through male eyes as a sex object, as a passive figure to be viewed but lacking the power of viewing or ultimately the power of her own as subject.

Laura Mulvey, a feminist film critic, defines this passive role of female representation in her analysis of the male gaze: "The determining male gaze projects its fantasy onto the female figure, which is styled accordingly. In their traditional exhibitionist role women are simultaneously looked at and displayed, with their appearance coded for strong visual and erotic impact so that they can be said to connote *to-be-looked-at-ness*." [22] Sue-Ellen Case explains that "the gaze is encoded with culturally determined components of male sexual desire, perceiving 'woman' as a sexual object," and so both the male characters and all the spectators perceive her in the same way.[23] These characteristics are clearly evident in this first scene. From the beginning, Flo is displayed as object passed for viewing from the stage to the auditorium, and while she is the most prominent, she is certainly not alone. The overweight Josie also strips down for erotic viewing as she taunts, "Cheap thrills," and the stage directions actually read "wears lacy bra; 'flashes' the men" (187). Each of these women, from the moment of her entrance, provides a clear example of a woman who has interiorized the male gaze, who has placed herself in the position of erotic icon available for visual consumption. John Berger, in *Ways of Seeing*, explains, "*Men act* and *women appear*. Men look at women. Women watch themselves being looked at. This determines not only most relations between men and women but also the relation of women to themselves. The surveyor of woman in herself is male: the surveyed female. Thus she turns herself into an object—and most particularly an object of vision—a sight."[24] Flo and Josie know that they will be looked at and construct their image to satisfy male desire. That act takes away their freedom, their subjectivity, their ability to act for themselves, and thus it firmly implants them within a male-derived narrative in which they are defined in relation to men. De Lauretis explains,

Concepts such as voyeurism, fetishism, or the imaginary signifier, . . . are directly implicated in a discourse which circumscribes woman in the sexual, binds her (in) sexuality, makes her the absolute representation, the phallic scenario. It is then the case that the ideological effects produced in and by those concepts, that discourse, perform . . . a political function in the service of cultural domination including, but not limited to, the sexual exploitation of women and the repression or containment of female sexuality.[25]

The constant bantering among the women (which alternates between sexual nuance and outright "dirty talk" as Arlyne, the self-appointed prude, calls it) and the foreman's incessant patting of their behinds, pinching of their cheeks, and stealing kisses or more also keep the women on display as sex objects. Women outside that paradigm are simply not women. The inspector, Catherine Shimma, so frustrates Sal with her rejection of his sexual advances and her apparent masculine authority over his future that he "trans-sexes" her through name calling, labeling her a "bull-dyke" and endowing her with "dyke-balls." Horovitz, however, undermines this empowered woman by clarifying her actual powerlessness within the system when she angrily shouts to anyone listening, "You tell him I got people lookin' over my shoulder . . . and I'm covering my own ass, no matter what. Even if I have ta' close this plant down. If I hav' ta, I hav' ta! I'm just doin' a job" (226). Catherine Shimma's plaintive justification of her actions depreciates her position of authority with the stage "audience" (the characters watching her "show") and also with the house audience.

Costumes, lighting, and blocking direct the spectator's vision, male or female, to see through male eyes, and the male-oriented presentation of woman as other denies the female character any real desires or goals of her own distinct from those desired by the male subject. This presentation of woman as other not only denies the female spectator a reaction distinct from the male one but forces her into an imagined feeling of superiority over the female character that precludes identification with that character and thus subliminally coerces the female spectator into becoming an agent of her own oppression. Horovitz provides a flagrant example in a scene in which the women are evaluating male decency by nationality. Having rejected Jews, Italians, Portuguese, Irish, and English, one suggests that Frenchmen might be decent, but Marlena quickly denies their eligibility with an anecdote. She and her husband were having a shed built by French workers, and one morning two asked to enter the kitchen for a glass of water. She confides so that we can almost hear a panting in her voice: "One . . . comes up behind me and like presses himself against me. The older one—with the muscle shirt—he presses himself against me, in front, kisses me. The younger one reaches under and up, around front" (220), but she cannot make a sound because her husband is shaving in the next room, and he would beat her up if he found out. That response alone calls into question her reaction to the incident, but just in case the audience misinterprets her represented desire, Horovitz has Porker break the silence after the story with the question, "So, what did you do?"—a question Marlena never answers. The impression is that this experience actually aroused her, the reaction desired by the male subject. It is important to emphasize that female as well as male audience members assume Marlena's titillation. Stripping the woman of her ability to represent a distinct point of view trivializes her and denies her a voice, and it reinforces a profoundly conservative patriarchal ideology—a monoglossic worldview. This scene demonstrates that not only is the female character denied a voice; the female spectator is silenced as well.[26]

Park Your Car in Harvard Yard offers a more complex instance of what Mulvey has labeled "to-be-looked-at-ness." While not presented physically on stage as an erotic icon like the women in *North Shore Fish*, Kathleen Hogan is presented erotically in the imagination. Not long before his death, Kathleen asks Jacob if he has any regrets, to which he answers, "Yup. I regret never sleeping with certain women" (57). The conversation eventually turns to Jacob's affair with Kathleen's mother and his confession that he "adored her." Kathleen, perhaps jealously, asks, "If I walked into your class today, would ya' . . . you know . . . feel a little blind and dumb? Hard ta breathe kind of thing. Would ya'?" (60) His answer clearly indicates that he sees the younger woman: "Oh Kathleen . . . if I could live my life over, I would have you walk into my class and I would behave like an animal! I would choke for oxygen . . . you would cause spontaneous pneumothorax . . . blindness, deafness, mental lapse . . . I would deliquesce: melt" (60). Kathleen has put herself in her mother's place as an object of Jacob's desire and encourages the audience to create a mental picture of a blossoming and seductive high school girl. Berger explains this disturbing behavior of apparent self-evaluation in terms of arousing desire in another by postulating that a woman "has to survey everything she does because how she appears to others, and ultimately how she appears to men, is of crucial importance for what is normally thought of as the success of her life. Her own sense of being in herself is supplanted by a sense of being appreciated as herself by another."[27] Caryl Churchill draws attention to the need to define a woman in relation to a man and to the inability to see a woman as a separate individual when Betty in act 2 of *Cloud Nine* confesses the thoughts of Betty from act 1: "I thought if Clive wasn't looking at me there wasn't a person there" (316).

Kathleen is not primarily an erotic icon, however, but she is certainly highlighted, almost theatrically framed, as an object for viewing. She

practically becomes a specimen confined to small quarters under the bright
lights of an experiment as the audience is coerced into seeing her through
Jacob's eyes.   Assuming her former teacher is deaf without his hearing aid,
Kathleen allows herself verbal revenge.   However, she loses her independence
and clearly becomes an object to-be-looked-at when, early in the play, the
audience learns, before Kathleen does, that Brackish feigns his deafness and
goads her into exposing herself.   The knowledge that Brackish hears and
evaluates each word prevents the spectator from watching her revenge from her
perspective and instead forces him or her to view Kathleen from Jacob's
perspective, with Jacob's eyes and ears.   Her actions, thus placed on display,
become a source of amusement rather than of power as we wonder what she
will do when she finds out that he can hear.   Like a rat in a maze, Kathleen has
lost her freedom and acts in response to stimuli orchestrated by Brackish; after
she finds out that he can hear, her apology for her "swearin' and sayin' bad
things" (58) seems not only polite but suitable.   His very interesting
reaction—"Don't apologize. I deserved every word of it. Any man who peeks
through a keyhole deserves ta get a key in his eye" (58)—highlights her role as
object on view as he not only equates the aural and the visual by switching
metaphors from "hearing" to "seeing" what was not meant for him but also by
firmly locating him in the role of voyeur.   While, on the surface, Brackish's
lines indicate an awareness (both on the part of the character and the author) of
how women traditionally have been put on display, the words offer only a
hollow pardon since the rest of the play justifies his deception.   Brackish
continues to "act," Kathleen to "react."

    In spite of foregrounding female characters, Horovitz reaffirms the
dominant ideology by essentially establishing it as a nonideology, as
natural—the only option, a given.   Events happen in the play, but there is no
real movement in terms of awareness, understanding, or beliefs, and that static
situation reinforces the status quo, the domestic ideology.   The women in *North
Shore Fish* look to the home for salvation: the possibility of a new husband or
of luring a wandering husband home, a new baby, a first vacation after several
years of marriage.   Kathleen, in *Park Your Car in Harvard Yard*, finds "true"
fulfillment in her caretaker role as she makes Jacob's last weeks comfortable,
heals the rift between them, and convinces the outside world of his worth.
These women live in stories defined by the male perspective and speak the
words that a man would expect or wish them to speak.   They, like Betty in
Cloud Nine, are men in women's clothing and thus reinforce the dominant
patriarchal ideology.

    "Ideology," writes Jill Dolan, "defines a way of thinking, a particular set of
world views that works as its own hermeneutics. No one is without ideology;
people are raised with and cultivate certain ways of thinking and seeing that
help them make sense of their culture. Ideology is based on assumptions about
how the culture operates and what it means."[28]   Ideology not only helps

organize what we see, hear, and think into coherent and comprehensible patterns that we then use in daily life but also, according to Michelle Barrett, represents "a generic term for the processes by which meaning is produced, challenged, reproduced, transformed."[29] Art plays a significant role in that process because "ideology is implicit in perception, and therefore in any critical or creative act—analysis, description, or interpretation."[30] Thus, it is of crucial importance to uncover the ideological assumptions that saturate a particular work—a task that is often very difficult since art that reflects the "truths" of the dominant culture may appear "ideologically void," but, in actuality, such art is ideologically laden and reaffirms the status quo.[31] As Claire Johnson insists, "The idea that art is universal and thus potentially androgynous is basically an idealist notion: art can only be defined as a discourse within a particular conjuncture."[32]

When the author creates a nonideology, Jill Dolan warns, "the perceptions of the more powerful have come to serve as standards for the less powerful, who do not have the same access to the media and artistic outlets that create public opinion . . . [so] less powerful people are subjected to social structures that benefit the interests of the more powerful."[33] The danger with these plays by Horovitz is that we fail to recognize these "perceptions." If "all representation is inherently ideological," as Dolan asserts, and ideology provides us with a way of seeing, knowing, and understanding our world, then we have a responsibility to know what is being taught.[34] And to take this notion one step further, if ideology, and by extension art, is knowledge making, it is of crucial importance to understand what is being constructed. Foregrounding female characters, as does Horovitz, does not necessarily valorize gender differences and can, in fact, reinforce the dominant culture. Only by challenging hidden ideological assumptions can knowledge be reconstructed to celebrate otherness.

NOTES

1. Caryl Churchill, *Plays: One* (New York: Routledge, 1985), 251. All subsequent references to this play will appear parenthetically in the text.

2. Shoshana Felman, "Rereading Femininity," *Yale French Studies* 62 (1981): 21.

3. Mary Jacobus, *Reading Woman: Essays in Feminist Criticism* (New York: Columbia University Press, 1986), 10.

4. J. P. Cholakian, "The Itinerary of Desire in Moliere's *Tartuffe*," *Theatre Journal* 38 (May 1986): 167.

5. Simone de Beauvoir, *The Second Sex*, trans. H. M. Parshley (New York: Vintage Books, 1989), xxii.

6. Ibid., 267.

7. Ibid., xxx.

8. Mikhail M. Bakhtin, *The Dialogic Imagination: Four Essays*, trans. Caryl Emerson and Michael Holquist (Austin: University of Texas Press, 1981), 271.

Bakhtin clarifies the concept of monoglossia when he writes that a unitary language "makes its real presences felt as a force for overcoming this heteroglossia [within which the unitary language must operate], imposing specific limits to it, guaranteeing a certain mutual understanding and crystallizing into a real, although still relative, unity—the unity of reigning conversational (everyday) and literary, 'correct language' " (270).

9. Ibid., 271.

10. Ibid., 259.

11. Patrice Pavis, *Languages of the Stage: Essays in the Semiology of the Theatre* (New York: Performing Arts Journal Publications, 1982), 86.

12. Bakhtin, *Dialogic Imagination*, 332.

13. Teresa de Lauretis, *Alice Doesn't: Feminism, Semiotics, and Cinema* (Bloomington: Indiana University Press, 1984), 5–6.

14. Janet Wolff, *Feminine Sentences: Essays on Women and Culture* (Berkeley: University of California Press, 1990), 12–28.

15. Ibid., 13.

16. Carolyn G. Heilbrun, *Writing a Woman's Life* (New York: Ballantine Books, 1988), 37.

17. Israel Horovitz, *Three Gloucester Plays* (Garden City, N. Y.: Fireside Theatre, 1992), 243. All subsequent references to this play will appear parenthetically in the text.

18. Heilbrun, *Writing*, 58.

19. Gayle Rubin, "The Traffic of Women: Notes on the 'Political Economy' of Sex," *Toward an Anthropology of Women*, ed. Rayna Reiter (New York: Monthly Review Press, 1975), 174.

20. Luce Irigaray, *This Sex Which Is Not One*, trans. Catherine Porter (Ithaca, N. Y.: Cornell University Press, 1985), 157–58.

21. In Horovitz, *Three Gloucester Plays*, 19. All subsequent references to this play will appear parenthetically in the text.

22. Laura Mulvey, *Visual and Other Pleasures* (London: Macmillan Press, 1989), 19.

23. Sue-Ellen Case, *Feminism and Theatre* (New York: Methuen, 1988), 118.

24. John Berger, *Ways of Seeing* (London: Penguin Books, 1988), 47.

25. de Lauretis, *Alice Doesn't*, 25–26.

26. See Dolan, *The Feminist Spectator as Critic* (Ann Arbor: UMI Research Press, 1988); Mulvey, *Visual and Other Pleasures*; de Lauretis, *Alice Doesn't*; and E. Ann Kaplan, *Women and Film: Both Sides of the Camera* (New York: Methuen, 1983).

27. Berger, *Ways of Seeing*, 46.

28. Dolan, *Feminist Spectator*, 41.

29. Michelle Barrett, "Ideology and the Cultural Production of Gender," in *Feminist Criticism and Social Change: Sex, Class, and Race in Literature and Culture*, ed. Judith Newton and Deborah Rosenfelt (New York: Methuen, 1985), quoted in Dolan, 15.

30. Dolan, *Feminist Spectator*, 15.
31. Ibid., 44.
32. Claire Johnson, ed., *Notes on Women's Cinema* (London: SEFT, 1974), 28.
33. Dolan, *Feminist Spectator*, 15.
34. Ibid., 41.

12

Machismo in Massachusetts: Israel Horovitz's Unpublished Screenplays *The Deuce* and *Strong-Men*

Ann C. Hall

Macho men quite literally wrestle with issues that threaten their manhood in Israel Horovitz's two unpublished screenplays, *The Deuce* (1991) and *Strong-Men* (1991).[1]   Set in Horovitz's adopted home, Gloucester, Massachusetts, both pit "lumpers" or stevedores, the home-town favorites, against a number of literal and existential opponents. In *The Deuce*, for example, the heroic lumpers clash with evil land developers, one-time stevedores who have sold out for quick profits and easy morals. The lumpers must also struggle with less tangible enemies: economic difficulties, family trials, and their own perceptions about themselves and their abilities. *Strong-Men* finds the heroes struggling with many of the same issues, but in this screenplay mortality or death is added to the list of existential contenders. In both works, the lumpers may not beat their opponents, but they do come out looking better than the competition; they may not overcome death or economic difficulties completely, but they do struggle nobly. More important, when the men reevaluate, compromise, and sacrifice, they undergo significant transformations. They realize the error of their macho ways and revise their views of the world and women.   Such dramatic action nearly reaches Aristotelian perfection: Blind to their own weaknesses, Horovitz's warriors gain understanding through their tragic losses and struggles. Unlike Sophocles' Oedipus or Shakespeare's Lear, characters who realize their weaknesses too late and therefore must suffer and die, Horovitz's characters awaken just in time for a Hollywood happy ending. And it is this movement—from tragedy to tinsel town—that causes many of the weaknesses in the screenplays. The characters' transformations come too easily, and they demand so much compromise on the part of the female characters that many of the feminist gains made in the screenplay are finally lost. Despite the screenplays' clear condemnation of macho, sexist behavior, many of the female characters are still objectified and marginalized, not as a result of some hidden misogynistic tendencies on the part of Horovitz but because of the Hollywood screenplay form.

From a feminist perspective, it is refreshing to see the issue of machismo or patriarchal biases treated as, in effect, a character's tragic flaw. To put it in terms of female, not necessarily feminist, popular culture, it is unusual to see that there are consequences to macho biases and behavior. The Horovitz screenplays illustrate that the consequences of this behavior cripple men as well as women. As the recent popularity of self-help books demonstrates, women have been approaching the problem as one that they must cope with in order to get or stay with a man. Strategies abound on how to cope, manipulate, or transform men who will not commit, marry, treat women decently, and so forth. Horovitz, however, clearly places the responsibility of macho behavior and its consequences where it belongs: on the shoulders of the patriarchal stevedores.

As insightful and refreshing as this strategy is, it creates problems for the female spectator of these works. As in many other Hollywood screenplays, the Horovitz works marginalize female experience. The fates of the lumpers supersede the fates of the female characters. Moreover, the macho transformations at the end of both works are founded upon or precipitated by the death of a female character. In this way, the female characters are merely facilitators of the more important male action of the dramas. This line of thought is not meant to imply that Horovitz should abandon his subject material for more politically correct issues, but it is a call to greater sensitivity to the female characters in the screenplays and the female condition in general. Horovitz's treatment of the macho behavior throughout the screenplays is particularly problematic. While the men realize that their macho attitudes limit their lives, they frequently shift these attitudes to more politically correct ones but pursue them in the same macho ways. In *The Deuce*, for example, both male characters realize that they and others have treated the women in their lives badly, but rather than depicting the men treating the women better, the men brutally beat other men who have not seen the error of their macho ways. This strategy fulfills Hollywood cinema's requirements: action is brutal, and there are clear winners and losers. Despite their new attitudes, ideals, and identities, the men in the screenplay continue to prove these ideals, attitudes, and identities in stereotypically macho ways. Consequently, the political or ideological transformation is undercut.

The Deuce opens with a stereotypical representation of gender roles. It is initially set twenty years in the past and depicts this era as idyllic: Men were men, and women were Madonnas. The first image of the film confirms this idealism: A statue of the Madonna, the Virgin-Mother of God in Catholic tradition, guards the town, the harbor, and the people. The ultimate woman, the ideal woman, is a statue. Furthermore, as mother and virgin, this ideal is unattainable for human women and it denies female desire: The Madonna is there only to bear the father's son and serve the father's children.[2]   The men in this opening scene are just as stereotypically presented. Two brothers, Franny and Philly Shimma, demonstrate their physical prowess through a number of competitions. With phallic imagery that is difficult to miss, the men climb to the top of a greasy pole, while their competitors fall impotently into the realm of the female—the calm, warm sea. The two brothers, "the deuce" as they call themselves, are unbeatable and inseparable, dedicated servants to the prowess of patriarchy.

The next scene, however, quickly shatters such gender idealism. Lumpers' work is not noble; it is backbreaking and even fatal. The deuce's father is even mortally wounded during an accident.   True to patriarchal form, Salvatore Shimma, who is on his deathbed, must nominate his successor as boss lumper. Traditionally the honor goes to the eldest son, but Salvatore names Philly because—much to both sons' surprise—Franny is not Salvatore's natural-born son. Franny recovers from the shock enough to suggest that the deuce work as a team, but at this point, both Philly and the screenplay reject such a collaborative compromise. Consequently, the deuce splits, and the dramatic conflict begins.

The lumpers' means of succession is nearly primal, and the disruption of this family's means of inheritance also disrupts patriarchal structures in general.   As Claude Levi-Strauss and Friedrich Engels illustrate, patriarchy depends on either the cooperation or oppression of women. Men need to know that their offspring are in fact their offspring, so controlling female sexuality is of the utmost importance. Franny and Philly's mother, however, has violated patriarchal strictures, in the process disrupting this family and splitting up the unbeatable deuce. Paradoxically, her transgression is also a catalyst for the drama itself; her "sin" creates. What is surprising, however, is how little the mother is involved with the action of the play. She remains in the margins, on the sidelines. She is not hated by her sons, but it is difficult to see her as anything more than a stereotype. The glimpses the screenplay offers of her make her past passion and transgression unbelievable. In this way, despite the screenplay's presentation of female transgression and its clear threat to patriarchal order and culture, female representation remains stereotypical. In the end, she dies, is neatly buried; she merely facilitates the male action.

Horowitz then moves the screenplay to the present. Times are hard, there is not enough work, and land developers attempt to turn the harbor into a shopping mall by strong-arming the stevedores. More important, Franny now works for the biggest land developer in the area, Laddie Powell.   Philly Shimma, however, remains true to his roots and tries to defend the harbor against such change. Such showdowns are popular in and typical of both Hollywood cinema and patriarchal culture: one man against another, winner take all. Recent studies in critical theory argue that such dialectical opposition earmarks phallocentrism, the patriarchal nature of language and culture.

Theorists such as Jacques Derrida, Jacques Lacan, Luce Irigaray, and Jane Gallop, as well as numerous film critics such as Stephen Heath, Teresa de Lauretis, and Laura Mulvey, argue that such dialectical opposition ensures patriarchy's continuation through "its false division of issues." [3]

In the Horovitz screenplay, the opposition between the two brothers mimics the mythic feud between Cain and Abel, but the screenplay complicates and thwarts this easy opposition by demonstrating that the families, no matter how much hostility exists, are inextricably intertwined. Philly's daughter, Ruthie, is dating Laddie Powell's son, Ricky. Philly has been having an affair with Roseanne Powell, sister to Laddie, for twenty years. And Franny still sees his mother and is close to his niece, Ruthie. Through this familial puree, Horovitz skillfully redefines the family in terms of social and emotional relationships rather than biological determinism. In terms of patriarchal lineage, such redefinition is quite revolutionary. The "real" father does not matter and may be replaced by another. The mother's connection to her offspring—no matter how the children were "got," no matter what her sin—remains not only intact but the primary parental relationship. In the end, Franny must choose between his biological family and his emotional family, the Shimmas, but this choice is not the easy dialectical opposition of phallocentricism, for his choice—to remain with the emotional family—disrupts the entire patriarchal chain of command. He goes against his natural father in order to recreate a new family.

Furthermore, Franny's choice is precipitated by a woman. Ruthie decides she does not want to date Ricky Powell any longer, so feminine desire once again creates conflict. This desire is so threatening to Ricky that he kills Ruthie. And it is at this point that Franny's loyalties to a natural or an emotional family are tested. Franny initially sides with the Powells; he believes that the murder was an accident and agrees to testify as long as the defense does not tamper with Ruthie's memory. The defense, of course, does more than tamper with her memory; they begin to revise it, arguing that Ruthie deserved to die because, in effect, she violently violated patriarchal codes of conduct for women: she was promiscuous, and she bit Ricky's testicles during sex.

Franny's loyalty to Ruthie, as well as the ridiculousness of the defense's statements, prompt Franny to undergo a transformation. He now vows to protect Ruthie's memory, fight for justice, and reestablish his relationship with Philly. He discovers that Ricky killed Ruthie intentionally, that Laddie paid off the prosecution and the defense, and that he helped cover up his son's crime. More important, he discovers that Laddie Powell is his real father, but this knowledge only strengthens his resolve to avenge Ruthie's death. In the end, the deuce reunites, and the two brothers combine forces to bring the case to justice and gain control of their lives and families. Philly ends his affair with Roseanne, returns to his wife, and decides to share the title of boss lumper with his brother, Franny.

Through an almost mythic structure of return, Horovitz illustrates the lessons the men learn by leaving their original relationship and then returning to that relationship wiser, stronger, and better. There are struggles, of course, but the men eventually learn to work together and with the women in their lives. By focusing on the male characters and the male experience in this way, Horovitz creates a vision for masculine collaboration that does not demand cutthroat competition, as well as a hopeful conclusion that illustrates that men can change, forgive, and relinquish their macho attitudes.

Although these images certainly challenge traditional representations of men, Horovitz does not entirely exorcise many macho myths from the screenplay. The men, for example, frequently resort to violence as a means of problem solving. Though their causes may have changed, their strategies for promoting these causes or attaining their goals are the same. The defense of Ruthie, for example, appears noble and different from the other patriarchal strategies in the screenplay, but in the end, all the men attempt to control her memory. The Shimmas wish to objectify her as a Madonna, while the Powells seek to objectify her as a whore. Both roles, however, transform a female character into an object and deny the character any desire.[4] While the Horovitz screenplay does not celebrate such methods, it does not entirely condemn them either. The men are rewarded by the film for their efforts. In the end, their collaboration is not that different from the traditional Hollywood buddy film in which two men save an innocent child, wife, woman friend, or someone else at the expense of female experience, which remains always in the hands of the male characters.

To a great degree, the Hollywood screenplay form itself dictates such conclusions and imposes such restrictions. As Laura Mulvey's important study of traditional Hollywood narrative cinema, *Visual and Other Pleasures*, demonstrates, traditional narrative cinema offers no place for the female spectator.[5] In essence, women are objectified in these films, frequently playing victims or sex objects and never affecting the plot. Women are merely props for the male performance. Action in the Aristotelian sense is reserved for the male characters. Consequently, female viewers are forced either to identify with the female victim–sex object or the male protagonist. Such identification is problematic, for the female viewer must either deny her sexuality or embrace it as victim. Female, essentially means passive here. Femininity is equated with passivity.

At the same time, the female figure as object is also a matter of great anxiety to the male viewer. As Mulvey argues, the spectacle of the female at once titillates and produces anxiety. Using the classic Freudian theory of the castration complex, Mulvey argues that the female—that which represents castration—will provide the male viewer with a sense of potence as well as the threat of impotence.[6] This ambivalence is clearly demonstrated in *The Deuce* through both Ruthie and Philly and Franny's mother. The mother's "sin" at once creates and destroys familial structure. Her affair destroys the traditional, patriarchal family structure and by association the chain of command, the social order of the stevedores.[7] This transgression, however, forces Franny and Philly to revise their entire understanding of family, and, to their credit, they do create a new family, one that affords collaboration and community without the rigid patriarchal line of command.

The mother's perspective on these events is never entirely illustrated. It is clear that she wants the boys to love one another, but her opinions, views, and desires are never articulated, and she dies before the screenplay ends. Ruthie, who is also a very vibrant female character initially, is not permitted to exist long enough to offer a female perspective on the action of the play. She attempts to bring the family together in order to overcome the hostilities and encourage community, but the depiction of her throughout the screenplay borders on idealization. When, for example, Franny and Philly meet for the first time in years at their mother's birthday party, a symbolic return to the womb, Horovitz describes Ruthie as the peacemaker, "born to play this role." While such compassion, healing, and communal actions are necessary at this point in the play, it is a role that women have played for centuries and a role that casts them as mediators rather than actors. Essentially Ruthie, like Philly and Franny's mother, becomes a conduit for the male-male relationship. According to Luce Irigaray, women's roles within a patriarchal structure are limited in this way. As objects of exchange within patriarchy, women merely serve male homosocial relationships.[8]

Ruthie's own death and later the death of another female character in Horovitz's *Strong-Men*, moreover, are not merely the deaths of innocent female victims. They reflect the ambivalent status of the female figure in traditional narrative. In her critique of traditional, dramatic narrative, Helene Cixous asks an insightful question: "How, as women, can we go to the theatre without lending our complicity to the sadism directed against women, or being asked to assume, in the patriarchal family structure that the theatre reproduces *ad infinitum*, the position of victim?"[9] Admittedly, Ruthie's death and the subsequent resolution between Franny and Philly may merely show that out of pain comes growth, but from the point of view of a female spectator, it is difficult to watch, in both screenplays, the death of two important female characters for the sake of masculine relationships. In terms of Ruthie, the screenplay denies the existence of a strong, female character. While it clearly condemns the actions of the killers, the plot itself demands her death in order to facilitate the reconciliation of the brothers. In this way, the screenplay itself becomes an accomplice to Ruthie's murder.

Strong-Men offers an equally complicated representation of masculine behavior by aligning masculinity and patriarchal behavior with body image. Such a relationship is certainly clear, but its implications have only recently been the subject for much discussion by feminists and their critics. Does the body affect social relations? Do such claims fall into the trap of essentialism? In *Strong-Men,* the relationship between the body and socialization is a matter of control; men, specifically the lumpers, try to control the shape of their bodies when they cannot control anything else. This image is a unique and ironic one. First, Horovitz's presentation focuses predominantly on the male body. As many have argued, cinema generally fetishizes the female body, but here Horovitz makes a shift in gender representation.[10] Second, the image of a strong, muscular male body generally evokes images or feelings of power, potence, and formidable achievement. Through this screenplay, however, Horovitz transforms the image of the bodybuilder into a Sisyphus-like one: Men lift weights, attempt to shape their bodies, and compete for trivial prizes because they have no power over their lives, death, or economic and familial crises.

Based on a play by Horovitz, *Strong-Man's Weak Child* (1990), *Strong-Men* again depicts the hard life of the lumpers, and once again land developers eat away at their harbor and livelihood. The screenplay opens with the appearance of Fast Eddie who returns home after years of rambling in order to compete in a bodybuilding contest. As was true with the depiction of Franny Shimma in *The Deuce*, Fast Eddie's characterization is initially far from flattering. He is a wise-cracking, self-centered, bodybuilder who took steroids at one time. As the screenplay progresses, Horovitz attempts to temper Fast Eddie's characterization. His sister, Mary Ellen, for example, is married to a man who beats her. After several evenings at home with his sister and brother-in-law, Fast Eddie comes to Mary Ellen's rescue and beats up his brother-in-law. The violence, of course, is much more dramatic and probably ultimately more effective than a trip to court, but it is difficult to ignore the implications of this image. First, although Fast Eddie's intentions are noble, his means for achieving his ends are still extremely violent. Second, and more disturbing, the screenplay implies that Fast Eddie's intervention has helped the marriage continue. Thanks to her brother, Mary Ellen can now stay at home with her husband. As in *The Deuce*, despite Eddie's "politically correct" motives—to condemn and stamp out domestic violence—he creates more violence. The female character, too, remains the vehicle for male characterization. The issue of domestic violence is used to illustrate the good-heartedness of Fast Eddie. Mary Ellen's desire and her viewpoint are sacrificed to the needs of this man's story. And although it is unfair to expect Horovitz to change his screenplay into one about domestic violence from a woman's perspective, it is difficult for a female viewer to see such an issue raised only for the sake of male character development.

Like *The Deuce*, *Strong-Men* also provides a double for Fast Eddie through the good-hearted, hardworking Franny. Unlike Fast Eddie, Franny has remained true to neighborhood, family, and heritage. Moreover, according to the female characters in the play, he is the ideal man: He helps with the housework, does the grocery shopping, and has even left a lucrative but very competitive engineering job in order to be with his family. He now works when he can as a lumper, making extra money as a weight trainer in his garage. Through a rather steamy sex scene with his wife, Evvie, the screenplay illustrates that Franny is also a romantic, passionate husband. Furthermore, the daughter he dotes on so much throughout the screenplay is not even his own. As in *The Deuce*, emotional parenting is pitted against biological parenting as a result of female sexuality. And like *The Deuce*, female desire at once transgresses the patriarchal family structure while creating a new one. In this case, it also serves as a means for highlighting Franny's already saintly status as the perfect husband. We learn later, of course, that the child is Fast Eddie's who, until the very end of the play, is unaware of his paternity. Franny, on the other hand, knows that Fast Eddie, his one-time best friend, is the father.

While the two men do not feud as ferociously as do Franny and Philly Shimma in *The Deuce*, their relationship is strained, and they are finally reconciled through a dead female character. The young child, Dede, is dying of bone cancer, and there is the outside chance that a donation of bone marrow from her real father could save her. Because of Fast Eddie's previous selfish behavior and his obsession to compete for the title of Mr. Massachusetts, Franny is skeptical that Fast Eddie would contribute because, as Franny explains, "They go in with these thick double-needles, to suck the stuff out. Once you're missing bone-marrow, no blood gets made right for weeks. You can lose all your conditioning" (72). Franny then sets up a competition of his own: He will take on Fast Eddie, and the loser must donate his bone marrow to Dede. In the end, Fast Eddie throws the competition in order to save Franny's pride and Dede's life, but his bone marrow does not help. Dede dies, but he discovers that he is her biological father. In a tearful death scene, Eddie tells Dede that she has a great father and thereby relinquishes any control over the child. After her death, Eddie is transformed. He plans to take another westward trip, while Franny and a friend decide to open a gym in an old fish warehouse, and Evvie plans to go back to school. To solidify the images of rebirth in the face of disaster, Evvie and Franny even talk of having another child.

The men in the play cannot control death or many of the other changes life brings, but they do have the power to change, adjust, and face the times. Their bodybuilding may seem hopeless in the face of death, but in the end, it becomes noble activity that brings some small relief. It is refreshing to see men having to experience change and to accommodate themselves to such changes rather than attempting to beat the reality of their lives or wives into submission. In this way, the screenplay celebrates masculine flexibility rather than macho rigidity or patriarchal paralysis. Nevertheless, the female characters remain somewhat disappointing. As in *The Deuce*, the women appear strong and sane, clearly the stabilizing and life-affirming forces in the plays. Even the women who made mistakes in the past recover and carry on. But we never see their struggles; they remain marginalized, left in the shadows or in the grave in order to highlight male performances.

NOTES

1. Israel Horovitz, *The Deuce*, unpublished screenplay (April 1991), and *Strong-Men*, unpublished screenplay (August 1991). All subsequent references to these plays will appear parenthetically in the text.

2. For a more detailed discussion regarding how such roles deny feminine desire but serve male pleasure, see Luce Irigaray *This Sex Which Is Not One*, trans. Catherine Porter (Ithaca, N. Y.: Cornell University Press, 1985).

3. See Derrida, *Of Grammatology*, trans. by Gayatri Spivak (Baltimore: Johns Hopkins University Press, 1967); Jane Gallop, *Thinking Through the Body* (New York: Columbia University Press, 1988); Stephen Heath, "Difference," *Screen* 19, no. 3 (Fall 1978); Jacques Lacan, *Feminine Sexuality*, trans. by Jacqueline Rose (New York: Norton, 1985); Teresa de Lauretis, *Alice Doesn't: Feminism, Semiotics, and Cinema* (Bloomington: Indiana University Press, 1984); and Laura Mulvey, "Visual Pleasure and Narrative Cinema" in *Visual and Other Pleasures* (Bloomington: Indiana University Press, 1989), 14–28.

4. Irigaray, *This Sex*, 184-87.

5. Mulvey, "Visual Pleasure," 14–28.

6. Ibid. See also Freedman, *Staging the Gaze: Postmodern, Psychoanalysis, and Shakespearean Comedy* (Ithaca, N. Y.: Cornell University Press, 1991); Jill Dolan, *The Feminist Spectator as Critic* (Ann Arbor: UMI Research Press, 1988); and de Lauretis, *Alice*.

7. Friederich Engels, *The Origin of the Family, Private Property, and the State*, ed. Eleanor Burke Leacock (New York: International, 1973); Claude Levi-Strauss, *The Elementary Structures of Kinship*, trans. James Harle Bell et al., rev. ed. (Boston: Beacon Press, 1969).

8. Irigaray, *This Sex*, 170–91.

9. Helene Cixous, "Aller a la mer," *Modern Drama* 27 (1984): 546.

10. Many important and insightful studies have appeared on this subject. To begin, see Gallop, *Thinking Through the Body*, and de Lauretis, *Alice*, as well as Rose Braidotti "The Politics of Ontological Difference," in *Between Feminism and Psychoanalysis*, ed. Teresa Brennan (New York: Routledge, 1989), 89–105.

13

Israel Horovitz's *Strong-Man's Weak Child/Strong-Men:* From Stage Play to Screenplay

Steven H. Gale

The creation of three versions of the stage play *Strong-Man's Weak Child* by Israel Horovitz presents an opportunity to examine how the creative process functions for this author. The fact that Horovitz has also written a screenplay adaptation of his drama extends this opportunity as well as allowing for an examination of the differences between the stage and cinematic media.

The four versions of *Strong-Man's Weak Child* (none of which had been published as of March 1994) are the script for the Los Angeles premiere; an actor's script for the Gloucester, Massachusetts, staging; a post-Gloucester variation (copyrighted by Horovitz in 1991 and represented through the William Morris Agency); and a revised cinematic adaptation titled *Strong-Men* and dated August 1991.[1] The Gloucester script includes hand-written notations indicating that it was altered during rehearsals or perhaps even during the production run, not an atypical procedure.[2]

Strong-Man's Weak Child is the eighth of the dramatist's series of plays set in Gloucester.[3] In trying to capture "the flavor of speech and emotion in a specific place and time," according to Peter Sagal, Horovitz says that "working to write about specific people, a specific community, is much more satisfying—and more difficult" than writing about the abstraction of the human condition.[4] Horovitz goes on to say, "With these plays, I have taken the position that changing times in Gloucester, Massachusetts, is an essential metaphor for changing times in our country and our world . . . My goal with this body of work is to create a sublimely detailed view of what life is like in our time, on this tiny dot on the planet earth. I hope that if I have gotten it right for Gloucester, I have gotten it right for the world."

A native of Wakefield, Massachusetts, Horovitz founded the Gloucester Stage Company in 1979, serves on the organization's board of directors, and is the company's artistic director, and he had planned to open *Strong-Man's Weak Child* in Gloucester. However, he had sent the script to artistic director Bill

Bushnell at the Los Angeles Theater Center (where several of his plays have been staged). Bushnell had intended to mount a play about an artist trapped behind the Berlin Wall, but when the Wall came down he asked Horovitz if *Strong-Man's Weak Child* could be substituted in the schedule. The Horovitz play premiered in Los Angeles in May 1990 with the author directing. On August 17, it began a two-month run by the Gloucester Stage Company, again under Horovitz's direction.

The two-act, five-character play is about a trio of thirty-something weight lifters who went to high school together and the wife and daughter of one of them. It opens in a makeshift though "reasonably well-equipped weight-lifting gym" in the garage of the home of Francis "Franny" Farina, "A former bodybuilder, late thirties, medium height, powerful," of Portuguese descent.[5] The action takes place over a "succession of early mornings, just after dawn, spanning four weeks in Fall, the Present," and the author notes that "the same North Shore Massachusetts 'Pa'hk Yo'r Ca'h In Hav'id Yah'd' accent [is] required," as in the earlier plays in the series.

August Amore, "significantly fatter than Farina, less muscular; same age, same height," joins his buddy in workouts in the gym. Fast Eddie Ryan (played in both the Los Angeles and Gloucester productions by Don Yesso), "a Body-builder, same age as Farina and Amore but shorter than others, and with much more significantly defined musculature," appears after an extended sojourn in southern California. He has returned to Gloucester to prepare for the Mr. Massachusetts bodybuilding competition.

At first it appears that the play is about a rivalry that has persisted between Franny and Fast Eddie since their school days. In part, the differences in their philosophies of life are evidenced in their approaches to weightlifting. Franny is consumed with the sport as a means of achieving a balance in life; his focus is on the weight lifted and the health aspects of lifting. In contrast, Auggie has let himself go; he enjoys eating unhealthy foods such as doughnuts in as great a quantity as he can, and his body and weight-lifting ability have been noticeably altered by his passion for food.

There is an even greater contrast between Franny and Fast Eddie, though, for Eddie is a bodybuilder as opposed to a weightlifter. For Franny, the difference is important: Fast Eddie and bodybuilding represent image as opposed to substance, the sculpting of muscles compared to a Zen-like meshing and expansion of body and soul in the creation of muscles during a lifetime of continually moving to a higher plane. Later it is disclosed that Franny's wife, Evvie ("same age as Farina, small, thin, beautiful"), was Fast Eddie's girlfriend when they were all in high school.

Into this mix comes Dede Farina ("nine years old, small, sickly, in a wheelchair"), Franny and Evvie's daughter who is suffering from terminal bone cancer. Bone marrow transplants, which can come only from blood relatives, have proved unsuccessful in stopping Dede's disease. The audience's consciousness becomes split three ways: on Eddie's mental attention to and physical preparation for his goal of becoming Mr. Massacusetts (a step on the way to becoming Mr. Universe or Mr. Olympia), on the animosity between Franny and Fast Eddie that is demonstrated competitively, and on Dede's fate and the ordeal that the others undergo as they suffer with her while awaiting the inevitable.

Along the way we learn that Franny is out of work, a victim of the economic depression that is slowly destroying Gloucester and similar cities in New England. Evvie is stuck in a fish processing plant job with no future. Fast Eddie is one of thirteen children who were abused by a drunken father and who have a low intelligence matched only by the lowness of their self-images; it was through bodybuilding that Eddie found a means of defining himself psychically as well as physically. He frequently refers to himself in the third person ("Fast Eddie is out of here. Fast Eddie Ryan is history.") as though to distance himself from who he was and to make who he is, or the image of who he thinks he is, seem more credible if his actions are related by an omniscient observer in the tones of a television anchorperson. Eventually, it is revealed that Dede is actually the daughter of Evvie and Fast Eddie, who left for California unaware that Evvie was carrying his child.

The details of the weight-lifting world are faithfully presented, as is the language of the class of people who populate the dying New England blue-collar neighborhoods (a multitude of four-letter words, contemporary slang expressions such as "wicked awful," the disparagement of the bizarre place called California where someone with Fast Eddie's personality—he is an "asshole" everyone agrees, even Fast Eddie himself—might feel at home). These details supply a sense of reality to the action, and when they are combined with the dramatic situations and natures of the characters involved, the result is a picture of humanity buried in a morass of circumstance. Each of the characters becomes more human and humane as the play progresses. Fast Eddie is willing to donate his bone marrow to his daughter, but Dede dies anyway. Affecting as it is, the play at this point comes perilously close to bathos in the figure of the brave young daughter, like Tiny Tim, who is less concerned with her own death than with her parents' being upset about it.

In directing the Los Angeles production, which ran ninety-one minutes, Horovitz learned several things about his play. In "A Note to the Director" written in Los Angeles in June 1990, the playwright indicated that "it is advisable to cast this play with male actors who are hobbyist bodybuilders, rather than with bodybuilders who are hobbyist actors."

In a "Post Script" to "A Note to the Director" written in January 1991, the dramatist says, "during the Gloucester Stage production, I determined that the play was better contained with Evvie, Franny's wife, cut from text" (3).[6] His reasoning was that he could thus center "the action on Dede and her essential [three] strong-men." Obviously this is an important deletion, and it makes thematic sense. After the Gloucester mounting, Evvie has only a few off-stage lines, and she is seen once, momentarily in the doorway between the garage and the house. Interestingly, Evvie is reintroduced in the screenplay, along with a number of new characters. Before examining the significance of this reversal, however, it is instructive to compare the Gloucester (hereinafter designated G-1) and post-Gloucester (G-2) scripts.

Although essentially only a cosmetic change, whereas G-1 is written in two acts, G-2 is divided into seven scenes. It may be that this change indicates a more connected story in the writer's mind. That is, instead of a structural break in the action at the end of act 1, Horovitz came to see the plot as having a straight linear flow.

Horovitz establishes several of the drama's major themes in the opening scene. First, in the opening dialogue, Franny's and Auggie's attitudes toward food are differentiated (especialy Auggie's penchant for junk food, represented here by his Dunkin' Donuts Munchkins purchase and Franny's linking of Auggie's last name, Amore, with a line from a popular 1950s song; "When the moon hits your eye like a big pizza pie," the original line continues, "that's amore!" (7–9). Then the differences in their approaches to lifting are illustrated:

Franny: If you want to . . . soar to new heights . . . You gotta ' hurt yourself.
Auggie: My water level's off. (9–10)

Horovitz also focuses on Dede and her illness immediately when Auggie asks, "How's Dede doin'?" (6). Finally, the character of Fast Eddie is introduced, although he does not appear onstage until the next scene.

Eddie comes into the conversation when Auggie refers to Eddie's comments about water level. Franny's response is that "Eddie Ryan don't know dick . . . The man's a known juicer" (10). He goes on to detail Eddie's failings: "Fast Eddie Ryan's nothin' but storebought health-club fancy bullshit technique from California muscle magazines and Joe Weider send-away books." More important, Franny claims:

the man's not a real *lifter*, Auggie. The man's got no strength any more. The man's got nothin' but a fashion-model-bodybuilder's mentality! And, as a body-builder, just look at him: he's a fuckin' joke! He poses like a fish: no grace, no form, no soul, no originality . . . That's not *lifting*, that's *posing*. (11)

Later in the scene Franny applies the appellation that is attached to Fast Eddie throughout the drama: He is an "Asshole" (12). In addition, Auggie offers some obvious clues to the reasons for the rift between Franny and Eddie when he wonders if Franny is "just pissed off at Eddie 'count'a old scores" having to do with Evvie and a Mr. North Shore championship. Before the audience sees Fast Eddie, then, an image of his character has already been implanted in their minds.

Furthermore, Franny mentions the possibility of a power-lift contest between himself and Eddie, a foreshadowing that sets up the contest at the end of the play. In the film, this portion of his dialogue has been cut. In another deviation between the play and the motion picture, Franny calls attention to Eddie's small stature, "We're talkin' midget class here," to which Auggie responds, "The man can't change his *height*." In the movie, it is Eddie who brings up the subject of his shortness. In terms of impact, the film version is more effective because it does not diminish Franny for alluding to a physical attribute that cannot be controlled while it simultaneously demonstrates that Eddie's height is a matter upon which he is fixated. Eddie's sensitivity about his stature thereby becomes a factor in understanding some of his motivations.

Along the same line is the expository information that Eddie affects a southern accent and that he picked up the accent while he was in prison. Again, even before he appears onstage, Eddie's outline has been drawn by the others' observations about him.

None of the changes in the first scene of the play has much impact on the action. Auggie's suggestion that the inventor of coffee cup sip-lids was "the same Nazi who came up with the idea for hot-air dryers for hands" (6) is eliminated, for instance, and Horovitz seems less concerned with trying to replicate dialect on the typed page in G-2 than he had been in G-1.

There are a few additions. Auggie tells Franny that the "powdery white Munchkin-sugar's loaded with testosterone. It'll grow a beard on your mother" (8). After Franny replies that he will call his mother to tell her because "she's always wanted a beard," a new line is inserted: Auggie's "She's *got* a beard!" (G-2, 8). Clearly this addition is intended for humorous effect, to lighten the dark mood that has been building and to make the characters more human. In the screenplay "mother" is changed to "Madonna," a more topical allusion and one that is intended to involve the audience's sense of humor even more. Similar humorous additions are included throughout the G-2 script, and more are added in the film script.

One other area that receives more emphasis in the later versions is the attack on the concept of California. In another segment of added dialogue, for example, Auggie says, "Eat your heart out in Venice, California, Arnold [unquestionably a reference to Schwarznegger] . . . You are looking at the Testosterone Terminator: August Amore!" (In an addition that answers Franny's pizza equation, he goes on to claim, "That is Amore . . . as in Italiano for *Love*! [12]).

Scene 1 ends with Franny's declaring that Dede has suffered from the treatments to combat her cancer at Children's Hospital (unidentified in the film) to the point that he is going to pull the plug.

The opening of scene 2 is signaled by music, as are all of the other transitions between scenes in the play. In his "A Note to the Director," Horovitz calls for all scene changes to be "executed in transition lighting," and he calls for music to indicate the scene changes, music that he chose that "people of this play would have listened to—and loved—whilst together in high school." Although the music is specified in the film, it is not used as an indicator of a scene change but rather to reinforce the mood of the scene in which it appears, to give another dimension to the characters who are interacting by placing them in a cultural and period context. At the same time, Horovitz calls for the added sound of a dog's barking to "precede *every* Fast Eddie scene" in the movie.

At this point in the play, Fast Eddie enters, and he confronts Franny. Ironically, he declares that "nothin' and nobody" can stop him from going after the title of Mr. Olympia.

A seemingly innocent question near the end of scene 3 (scene 2 in G-1) brings an interesting response:

Fast Eddie: Evvie come in here much?
Franny: No women are allowed in the gym here, 'less they pay five bucks to train.
Fast Eddie: You get many women training here?
Franny: Not many, yet, no.
Fast Eddie: How many?
Franny: So far? None.

Well, none is certainly not many, as Fast Eddie notes. Thus, the dialogue is humorous in its diminishment. Franny's comment about no women seemingly extends to his family, for when Dede calls to him from the house, he reacts quickly, telling her to stay where she is. He obviously does not want her or her mother in the gym (that Evvie is "not allowed in" is disclosed later; G-1, 46). When scene 4 opens, Dede can be seen in her wheelchair just inside the door to the house. The scene is retained in the movie, but the cost of working out goes from five dollars to ten, the introductory music (Joe Cocker singing "You Are So Beautiful") is cut, and the next scene, instead of consisting of Franny's recitation of Esmerelda the Seagull story, shifts to Evvie's work station at the Gloucester Fish Company. There are several simple insertions in G-2 that make the dialogue during the storytelling work better: Dede asks "Why" several times about questions raised in the story (why doesn't Esmerelda's parents want more children? why was their family "special"?), which allows Franny to continue in a sensible manner. In G-1 he merely kept talking.

Similar effects are achieved when lines are reassigned to other characters, which makes better sense in the context than did the original assignment. One whole page of dialogue is moved as well—the section in which Auggie and Fast Eddie talk about the fact that "Gloucester's changin' wick'id" (48), as evidenced by the closing of the North Shore Fish Company. In G-2 the conversation is inserted into the dialogue when Eddie asks why Franny has gotten out of shape. Originally Eddie's question was followed by the hint that Franny had a major problem on his hands in Dede's health. Structurally the alteration works because it creates a logical flow of themes in the conversation   and by establishing a symbolic connection between the child's illness and the economic malaise that has struck the community.

Although there is no question about the applications of the metaphor of affliction, the title of the play is ambiguous. Given that Franny appears to be the strongest of the men, at least in the beginning of the drama, and that Dede appears to be his daughter, the strong-man alluded to could be him. Of course, since it turns out that Fast Eddie is actually stronger than Franny and that Dede is *his* daughter, the title more appropriately applies to him. At the same time, in the G-2 "Post Script," Horovitz suggests that all three of the men are referred to. The title of the film is more inclusive; not just the father or the stepfather but both, and maybe all three, of the lead males fit. But with the introduction of new characters, settings, and scenes, the subject of the movie becomes the people of Gloucester, not three or four individuals.

There are other alterations that may be meant to make the film more generic, and presumably more generally applicable and appealing to a wider audience than that which was the target for the stage play. Films normally attract larger and more diversified audiences than do plays, and it might be that this is what Horovitz had in mind when he changed the name of Dede's doctor from Goldbaum to Bowman (17/27). Interestingly, although he retains Auggie's observation that "he's just one Jew doctor, right? Out of *how many*?" the author adds Franny's reply, "Henry Bowman's not a Jew. He's in my Parish . . . He's a definite Catholic!" One ethnic stereotype is replaced by another. Perhaps Horovitz, who is Jewish, felt that there could be some stigma attached to the figure of a Jewish doctor that would not function in the same manner with a non-Jewish doctor, something of particular note since the treatment fails.

The screenplay adaptation of *Strong-Man's Weak Child, Strong-Men*, is completely different from any of the stage versions. Partly this is a function of the opening-out effect of moving from the stage to the screen, and partly a result of a shift in Horovitz's focus, a permutation in his dramatic examination of the concept of strength as he moves from probing its operation in individuals to exploring how it applies to geographical communities.

The August 1991 revised draft of *Strong-Men*, contains eighty-eight scenes. The most obvious changes in the script are the addition of scenes (most notably in Eddie's sister's house, in the gymnasium, and in the fish-processing plant) and a concurrent addition of characters to fill these scenes.[7] The ability of a film director to cut from scene to scene is also utilized for dramatic effect to strengthen the parallel plots and subplots through cross-editing.

The first major change is in the opening. Instead of beginning with Franny and Auggie in Franny's garage, the movie opens at 3:00 A.M. on a July morning on Route 128 leading into Gloucester. The first image is of a truck with a California license plate pulling to a sudden stop, an action that elicits an obscene gesture from the driver of a folling car, which almost rear-ends the truck. The reason that the truck has come to such an abrupt stop is that the driver is ejecting Fast Eddie from his cab. Fast Eddie's first words are: "What the fuck are you doin'?" The truck driver forces Eddie out with the threat of a handgun and calls him the "*king* asshole." As the truck drives off, Eddie scratches its side with a jagged rock while a stray dog barks at him.

This scene introduces Eddie to the audience directly and immediately. No one talks about him before he appears; his personality is self-evident from his actions rather than from what someone says about him, although the "asshole" motif is established from the first as well. An interesting addition to the film script is the stray dog's barking. In fact, according to a later stage direction, "Dog Barking should precede *every* Fast Eddie scene . . . wherever Fast Eddie Ryan goes in life, dogs nip at his feet" (3).

Besides letting Eddie expose himself, the opening shifts the emphasis from Franny and Auggie to Eddie. Clearly, from the beginning he is a "strong-man"; indeed, given his appearance on the screen first, it is also implied that he is the protagonist. In the play, all three of the men exhibit strength, albeit a different kind of strength in each case. So it is in the movie, though Eddie's initial appearance needs to be balanced somewhat in order to keep the other two characters on a similar plane.

Scene 2 continues the opening-out mode. Whereas all of the action in the play takes place in Franny's garage gym, Horovitz takes advantage of the movability of the camera to draw the world into his plot. The second scene is set at a parking lot pay telephone as Eddie calls his sister. Scene 3 is a shot of the sister driving a pink pickup truck along the Gloucester harbor road, which introduces the city as a character in the film. The California truck driver is an addition, too, of course, as is Eddie's sister, who will appear in scene 5. Meanwhile, there is an intercut (scene 4) in which an event alluded to in the play is actually seen: Auggie is at the Dunkin' Donuts takeout counter, and the audience sees that rather than being impressed by his musculature as he claims in both the play and the film, and the ginger-haired counter-girl purposely places the slip-lidded cup upside down in the takeout bag, "knowing the coffee will soon be leaking on Auggie's leg." Thus, the author visually explains that the "accident" was not an accident while at the same time humorously illustrating that Auggie is seen by others as less than the paragon that he sees himself as being. Further, Auggie is described in the stage directions as being "fat, baby-faced," a more distinct physical difference between him and Franny than was described in the play (Franny is described as "strikingly handsome, muscular" in the film directions). The counter-girl is another added character, as is the waitress who is in the background and witnesses what happens.

Besides having introduced Eddie's sister, Mary-Ellen, thereby setting up a later sequence, Horovitz reinserts Evvie ("paper-pale, pencil-thin, beautiful") into the plot in scene 7. She is discovered "lying naked atop her bed, asleep." Evvie and Franny are quickly involved in a "sexual, hot" kiss, and then the topic of Dede is opened when Evvie asks if the child is sleeping. Her question is followed by a shot of the couple embracing as there is a "wipe" (pan?) "past framed photo of Franny, Evvie and their child Dede frolicking at beach" (6), a basic composition repeated live in scene 46.   This kind of comparative connection between the present and the past (a key theme in all of Horovitz's work), used repeatedly in the motion picture, is not available to stage directors.

Scene 8 takes place in Dede's bedroom.   She is a seven year old in the movie (removal of two years presumably makes her situation more pathetic and arouses additional sympathy, and it is easier to use a younger child in a motion picture than onstage because the action is not live, so it is more controllable), "skinny, pale, adorable."   Once again the camera holds on a photograph, this time of Franny and Dede weight-lifting.

Scene 9 is essentialy the first scene from *Strong-Man's Weak Child*—Franny enters his garage gym—five minutes into the film.   And even now the screenwriter intercuts with a shot of Auggie arriving at the house in his Cherokee.   The scene progresses much as it did in the play for a minute or two, and then the dialogue is delivered in a series of scenes (11–15) in which Franny and Auggie drive out to examine the health club facility at the closed North Shore Fish Processing Plant in which Franny hopes to set up a more professional gymnasium than the one in his garage.

Fast Eddie is brought to the characters' consciousness by virtue of a front-page photograph in the *Gloucester Daily Times* (seen by the audience).   At this point a new sequence is developed, revolving around Evvie and her worries about being laid off at work.   The following scene takes place in Mary-Ellen's house, where her husband, Dominic, and two sons, Little Dom and Donny, are involved in the action.   With a quick cut to the Gloucester Fish Company plant where Evvie works, five additional characters enter: Florence Rizzo,   Arlyne Flynn, Ruthie, and Josie, along with Mary-Ellen.   Soon another set of characters is presented, in still another setting; at Gold's Gym, Glen Asaro, Mick, Davey, Cooke, and Big Al are used to delineate Fast Eddie's character through comparison and their commentaries.

A quick glance at the film script reveals additional differences.   The time of the action is changed from July to the fall ("Changing leaves create [a] spectacular show of color," 5), and instead of taking place over a duration of a few days, the period is several months.   By moving the time to October through December, Horovitz evokes the family feelings that surround the holidays of the season (Thanksgiving, Christmas), which serves his enlarged thematic purpose and makes the timing of Dede's death more pitiable.   And extending the interval to months makes the introduction of the multitude of new places and people more reasonable while also allowing for further character development.[8]

Among the technical advantages of film that Horovitz utilizes is the camera as a means of focusing on an object or person in a way that is not possible on the live stage.   He usually does this in connection with his character development, as in scene 37 when a shot of Fast Eddie and Franny in live action is match-cut to a photograph of the two at age sixteen. The shot then widens to include Auggie, Glen and several others who appear in the film and is followed by a sequence of shots, first of a group of contemporary high school boys "enthusiastically" lifting free-weights in the gym, next of the photograph again (showing Eddie and Franny, arms entwined), and then a shot of Franny and Evvie, arms entwined. The screenwriter thus quickly moves from one shot to another, forcing the audience to see exactly what he wants to present—in this case, the parallels between past and current connections, with an ironic overtone that results from the contrast between the relationship between Eddie and Franny as schoolboys (reinforced by the juxtaposition of the photograph and the moving picture of the the contemporary boys) and their relationship in the movie.

Similarly, the inclusion of Franny and Auggie's visit to the closed fish plant's health club allows the author to introduce additional detailed conversations, as that between Eddie and Auggie in Maria's Restaurant in scene 39, that tie together some of the film's thematic threads. The two characters appear in a restaurant that did not exist in the play, a means of expanding the parallel and applicability of the sickness and financial devastation themes and at the same time furnishing the audience with images of the closed plant so that it is real to them when the characters refer to it.

There is another set of companion sequences in scenes 45 and 46. Scene 45 ends with Evvie and her fellow workers as she tells them that Dede is "definitely lookin' worse" (45); scene 46 is a long shot of the Farina family having a picnic on the wharf—"They are happy." This coupling of Evvie's words with the dialogueless shot has an affective impact. Another ironic note is interjected when the camera pans from the happy family to an equally happy Eddie and Auggie on the prowl for women at Good Harbor Beach, Fast Eddie clearly being unconnected with either the pathos of his daughter's condition or the happiness that comes with a family.

This ironic ingredient is intensified by virtue of the addition of characters. Ruthie, one of Franny's worker-friends, is expecting a child. Indeed, her due date passed thirty days earlier. As Dede's life is lost, another's replaces it. The same dialogue in which the past-due date is revealed, which takes place in a Stop and Shop grocery store (and what more prosaic and generalizing setting could there be?), includes commentary on Franny's character as a good father (48–49). This information is complemented in scene 49 when Auggie, riding with Fast Eddie in Eddie's sister's pink pickup truck, is discovered to be the Farina family helper.

By now, about halfway through the motion picture, Dede's plight is threatening to turn the film into a kind of television disease-of-the-week movie (as will be seen, the added elements extend the film's relevance so that this does not happen). In the meantime, Horovitz uses humor to break the mood, a humor that is abetted by the camera. At Mrs. Garagiola's, Eddie and Auggie carry an air-conditioner through her house and down the steps, and it falls through a wooden bulkhead. The humor is enhanced as the camera follows the two men as they strain through the move.

Another strain, intended to be humorous in the play, is dealt with differently in the film script. During an exercise session in the play, Fast Eddie is on his back doing bench presses with bar weights. He becomes trapped beneath the 315 pounds of weights, and Franny and Auggie, who are supposed to be spotting for him, have to help him out of his predicament. In the movie, Eddie is forced to extricate himself. The humor of the play is replaced by the serious threat of harm.

The introduction of Mary-Ellen in the film permits the script writer to show Fast Eddie extricating her from a bad situation as well, thus allowing for development of the protagonist's character. When Dominic slaps Mary-Ellen, Eddie comes to her rescue and threatens her husband (56–57). This protective action makes Eddie seem more human than the relatively narrow characterization allowed in the limited stage version (in part because the restrictions imposed by the set diminished by the filmmaker's freedom of movement through time and space, which do not have to be accommodated within a few minutes of real time during which stage sets are changed in live productions). Eddie's action on his sister's behalf also prepares the audience for his concern for his daughter and his willingness to help her. In the drama, his decision is more surprising because the selfishness of his character is emphasized, if for no reason other than that is is virtually the only side of him presented.

At this point in the film script, several pages are devoted to the layoffs at the fish-processing plant (68–69). These are followed by Fast Eddie's confrontation with Mary-Ellen in which he confirms that Dede is his daughter. The connection between the two plot lines is again the metaphorical connection between what happens to Eddie personally and the destruction of the area's financial and psychic well-being under the pressure of powers over which they have no control, expressed metaphorically as cancer. Eddie's character is further delineated when he says that if he had known Evvie was pregnant, he would never have left Gloucester. This sentiment fits his later statement to Franny that no contest is necessary to force him to provide bone marrow for Dede; he would be happy to do so—"All ya' hav'ta do is *ask me, nicely*" (80), a theme that he comes back to during the actual competition: "If you ever once come ta' me goin' 'She's *your* Daugher, Eddie . . . Come meet her . . . ' I would've been here in a fuckin' shot . . . Now everybody figures I'm s'pose 'ta' wreck my legs tryin' ta' save her . . . All you gotta' do is ask me, nicely" (87–88).

Two months later (in December) Fast Eddie is discovered sitting next to Dede's bed. She is now hairless because of her treatments; her physical condition is emphasized by contrast with the framed photographs of Dede with Franny and Evvie "from happy times past" (97) that are seen from Eddie's point of view. In added dialogue, Eddie tells Dede that while he "helped get [her] born," Franny is her "real daddy." He also finds out why Evvie did not tel him about the child: "I didn't wanna' risk bringin' you back because of it. If you wanted to stay around for *me*, you would'a stayed." He learns, too, that if he had been there to give Dede some of his bone marrow "a long time ago," the result would not have been any different (99).

The final minutes of the motion picture are very different from the stage versions. First, Dede's funeral is visited (Eddie tosses into the grave a small, gold Catholic medal that was his mother's [100]). Next, Franny and Evvie reveal the fears that have existed throughout their marriage because of the ghost of Eddie in the background. Franny has always felt that he had "borrowed" Evvie and Dede from Eddie, and he tells Evvie that she does not have to remain married to him (101). Evvie philosophizes about what is important in life: "The things we think we own—houses, cars, children. . . . We don't own these things . . . It's only our memories that we end up owning. . . . Our memories and our dreams. These are the only things that live with us and get buried with us" (104). Then Franny philosophizes: *"We're all dying . . . The only difference . . . is that the doctors named what Dede got. . . . Once we all knew the name, then it was all this* love, *all this* gentleness, *all this* kindness *and* thoughtfulness, *all this phoney* caring. *. . . We shouldn't be waitin' for the name of what we got . . . We're all terminal cases . . . Everybody who's on their feet, movin', needs carin', understanding"* (105).

In the final scene, Franny's dream of turning the abandoned North Shore Fish Plant into a gymnasium is to be realized, and Franny and Auggie invite Fast Eddie to join them in the enterprise. Amends have been made. Nevertheless, Fast Eddie announces that he returning to California. The movie ends with Eddie's lifting a barbell carrying 420 pounds, the best lift in his life, as he salutes "Dede . . . and . . . everybody else I ever loved in Gloss'tah, Massachusetts, U.S. of A. . . . and all the other son'a'bitches, too!" (110). The bleakness of December mirrors the loss represented by Dede's death, yet a new child has been born, a new year is on the horizon, and the characters are meeting the challenges of life by moving on, advancing into new areas and with new accomplishments.

The tone in these last sequences is more maudlin than it was in the play. There are more important differences between the two media presentation of Horovitz's tale, though. To some extent, the differences reflect those in the media themselves, and to some extent the change in media reflects a change in the author's thematic explorations.

In the film, cross-editing is employed to weave together the plots and subplots. By moving back and forth between Franny's garage and Gold's, the Farina household and Mary-Ellen's, and inserting interior and exterior scenes at the fish processing plant and other locales around Gloucester[9] with added characters,[10] the screenwriter accomplishes more than merely supplying an enormous expansion of the number of settings and characters. The author's purpose is not just to open out his drama cinematically or to round out his characters; it is an inclusive impulse that widens his thematic application, generalizing and encompassing the community.

Additionally, Horovitz uses cinematic juxtapositions to make his points, to provide contrast, and to emphasize and refine his interrelated themes. He uses both slam cuts and match cuts to create visual bridges between scenes and connections between thematic elements that are much more striking than he was able to accomplish with audile transitions in the drama.[11] The movement from scene 31 to scene 32, for instance, is a cut from Fast Eddie's naked back as he walks away from Evvie toward his truck to Franny's naked back as he and Evvie are wallpapering their living room (32). There is a connection when the sound of Evvie's whacking her fist against a hollow metal file cabinet during the confrontation with Sal at the fish plant in which he stares at her chest is matched to Franny's hammer hitting a nail as he works on the addition to his house. Unquestionably, the subplots generated along with the incorporation of new settings and characters operate to underscore the theme of strength. Eddie trains for the upcoming Mr. Massachusetts competition while becoming involved in Dede's plight; he and Franny compete against each other verbally and physically; the masculinity of the weight lifters is matched with the sexual harassment of the fish company managers; Dede's illness is a symbolic reflection of the economic disaster befalling Gloucester, both of which are topics of conversation among the women at the processing plant. In each case there is a certain amount of control: Eddie determines how and when he will train; the contest is agreed upon; the managers hold the power to fire; bone marrow transplants may save Dede. Concurrently, and conversely, in each case there is also a lack of control: Eddie is sidetracked from his quest; Franny breaks his arm during the competition; Evvie stands up to the bosses, whose power is thereby diminished; the transplants are ineffective.

Ultimately, perhaps, Eddie demonstrates the greatest amount of control: He returns home, he trains, he accepts Franny's challenge, he adjusts to Franny's predicament so that Franny can win. In setting his own terms of adjustment, Eddie is the most capable of the characters. Ironically, despite initially seeming the least stable, he, better than anyone else, accepts what comes his way and deals with it the best he can under the circumstances. To some extent, however, this ability to take the worst that fate deals and accommodate to it in a meaningful way, to exercise some minimal self-direction, is present in all of the inhabitants of Gloucester. How the characters react to this second set of circumstances is definitive of their strength. That they all continue is the measure of that strength.

Since Dede's disease is a focal point in the first produced version of the play, it made sense to involve the family, including Evvie. When Horovitz's focus shifted to a consideration of the nature of strength, symbolized in the bodybuilding, it made sense to foreground the men and to remove Evvie's character. On the stage, either of these approaches works. Following the Gloucester production, however, either because probing the nature of strength led him to expand the community elements that were present even in the earlier versions or because the opening-out nature of film called for broadening his focus and thus led to expanding those elements, the metaphor became not just the three men and the child, not just the inclusion of the mother, but a representation of the people of the Northeast beset by an economic cancer beyond their control.

The variations between the version of *Strong-Man/Strong-Men* illustrate the author's movement from the exploration of the character of a few individuals to the exploration of the character of a community. In those variations there is also evidence of how Horovitz's creative processes operate and of how the differences between stage and film function to allow for or invite shifts in approach and perspective.

NOTES

1. From a note at the end of the typed filmscript (supplied by Horovitz) it is apparent that Horovitz worked on the various versions over a period of time from July 1989 to August 1991 in a variety of locations—Gloucester, Los Angeles, London, Paris, New York City, Key Biscayne, and Gloucester again. Incidentally, it would be typical for changes to be made in the script during the shooting of the movie, which is scheduled to be produced by Ned Tannen at Paramount.

2. Most of the changes made for the Gloucester production were not retained in the post-Gloucester version. This even includes some that clearly should have been, as in the line, "Why are you sayin' here ?" which should read, "What are you sayin' here?" (p. 65 in the Gloucester script/p. 66 in the post-Gloucester script). Horovitz's scripts were composed on a computer, and when he made changes, apparently he merely altered what was on the disk rather than retyping the whole manuscript; thus, some of the changes were not entered, and obviously errors have been retained since they were on the script originally.

3. Those in the cycle series are *Henry Lumper, The Widow's Blind Date, North Shore Fish, Year of the Duck,* and *Park Your Car in Harvard Yard.*

4. Peter Sagal, "Strong Men in Tough Times," in the playbill for the Gloucester Stage Company's production of *Strong-Man's Weak Child,* 17 August–14 October 1990.

5. Actor's copy of the typescript of the version of *Strong-Man's Weak Child* staged by the Gloucester Stage Company, n.d.

6. Attempts to locate a copy of the Los Angeles script, including from Horovitz and Bushnell, proved fruitless, and reviews of that production are not sufficiently detailed to be of any help in establishing either the extent to which the Evvie character was involved or the nature of that involvement.

7. There are a few other minor differences between the stage scripts and the screenplay that are peculiar to film. For instance, in the movie version, the stage directions specificaly call for particular thermoses (Elvis Presley), coffee mugs (with Arnold Schwarznegger as "Terminator II," "Rocky IV," and Madonna or Dolly Parton pictures on them), and brand names are used in describing Fast Eddie's clothes, mentions of Kotex, Chlorox, and *TV Guide*, and the like, whereas in the play they are identified generically ("Fast Eddie wears California weight-lifting togs"). While this may be a means of demonstrating the class level of the characters, it may serve a practical purpose as well, since advertisers pay film companies to include their products.

8. Interestingly, in the screenplay Horovitz adds personal comments as well. In the description of one shot (scene 24), he writes: "Angle On: Lumpers unloading live fish from Dragger's 'hold'. Close Shot: Huge vat of live fish flopping about, anxiously. (Do the fish know what's coming?)" This observation/query is related to the movie's theme in that there may be a Ledaesque comparison between the fish and the populace of Gloucester, who are uncomprehendingly caught in situations beyond their control that have a potentialy deadly consequence.

9. These include Franny and Evvie's bedroom, the street, Good Harbor Beach, a pizza parlor, Maria's Restaurant, a Stop and Shop, Mrs. Garagiola's house, the Rigger Bar, Arlyne's house, Sal's house, the high school track, Seaside Cemetary, Stage Fort Park, Dede's bedroom, and others.

10. Various lumpers, Marlena, Reenie, Florence, Sal Morella, Porker, fifty bikinied women, assorted boyfriends, the longshoreman Maxie, Butchie, Toughie Chincilla, a stockboy, Earl, a cashier, Mrs. Garagiola, a kissing couple, a crowd, Carmella Morella, Frankie, Manny, Tommy T., a baby, "hundreds of townspeople," two gravediggers, schoolchildren, and a priest are encountered in the additional scenes and additions to scenes.

11. Sometimes called dynamic cutting, slam cuts are an abrupt, obvious cut from one shot to another, a conscious jamming together of images; mash cuts, also called invisible cutting, are a smooth, seamless joining of images based on continuity and are often "hidden" by cutting on action.

14

Ed Lemon: Prophet of Profit

Martin J. Jacobi

Israel Horovitz has written dozens of plays and been translated into more than twenty languages. Early in his career, he had already won an Obie for the realistic play *The Indian Wants the Bronx* and "staked out his claim to a share in the Beckett-Ionesco tradition of modern absurdity."[1] In these early works—such as *The Indian Wants the Bronx* and *The Honest-to-God Schnozzola*, as well as absurdist works such as *Line* and *Rats*—Horovitz often focuses on senseless violence and inarticulateness. Things happen, but neither the characters nor the audience are clear about the motives. Nor do we in the audience see clearly the connections between the play's action and Horovitz's attitude toward his social and political environment. Critics who praised the potential they saw in the young playwright nonetheless saw these plays as flawed. Richard Watts thought that *Line* was more concerned with befuddling the audience than with telling a recognizable story, Dan Sullivan asked of *Indian* if Horovitz had done more than to drag a street fight into the theater, and Martin Gottfried thought that the play showed his lack of "ability to create characters and situations."[2] And of *The Primary English Class* Clive Barnes claimed that "Mr. Horovitz is better at setting a situation than plotting a play."[3]

The charge of these critics is that the plays lack breadth and depth; like many other plays or movies or television shows, or for that matter like crossword puzzles, they entertain but are neither instructive nor persuasive. They provide the emotional release of laughter or at least help time pass pleasantly, but they do little more; they do not coherently address major issues of life. Horovitz's later plays, lengthier and often more realistic, continue to portray actions centered on the threat or appearance of violence and on the lack of communication, but they also provide other dimensions, including a look at the problems' origins, which in turn gives us a better appreciation of their effects on plot, characters, and context. For instance, of *North Shore Fish* Mel Gussow says that Horovitz "is artful in his delineation of a dying economy and in his small but sensitive group portrait of people allied by geography, their Roman Catholic upbringing, and their limited aspirations."[4]   Gussow also notes that Horovitz "performs the double obligation of humanizing his characters and of making a statement about the troubles of the American economy."[5]

The later plays still capture the rage and inarticulateness, corruption and selfishness, that permeate his vision of American society, but they also point at what he would have us, his audience, do about these problems. Kenneth Burke says that the artist attempts to present his or her concerns and problems in a drama so that the concerns and problems can be worked out; the artist figures out a way to adjust to the social and political environment, or to adjust the environment to himself or herself, or to coexist with the environment at some level of tension. Further, claims Burke, the play's function as authorial catharsis is joined by a rhetorical function, literary works are "proverbs writ large."[6] Particulars of an author's problem are unique, but due to our common heritage and culture, the play is a personal individuation of a pattern of experience shared somewhat by all people.[7]   In the headnotes to *North Shore Fish* and *Henry Lumper*, Horovitz says that "all knowledge flows through the trunk of the tree." He means that a play can be interesting and effective to a larger audience even though it is about a specific locale or group of people or about a particular person's vision of the locale or people. Thus, "if I am truly successful in my dramatising of life as it is really lived . . . then the play will have meaning and will touch people throughout the world."[8] As Burke puts it, a work of art is understood by the audience because they share this common ground; thus, the strategizing by the author is also strategizing for the audience, so that the work can become "equipment for living," advice to its audience on how to act in similar situations.[9]

Horovitz's *Mackerel* is an absurdist play that does more than entertain. It depicts the corruption in modern American family, religion, and business; it asks us to accept its particular vision; and it asks us to consider certain issues in certain ways because of our acceptance. The play shows a father who sees his family as subjects in his kingdom and for whom he may be benevolent or autocratic or capricious as he wishes while assuming total control; it shows just how undeserving of this position he is. It also shows American business as a heartless, corrupt and corrupting, sometimes evil system, and religion as either the refuge of the mad or the cynical resort of scoundrels. It replaces Joyce's triad of Mother, Church, and Ireland with what can be described as Father, Prophet, and Profit, with the play's development being the Father's becoming the Prophet of Profit. The critique, as do all other dramatic critiques of this sort, asks that we believe it to be "accurate" regarding the shortcomings of our culture and that we consider people who act like Ed Lemon to be psychopaths or sociopaths, or both. Although it suggests the need for change, it does not suggest what changes we should make in our familial, economic, and religious lives.

Stories of selfishness and avarice in the family, society, and business have been told by Horovitz through realistic drama; *North Shore Fish* and *Henry Lumper*, for instance, touch on similar themes. When we view or read *Mackerel*, we laugh at the clever jokes and puns in the characters' dialogue, which underscore their follies and foibles, their foolishness and knavery. We laugh as we watch characters who are faced with issues that face us in real life but who perform miserably. We laugh because their weaknesses and their confrontations, while making them like us, are so much more pronounced than ours as to make for absurdity. We laugh, and we realize that the weaknesses in ourselves are not to be feared and avoided but laughed at and improved. The play presents American business and, to a lesser extent, religion and the American family, as rapacious, selfish, and immoral, but the events are so fantastic, the family's intentions so banal and their actions so horrific, the comic plot developments and dialogue so disarming, that we see quite clearly a rather revolting human condition and can believe in our ability to improve on it in our familial, economic, and religious lives. Thus, as absurdist drama, *Mackerel* uses our laughter to persuade us to look at and then examine a starkly and clearly drawn depiction of a truly ugly American, and to readjust our own perspectives on our attitudes toward these aspects of our lives.

In the following pages, I bring together under the aegis of Burke's critical theory the various strands I have introduced. First, I examine the degree to which *Mackerel* asks us to accept the accuracy of the picture it draws of the American family, American business, and American religion. Then I examine the play for what Horovitz offers us in the way of equipment for living—for himself and for us.

Mackerel begins with a hurricane that deposits a 250,000-pound mackerel on the Lemon family's front lawn and in their front room. This dysfunctional family—a father, mother, and two grown daughters—put aside their mistrusts and animosities long enough to package and market the fish, even though they have reason to believe that it is poisonous. In fact, the entire population of North and Central America and the Middle East, most of South America, and all but sixteen Chinese are among the victims, and at the end of the play, the world's remaining people are outside their house, across a field, demanding that the family surrender. The younger daughter, Edna, cuts a deal with the remaining world leaders to give up her family in exchange for her freedom. The play ends with Edna free and the other Lemons, ensconced in a glass bubble suspended from a helicopter, receiving what they take to be the adulation of the populace.

Ed Lemon uprooted his family from their home in Salina, Kansas, and transplanted them into their oceanside home in New England. Ed is a fisherman, but as his wife, Emma, complains, he is "a fisherman without a boat, without a pole, without a line, and, consequently, without a fish. . . . He hasn't earned a dime in nearly a year." [10] He spends most of his time alone in his room, refusing to interact with the members of his family. He led the Lemon women out of what they at least claim was a good home and a good life, and then he abandoned them. The marooned women fend for themselves as best they can after Ed relinquishes his autocratic control. They do not have much financial success, however, and two of them must resort to a traditional way women have of making money in a male-dominated economy. Emma, who does not work outside the home, pays the family's plumber, Mr. Fortunini, with her sexual favors (although it is not clear whether more than purely economic motives are involved in her adulterous behavior), and a daughter, Eileen, is a prostitute (although it is not clear whether she also has another job). As the play opens, the two women are the strong characters, holding the family together through work and, if not love, at least habit. It would seem that Edna, the other daughter, has had no romantic or sexual relationships, has perhaps never held a job, and—like her father—never leaves the house. Also like her father, she offers no economic or moral support to the family.

The appearance of the mackerel returns Ed to his previous role as the dominant force in the family. He immediately takes responsibility for the apparent good fortune of so much mackerel in their back yard: "A mackerel. A Guiness World Record mackerel. The *numero uno* mackerel! The over-the-top, the killer mackerel! The king of the mackerel! The *risus puris* mackerel! *He jumps again.* Me! I did it! Me! I did it! Me! I did it! Me! I did It!"(40). When Eileen observes that he did not catch the fish, that it in fact washed up in the storm, he first equivocates and then threatens her. "It's *my* record, Eileen! Mine! Nobody's taking it away from me. . . . *He leaps between Eileen and the fish.* What the hell do you think I've been waiting for? This is mine, Eileen! My record! My claim to fame. My *raison d'être*! My *fish*!"(44).

When he observes to the family that the fish can make them all rich, his status improves enormously. Emma and the daughters look upon him as heroic and are close to tears of joy at the thought of the wealth their man will bring (47). He blunders his way through the development of a marketing plan, suggesting at one point that they kill the fish with a kitchen knife and at another point that they market frozen fish fingers; of this latter suggestion Eileen observes, "We've only got eight hands and you're after ten billion fingers" (57). Left to his own devices, Ed probably would have been unable to realize any economic gain from the fish; the family, especially Eileen, develops the means to package and market it. It is Eileen, for instance, not Ed, who realizes that they must sell in bulk if they are to move the product quickly enough. Her parents momentarily cease their attacks on her morals and intelligence, with Ed acknowledging that she has saved the family and Emma saying, "I always knew you had the brains, *too*" (60). Yet ultimately Ed takes credit for the entire venture; when they are asked by the world's remaining population why they sold the poisoned fish, he cuts off Eileen, saying that "they're asking *me*" (124). He has restaked his claim to the position as the most important person in the family, the patriarch, the one who deals with the outside world.

To a great extent, the family relationships, which were never very familial, are replaced with relationships more suited for life in economic units. That is, the Lemon family is replaced by the Lemon company, purveyors of "Ed Lemon's Keg'o'Mackerel" (58), and Ed's familial concerns as husband and father are replaced by the concerns of a corporate executive. Just as we come to see that Ed is a ruthless family member, we see that he is a particularly ruthless executive, one who cares no more for the health and well-being of his corporate family than he does for his consumers. His lack of concern for his customers is shown in his willingness to sell the tainted food, and his selfishness toward his family/employees is clearly shown during the siege when he says to them, "What the hell do I care about *your* heads, huh? It's *my* head that's gotta be saved here . . . I'm Ed Lemon" (105). It becomes clear that he has been using the family all along for his own ends. While accepting, if not condoning, his wife's and daughter's prostitution for his economic benefit, he is quick to denigrate it as soon as his dominant place in the family is created by the mercantile concern he establishes.

Yet while the women are mostly responsible for the business's financial successes, Ed bears primary responsibility for the disasters. He has every reason to believe that his mackerel will harm his customers, but his avarice drives him to rationalize his actions by refusing to believe that anyone will be hurt. For instance, when the daughters point out to him that the flies circling the dead fish are themselves dying, he says, "I don't get it," and when Eileen begins to tell him that the fish is poisonous, he interrupts her by saying, "Don't say it!" (72, 73). He knows there is a problem but apparently wants what some politicians call plausible deniability for any problems that might later arise. When Emma joins Eileen in pleading with him to stop, he suggests that they can market the rest as cat food after testing it on Fortunini's cat. He says: "I have no intention in the world of poisoning or killing Angelo Fortunini's cat! I have every intention in the world of proving to you . . . once and for all . . . that our mackerel meat is safe and sound for cats to eat" (74). After eating some of the meat, the cat expands to the size of a lion, and Ed joyfully points out that "it's much more than a catfood, Emma. . . . It makes cats grow a thousand times their normal size and strength *and* . . . it kills flies!" (82). He claims that perhaps there will be a Nobel Prize for their creation of "a new race" of human giants who have eaten the mackerel, but before his fantasy goes too far, the cat dies.

He is thus to blame for the seemingly desperate condition the family finds itself in at play's end, although it is not clear just how desperate the conditions are. There are troops and cannons arrayed against the family home, but Ed believes, and he may well be right, that the remaining population of the world stands in awe of him. After all, he says, "I'm not just another maniac, God damn it! I've done more damage than any other maniac in the history of the world!" (115) Capitalism run amok has caused the world's greatest disaster, but for all we know, the population applauds the enterprising nature, the chutzpah, of Lemon's attempt to grab the golden ring. They lionize, if indeed that is what they do, a banal person who just happened to destroy most of the world's population.[11]

Ed's treatment of his womenfolk is similar to that of women in *North Shore Fish*. The women are victimized in that play as well, sexually, familially, and economically, in part by their sexist supervisor and their husbands and fathers, and certainly by the faceless Markie, who sells the plant out from underneath women who have worked there for thirty years and have had mothers and even grandmothers who worked there before them. After Ed assumes the dominant position, the self-confident and decisive Eileen begins to degenerate into the stereotypical quivering bundle of nerves while the erstwhile nerve bundle Edna exchanges places with her. Eileen takes the woman's traditional place while Edna becomes "little Ed," the male figure; she begins to order her sister and mother around as her father does (66–71), and she even begins to talk differently—more like a businessperson making a deal. Like her father, apparently, she needed the fish's arrival to shock her out of her reclusion. She shows herself to be daddy's girl when she beats him at his own game by selling out her family for her own freedom. The women are victimized by the man except in the case of Edna, who is, like her father, reclusive, asexual, and economically predatory—who almost seems to have become a man.

Horovitz's criticism of family and economics is accompanied by a critique of religion equally satirical. Ed had moved his family from Kansas because he had dreamed that "God had a fortune for him, in Lowell, Massachusetts, from the ocean" (23); he has been called to be, if not a fisher of men, at least a fisherman. Once there, he removes himself as Christ removed himself before his ministry, and the fish's arrival he sees to be God's answers to his "fasting and prayer." He says to Emma: "Now you understand . . . now you can *see*. This is why we sold the farm! This is the big cookie!" (39). And later he says, "God isn't gonna send you a mackerel like this and let you die!" (55). His messianic zeal is an extreme form of the New England Puritans' belief in the relationship between financial success here on earth and their predetermined success in the next world. In the play, business and religion coalesce. Ed believes that his economic plan will bring him "money . . . fame . . . a position in society . . . right up here with the gods of fishing . . . The *gods*! Me. Ed Lemon" (46). And when he is asked by the people outside why he sold them the mackerel, he responds in an oracular fashion: "You asked him why he did what he did? . . . Because he is Ed Lemon. . . . That's his answer. *He pauses.*

Anyone of you would have done what he did . . . only he did it better. That's
Ed Lemon for you . . . *He smiles.* He's just got to do it better" (124–25).

It is fair to ask whether Ed thinks he is godlike or whether he is using that
ploy as an escape from the responsibility of so grievously misusing the social
compact. Possibly he believes he is important and even godlike, and possibly
the enormity of his crimes has driven him to the monomaniacal madness of
extreme religious conviction. However, I suspect that he is a con man who
believes that he is only doing to other people what they have always tried to do
to him and that he is pursuing the American dream as others would like to, and
indeed would if they were in his place. He is willing to use whatever supports
he can think of for his practice. People are psychopathological if in their
monomania they believe themselves to be right and everyone else wrong, and
sociopathological if they take advantage of the weaknesses of the social bond.
To illustrate, some FBI people said that David Koresh of the Branch Davidian
religious cult in Waco, Texas, was a sociopath who would capitulate after he
had arranged his television and movie contracts; others said he was a
psychopath, capable of immolating himself and his followers. If Ed Lemon
believes that he is God's messenger or more, he is a psychopath; if he is
cynically using religion as justification for his acts, he is a sociopath. Ed, I
would say, is more conning others with his religious attributes than he is
conning himself. But as either psychopath or sociopath, he has problems.

Ed, as a father, "CEO," and "prophet," is irresponsible, or if not
responsible only so because he is too stupid to consider the probable effects of
his actions; he is either amoral or evil, and his actions are certainly not
justifiable, no matter how much he would like to make them appear to be so.
"Lemon Foul Disease" not only is the name of the disease that kills half the
world's population but also an accurate name for a family business that
practices all that is worst in American business; they have little or no sense of
responsibility for the customers nor do they exhibit any sense of a business's
role as a corporate citizen. Through luck and predation, Ed uses the fish as the
means to his success, showing that success is not limited only to those who are
smart, honest, decisive, and so forth.[12]

Burke would contend that the various issues raised by the play are
underpinned by events in Horovitz's life. He grew up in Wakefield,
Massachusetts, and he says that on his family's "special day," they went to
Gloucester. He owns a house now in Gloucester, which serves as the base for
his career and family life. Horovitz reports that developers buy up businesses
and convert them to condominiums, putting hundreds of people in the fishing
industry out of business and making it impossible for the rest of the local
residents and their children to find affordable housing. The Unification Church
began a fishing fleet and has used business practices alien to the traditional
residents, and the economic and social scourge of drugs has also devastated the
community.[13] In *Mackerel* (as well as in *North Shore Fish* and *Henry*

Lumper) the playwright reflects a dissatisfaction with the road his community has taken.

His dramaturgy, including plotting, style, and development of characters, as well as the comic frame, helps make this presentation. The plot is clearly fantastic. Mackerels of 250,000 pounds do not exist, nor do they turn their consumers into giants; people would not eat such foul-smelling fish, nor would they have "wanted to get the height" (113), as Ed claims they did, when they saw the mortality rates of their predecessors. I am reminded of the end of Mark Twain's *A Connecticut Yankee in King Arthur's Court*, when the knights attacking Henry Morgan are blown up by land mines. It may have been suitable as comedy when Mark Twain wrote it, because it was unrealistic and so unthreatening, but with the advent of real land mines in the twentieth century, this ending lost its humor. Now, while it might be absurd to imagine destruction of the magnitude brought on by Ed Lemon's Keg'o'Mackerel, we can still wonder how long it will be before the small outbreaks of tainted food are replaced with a much larger problem, especially since the loosening of governmental inspections has brought with it an increase in disease in chicken and beef sold in supermarkets; we can wonder how long it might be before our current environmental and health-related problems of garbage or smog or drug-resistant bacteria are replaced by food-related catastrophes.

Ed's adventure, Burke's theory contends, tells us something about ourselves and the way to live. It presents Horovitz's belief that our socioeconomic, and so our political, system rewards mindless and clumsy brutality and cynical manipulation to further selfish interests. First it asks us to identify, at least a little, with the Lemon family members. When Ed says that he just did what every other person in the world would have done, he exaggerates, of course—both as to how many people would choose to act immorally in such a situation and how many would go to the extremes this family has gone—but there is some truth in what he is saying. Ed Lemon and his actions say something about the human condition generally. We are asked to identify with Ed Lemon, if only to the extent that we objectify those around us in pursuit of selfish desires, or engage in unfair business practices, or refuse to accept, contrary to good evidence against us and for others, that we are not always correct and just in what we do.

From the point of view of economics, the play asks that we reconsider how we think of our business leaders if we accept that their claim to power is supported not by intelligence and hard work but by luck or lineage, that they are self-centered egotists willing to break civil and natural law for their economic and social betterment, that they do not even believe that they are doing wrong or, at best, rationalize their problematic decisions. We are asked to consider our willingness to make heroes out of our flawed leaders. When the remaining populace cheer the Lemons, the family believes that they are idolized as some sort of monstrous mass murder "record breakers." It is a ghoulish extension of the way in which Jeffrey Dahmer or Richard Speck or Ted Bundy or Jim Jones or other killers live on as celebrities long after their victims are forgotten by all but their families and friends. What, the play encourages us to ask, does this say about our attitudes toward the unfair deaths or economic destruction of our neighbors, associates, real or imagined competitors, in the face of our respect for the feats of people like Michael Milken and Charles Keating? How should we refigure our stance toward our clergy, our elected officials, business management—even perhaps our own family—if we perceive that they are willing to sacrifice us for their fortune and fame, willing to poison us for profit?[14]

The play asks that we reconsider both the presumption for leadership given to men in society and the subordinate status of women that society dictates. By showing Ed's incompetence as a father and as a businessman, it underscores the undeserving ascension to power that men can make simply because of their gender; by showing the subordinate roles taken by Emma and Eileen, it underscores the inadequacy of the traditional place of women; and by showing the development of Edna, it satirizes society's belief that women can succeed only if they act like men—if they treat their competitors, customers, and colleagues as ruthlessly as a man would.[15]

And the play asks that we reconsider the role of religion in our lives. *Mackerel* warns against messianic zeal and a cynical use of religion for personal profit. As I write these lines, the Branch Davidian compound has just burned, with scores of adults and children killed. Regardless of the complicity of the FBI in this disaster, the lesson here is similar to the one presented by Horovitz: whether one is a religious fanatic or just a con man whose con becomes religion, religion can be misused to terrible ends.

It is reasonable, *Mackerel* tells us, that we consider more carefully our roles in our family and economic life; it is reasonable also that we show more caution, be more suspicious, concerning our corporate and and religious leaders; and it is reasonable to consider more carefully what we are doing about such problems as tainted restaurant food, food preparations and additives that cause heart-related and other diseases, and such potential disasters in the environment as electromagnetic fields, water and ground pollutants, and so on. Since our own government seems as complicit in making heroes out of agents of destruction as does the surviving world government in Horovitz's play, it is reasonable to be suspicious of the intelligence and goodwill of our governmental leaders as well. To what extent are we willing to make heroes out of our governmental, corporate, and religious leaders, people who if not overtly monstrous and maniacal may well be irresponsible and stupid? To what extent are we willing to reassess our leaders' and our own attitudes toward gender issues in our personal and professional lives?

Like the popular television show, "Married with Children," *Mackerel* uses satire and slapstick to focus on the weaknesses of the late-twentieth-century

American male. Ed Lemon, like Al Bundy, is ready to do almost anything for his own selfish ends, and the Lemon family, like the Bundy family, plays a complicated game in following and resisting him. If Edna indeed does turn into a man, she would be even more like the Bundy son, who, like her, is the father's apprentice and, ultimately, competitor. My point with this comparison is to say that the use of a deprecating humor presents flaws in Ed Lemon and Al Bundy that we all share, although perhaps their flaws have much wider fissures than ours, because it holds up for ridicule what is most ridiculous in us: our willingness to allow ourselves to breach family trust and override the social compact in our pursuit of banal, selfish, and hurtful satisfactions. It *is* ridiculous to poison one's fellow citizens and humans just to make a buck, although we are aware that because of waste and pollution, our environment's future is in severe danger from just such catastrophes.[16] We can take it to mean that we ought not to ignore others in the pursuit of gratification, which in our society is displayed through economic improvement.[17] It is ridiculous to say that our actions are ordained by God when those actions harm our friends and our foes; it is either a maniacal belief or a cynical cover for selfish, personal preference. It is ridiculous to say that we can do what we wish simply because we want to and simply because we choose to see ourselves as the center of the universe, as Ed does when he offers as the reason for his actions that "I AM ED LEMON."

Mackerel asks us to consider all of this and to consider a change in our attitudes and actions afterward. In this play, Horovitz has moved beyond where Jack Kroll had earlier placed him, when he said that in *Leader* Horovitz "has his incoherent raucous say about the particular bankruptcy of the American political system."[18] Whether we choose to see Kroll's attack as accurate, Horovitz's *Mackerel*, while raucous, is also coherent and persuasive in its depiction of bankruptcy.

NOTES

1. Scott Giantvalley, "Israel Horovitz," in *Crticial Survey of Drama: English Language Series*, ed. Frank Magill (Englewood Cliffs, N. J.: Salem Press, 1985), 3: 958.

2. Richard Watts, Jr., "Five People on Line," *New York Post*, 16 February 1971, reprinted in *New York Theatre Critics' Reviews* (1972): 349; Dan Sullivan, "Theater: Two One-Actors," *New York Times*, 18 January 1968, reprinted in *New York Theare Critics' Reviews* (1968): 269–70; Martin Gottfried, "The Indian Wants the Bronx," *Women's Wear Daily*, 18 January 1968, reprinted in *New York Theare Critics' Reviews* (1968):268.

3. Clive Barnes, "Theater: *The Primary English Class* is Staged," *New York Times*, 17 February 1976, reprinted in *New York Theatre Critics' Reviews* (1976): 335.

4. Mel Gussow, "Stage: *Fish*, by Horovitz," *New York Times*, 12 January 1987, C20.

5. Mel Gussow, "When the Group Becomes the Star," *New York Times*, 25 January 1987, H4.

6. Kenneth Burke, *The Philosophy of Literary Form*, 3d ed. (Berkeley: University of California Press, 1973), 17, 296-97.

7. Kenneth Burke, *Counter-Statement* (Berkeley: University of California Press, 1984), 143.

8. Israel Horovitz, *North Shore Fish* (New York: Dramatists Play Service, 1989), 9.

9. Burke, *Philosophy of Literary Form*, 304.

10. Israel Horovitz, *Mackerel* (Vancouver, Canada: Talonbooks, 1979), 17, 25. All subsequent citations to the play are from this edition and will appear parenthetically in the text.

11. The possibility exists that they cheer because they have captured the Lemons; perhaps the cheers grow in volume as the Lemons introduce themselves because most of the world's population does not understand English. If this is so, we still have the Lemons believing that, as Emma says, "They don't just like us, they *love* us!" (125), a suggestion that people such as the Lemons cannot or will not come to terms with the magnitude of their crimes.

12. *North Shore Fish* and *Henry Lumper* also portray businesspeople who abuse and kill others—not with poisoned fish but with factory closings, narcotics, and murders. Business leaders quarrel within and between each other for political and economic control of the waterfront, and certainly the Lemon family.

13. Horovitz provides this information in the Preface to *North Shore Fish* (4–9) and the Author's Notes to *Henry Lumper* (New York: Dramatists Play Service, 1990), 90–95.

14. Given that this play was written in 1976, the geopolitical winner is the former Soviet Union; it competitors, China and North America, are nearly vacant. While Horovitz makes no explicit geopolitical statements, Lenin's observation about giving the capitalists enough rope to hang themselves and Khrushchev's promise to bury the West are worth mentioning.

15. Like *Mackerel*, *North Shore Fish* supports these suggestions in its portrayal of a factory closing that costs the town's women their livelihoods. Markie and the big city money that will make the factory into a fitness center never think of their traditionally female employees. The only "boss" who claims to have the women's interests at heart is Sally, their married floor supervisor who preys on the single women employees and even attempts to seduce the federal inspector. In *Henry Lumper*, the only woman character of note is a wife who is transferred from one young warrior to the other. The play simply does not address feminist issues directly. Horovitz has said that the play "does purposefully parallel *Henry IV—Parts 1 and 2*" (*Henry Lumper*, 95), and that too is a play about young and old male contestants.

16. A true story that sounds as if it could have been told against Ed Lemon instead concerns a person who, I believe, is an internation banker; this banker suggested that the more economic dump sites for toxic waste are in the Third World, particularly Africa, because the African government can make the needed money from the West that will otherwise not be invested in their countries. If there is a disaster, the official said, the insurance losses would be low, since the average earning capacity of a thirty-year-old East African is miniscule compared to that of a Western European or American worker. The economy requires the West's toxic dumps even as it protects Western insurance companies from exposure; is is quite a system.

17. *North Shore Fish* depicts more particularly, and more realistically, this same lesson through the closing and sale of the town's fish packing plant where the play's characters work. *Henry Lumper* also illustrates the lesson through deaths in the leadership struggles and economic ruin in the face of rising unemployment among the community, the threat of increased loss of jobs because of gentrification of their community by big city money, and the economic and personal scourge of drugs.

18. Jack Kroll, "Theater of Crisis," *Newsweek*, 5 May 1969, 118.

15

Interview with Israel Horovitz

Leslie Kane

Israel Horovitz's *North Shore Fish*, selected for broadcast on "New England Theatres on the Air," was taped in Boston in front of a live audience on March 21, 1993, as part of national project to revivify radio drama. I spoke with Israel Horovitz on the following morning in my home in Newton, Massachusetts, about the forthcoming premiere of *Fighting over Beverley,* parental responsibility, artistic influences, and his lifelong commitment to writing and running.

Kane: Eugene Ionesco has described you as "a tender American hoodlum who writes the cruelest things there are." Can you tell me something about your relationship with Ionesco and clarify his characterization of you?

Horovitz: We were close, oh, twenty years ago, I suppose, in the early to mid-1970s. In those days, Ionesco drank quite a lot, and he was purposefully nutty. He used to call me his "*fils spirituel.*" One night, during the Paris run of "le 1er" [*Line]* at Théâtre de Poche-Montparnasse, Ionesco actually came out on stage, reasonably drunk, screaming, "*Israel, mon fils spirituel, mon fils spirituel!*" The audience was rather shocked . . . as was I. I adored Ionesco. At the end of the day, I think he was far less interested in me and my work than he was in the possibility of my marrying his daughter, Marie-France, who was my friend but had no particular interest in marrying me, nor I her. It was a romance that existed completely in the tête d'Ionesco. So, I didn't marry Marie-France, but I did work with her on an adaptation of *L'Homme aux valises.* I had almost no written French back then, so Marie-France managed an odd text in literal, word for word dictionary English, which I then went through, word for word, and fashioned into the current American edition. In English, the play's called *Man with Bags.* It's a big, brilliant, but rambling play, which, I suspect, did not improve in translation. Grove Press published my version here in the U.S. *Man With Bags* had its U.S. premiere in Maryland. Glenn Close was in the cast, as was Dwight Schulz.

Kane: During more than twenty-five years in the professional theatre, you have worked with some of our finest actors, directors, producers, and composers—such as Michael Moriarty, John Cazale, Al Pacino, Robert Whitehead, Joseph Papp, Diane Keaton, John Heard, Scott Glenn, Mary Beth Hurt, Paul Simon, John Hall, Richard Dreyfuss, Jason Robards, Lenny Baker, Judith Ivey, Peter Reigart, among others. Many of these now-famous actors made their debut or honed their craft in your plays. To what do you credit these fortuitous collaborations?

Horovitz: I seem to write characters that actors want to play. In the end, that has been the key to my getting my work produced.

Kane: Have you changed much in the past twenty-five years, since *The Indian Wants the Bronx* first opened so successfully in New York?

Horovitz: God, I hope so! If I had to pull out one line from all of my writing to best describe the way I feel about myself these days, it would surely be Brackish's line from *Park Your Car in Harvard Yard*: "If the man I *am* met the man I *was*, there'd be a fist fight." I was such a dreadful person when I was in my twenties and thirties. But, really, what can anybody do about what you were other than to try like hell to not slide too far backward, at least not all the way. I've made so many enemies along the way. I was arrogant and combative—reeling from a more than difficult childhood with a more than difficult father. I was as likely to punch somebody in the jaw as not. I broke a director's jaw once, with one punch, and I'm not what you'd call a large man. Hard to talk about, really. It's all there in the early plays; admitting this shouldn't be a surprise to anyone who knows my early plays or to anyone who remembers me as a total son of a bitch.

Kane: How do you account for your apparent mellowing? Is this age or contentment?

Horovitz: I'm not sure whether age mellows you or whether it simply beats you down. Feeling one's own mortality is a big step toward health . . . and realizing, of course, the mortality of others. Also, for me, it was years and years of psychoanalysis. Psychoanalysis took a lot of panic out of my life.

Paul Simon rates a major assist in my particular life. We were quite close friends, some years back. Paul was, himself, in treatment, and was throwing many fewer punches than me. Paul was (and is) one of the few people I knew who could say to me, "Hey, Israel, you're totally flipped out, man! You ought to be in treatment!" without getting socked. His doctor found my doctor. Paul told me he'd told his doctor, "We have to find somebody for Israel who's old, male, intellectual, literary, tough, and lives close to Israel's house." They found the perfect doctor for me, the late, great Dr. Edward Harkavy, who lived less than a block away from me in Greenwich Village, with only one major street to cross.   Harkavy was actually a great man.   He'd founded the New York Psychoanalytic Institute. He was old, wise, and totally terrifying. I was late to my sessions probably three out of five times a week for the first year or two . . . and I fell asleep for a large portion of each session. Psychotherapy was tough for me for the first three or four years. I stayed with Edward Harkavy for nine years in all, until he died at age eighty-eight. I still hear Dr. Harkavy's voice, clearly, every day of my life. Have you ever been in treatment?

Kane: Yes, I have. After a divorce I experienced a tremendous amount of guilt that I had taken my daughter away from her father.

Horovitz: Isn't it awful, in the end, how we've all spent so much time of our lives feeling so guilty about so many things? I mean, how many bad things can you do in a lifetime, really? I suppose you could actually kill somebody, which would be a very bad thing to do. One can always find the time to be deceitful, hurtful. We do learn awfully well from our parents. But I'll tell you what I think the most treacherous parental crime is. It's the withholding of affection. I think the withholding of affection is the cruelest thing a parent can do to a child. The ultimate curse for a child is growing up with a sense that one's mother or father really doesn't care.   Even a truly bright person can spend an entire lifetime trying to please that parent . . . or anybody who even vaguely reminds you of that parent.   The withholding of affection is the subject I'm inspecting just now in a play I'm writing called *Unexpected Tenderness*. It's a play about, among other things, a sexually jealous father. We'll see how it turns out. The early drafts have been quite popular.

Kane: Relationships between fathers and sons is a paradigmatic theme that appears repeatedly in many of your plays.

Horovitz: Yes, it does. I don't exclude women. I try to write really good female roles. But, truthfully, I believe that the real plays for women—about the female experience—should be written by women. It's not a complicated notion. Being born in Massachusetts makes it so easy to write about being born in Massachusetts. It's not impossible to write a British character—as I have just recently done in *Fighting over Beverley*—it's just that it's such an astonishing amount of extra work. I found myself bogged down in stuff that would have come to me automatically if I'd been born British. I want to write some really great women's roles at some point in my life. I have it in my head that I have to do that. I feel I owe that debt to women . . . to my wife, to my mother, to my daughters, to my female friends. It's funny to actually say this sort of thing out loud, isn't it?

Kane: Where does that come from?   Increasingly, in your Gloucester plays—*Park Your Car, Sunday Runners in the Rain, Widow's Blind Date,*

Fighting over Beverley—women do emerge as formidable emotional, intellectual, and physical competitors. To what do you attribute your enhanced sensitivity to feminist issues?

Horovitz: It comes from being alive in America, just now. Women's issues sort of hang in the air we breathe. When I'm in France and I see all these French people lining up to see American movies, I think, "How did the Americans pull that off? . . . how did Americans get French people to truly believe that inspecting American culture is important?" I mean, it's lucky that we did that—fooled them—but how did we do that—get French people to care about American culture which is clearly inferior to French culture? Yet they're watching Spielberg movies set in the suburbs of California! It's utter nonsense! How did we ever do that? There are explanations. People say, "Oh, it's superior American marketing . . . or Americans bully the world." Well, perhaps, but to my thinking, Hollywood's getting people around the world to pay attention to American culture is kind of a twentieth-century miracle. And how did men ever convince women that they were more important than women? It's just absurd, absolutely absurd. Yet it's a man's world, and it's unjust. I think if I had stayed in Wakefield, Massachusetts, close to my parents, I never would have come to this realization. So, *North Shore Fish, Unexpected Tenderness, Fighting over Beverley*—my women's plays—are, in a strong sense, from this line of thinking. It's something transitional, which is to say that the women in my plays—in my life—are as much in transition, as I am in my thinking about women.

Kane: I find it fascinating, though, that at the end of *Fighting over Beverley*, when you have clearly positioned a character who can effectively change her life, there are allusions to *Our Town*. Although Beverley is only reflecting on her past, she has the possibility of looking to a future, if she has the guts to carry it off without the pressure of guilt.

Horovitz: If writers bravely put it out there in literature they create, then people will have the ideal in front of them to consider. That's our responsibility as artists. But there's a chilling line in *Fighting over Beverley,* at least for me, when Beverley talks about her mother. She says when her father died, her mother said, "I can hardly wait to call him up and tell him who died." And then, of course, she says to her husband, Zelly, "I could hardly wait to ring you up and tell you the most astonishing news: Beverley's left Zelly!"

Kane: In a sense he's been her only friend. She doesn't have a woman friend to call up and say, "Guess who's just died?" or, "Guess who's left Zelly?"

Horovitz: It's awful. It's an awful truth, people in loveless marriages have, for better or worse, 'til death do they part, a best friend who's a completely loveless, friendless drain on their supply of affection.

Kane: You, however, have been most fortunate in enjoying many supportive relationships and an especially close friendship with Samuel Beckett. How did you meet Beckett, and what was the nature of your relationship?

Horovitz: I was in Spoleto, Italy, in 1968, with [Al] Pacino, [Jill] Clayburgh, [John] Cazale—*The Indian Wants the Bronx* and *It's Called the Sugar Plum* casts–performing at the Festival Dei Due Mondi. There was a woman performing in the schedule, as we were, named Eléonore Hirt. She's a Swiss-French actress. She was doing a Beckett monologue. I don't know what it was—something taken from a larger work, out of context; it wasn't a complete piece. She was doing three monologues, and one of them was a Beckett monologue; one of them was a Giraudoux. I remember an image from it that I just stole and used in a production of my play *Stage Directions (Didascalies)* that I directed in Paris this past winter. It started me thinking about Eléonore Hirt again. She'd asked me, "Would you like to meet Samuel Beckett?" as simply as she might have asked, "Would you like a glass of wine?" I said yes, and she said, "Well, good. He would like to meet you." She told me to be in Paris on such and such a day at seven o'clock, at the bar of the Cloiserie des Lilas, on July whatever. She said, "He'll meet you for a half-hour. Be on time and don't ask him how he works." So off I went to Paris, and this odd, really odd kind of tourist restaurant, in Montparnasse, near the Jardin Luxembourg.

Kane: Didn't Beckett typically meet people where he wouldn't be recognized?

Horovitz: Not really. He just had spectacularly bad taste in restaurants. He liked this place. I mean, years later, he had me meeting him at the coffee shop in PLM Hotel. We used to meet often at the bar in La Coupole, where *everybody* would know him. Please, don't let me forget to tell you a great Beckett story set at Cloiserie des Lilas, from some years later. Anyway, we're talking about our first meeting . . . I went into this weird, tourist restaurant, 6:55 P.M., and there was Beckett, waiting. His cataracts were full blown then, so he had thick thick thick glasses, like inverted champagne bottles. He looked like an owl on anti-Prozac. I sat down, and he squinted at me. I said, "Bonjour, je m'appelle Israel Horovitz". . . and he said, "I prefer *Rats.*" I guess Eléonore Hirt had sent him a copy of my plays, *Rats* among them, and that's probably when he told her, "I'd like to meet him." Anyway, instead of "Hello," he said, "I prefer *Rats.*" I then told him something like I hadn't written anything worthwhile yet, but that I would surely be one of the great ones. Anyway, I sat, we drank, and we talked about playwriting and about life . . . for hours and hours and hours. When we parted, I was thrilled, he was charmed. I asked him if we could be friends. He said yes.

It became my mission, in later meetings, to make him laugh. I had this notion that he wouldn't laugh, ever, and it was my responsibility to crack his smile. Of course, he was a hilarious guy. We had a meeting at Cloiserie des

Lilas one night a few weeks later.   It was packed with French *fressers*.
Everybody knew who he was, wherever he went in Paris.   He was a star of
mammoth proportion, a superstar. Paris was and is a very literary place. His
plays were hits, so wherever he went—and he was such a specific-looking
character—people treated him as if he were a movie star.   He was like Jack
Nicholson walking in to any restaurant in Beverly Hills—but, less likely to be
stoned.

Kane: You have acknowledged that *Spared*, a play that you dedicated to its
sole actor, the late Lenny Baker, was a straightforward imitation of Beckett. Do
you consider your novel *Cappella* to be similarly imitative?

Horovitz: Beyond a question of doubt. I started writing *Cappella* when I was
in the hospital having a hernia repair. How's that for a romantic setting? I wish
I could say it was written when I had a collapsed lung! At least there would be
a shade of Chopinesque!   But life is life, isn't it?   I went in for a normal,
routine, nothing-to-worry-about hernia repair . . . and it was so incredibly
frightening! First of all, I went in and I had—like in the novel *Cappella*—a
hundred people around my hospital bed.   I was a graduate student back then,
and when you're in graduate school, you have a million friends.   It's an
obligation. Also, I was already doing movies. Can you imagine, I had three
movies out, and I was in graduate school?

Kane: Is this when you were teaching at City College in New York?

Horovitz: Yeah.   I also had about twenty produced plays behind me.
Everybody from my Ph.D.-level tragedy seminar used to come to my hospital
room to discuss the comedy of my hernia repair. I checked into my room at
3:00 P.M. with my friends Irwin and Margo Winkler and my late wife, Doris.
By 5:00 P.M. there must have been thirty of us crammed into this tiny double-
bedded hospital room, with an old, old guy sleeping in the bed next to mine.
There was champagne, a party, and I remember this one guy, Neil, reading his
poetry.   It was like a little bedside salon.   Everybody left, and the guy in the
bed next to me died. Died. Dead. No kidding around at all. Dead. I was in the
bed next to him, and I said, "Excuse me . . . are you all right?" And he was
still dead. I called the nurse, and people came in, and they were pounding his
chest, and it was indisputable: he was a dead old guy. They took him out and I
was there, alone, and it was awful.
  His bed didn't stay empty for long. About an hour after he died, they
brought his replacement, this old, old Jew named Mr. Capellner, who would
not shut his fucking mouth. He just kept talking day and night. A litany of
complaint that defined old Jews! I had no defense whatsoever, because if I
answered him or, God forbid, if I made actual eye contact, Mr. Capellner's
"conversation" would become nothing short of volcanic. If I *didn't* answer him,
he became angry and his "conversation" became mega-babble, so I started

writing it all down. He would ask, "What are you doing?" and I would say, "I'm a writer and I'm writing. Shhhh! Please leave me alone; I'm trying to concentrate." He would say, "Okay, I'll say nothing," and he'd keep on talking and talking, and I'd just keep writing down his amazing litany of complaint in pencil, filling an endless supply of notebooks . . . and my manuscript got bigger and bigger and bigger, because my hospital stay kept going on and on and on.

The recovery period from my normal, routine, nothing-to-worry-about hernia repair was endless. In those days they didn't do the surgery the way they do it now. I couldn't straighten up for a month. One summer day, four weeks after I'd been released from hospital, I was lying on a beach on Fire Island. And I wrote *Cappella* that way . . . on my belly, on a sandy beach, with my dozen beautiful Brown University pencils and my two dozen blue-lined notebooks . . . until, finally, I'd created an amazingly hulky, mound of a manuscript. There was a wonderful editor at Harper & Row, Frances Lindley, dead now. Dear old thing, legally blind, she sat with a magnifying glass, and she read that whole novel in its immense, 2,000-page pencil-and-notebook, little giant format, and she edited it down to book size. I went to Paris and boiled it down further, to a thinnish novel. I remember it was the loneliest thing, this damned novel, because I was used to writing plays . . . used to getting out of my lonely room and going to rehearsal . . . and there'd be actors and they'd say, "Oh, you're brilliant, it's great."

Kane: And, you'd get no feedback in this novel-writing experience?

Horovitz: Nothing, but for Frances, this mad old lady, who wanted to touch my flesh as often as possible and cook unflicked chickens for me to eat in the dark of her dining room. It was so crazy! The novel came out, and I remember going to St. Patrick's Cathedral. I was just walking around going from bookstore to bookstore saying, "Yup, there's my book." I didn't know what to do with myself. I hadn't had contact with a single living person in the entire novel-writing/publication experience except lovely mad old, Frances. Anyway, *Cappella* was quite well reviewed by the *New York Times,* but, in the end, nobody ever bought the book. Seventeen copies sold in foreign markets. The book is sort of an ipso facto Beckett imitation, so, why not have Beckett's sales? In truth, whatever unique voice I had found in *The Indian Wants the Bronx* in that early period of writing was suddenly being quietly criticized as being Beckettian. I was shocked, and I thought, "What are they talking about?" Then I looked at my work and I thought, my God, they're right. It *is* Beckett's voice. It was silly of me to be so concerned about the imitativeness, really silly. I was saying "I love you" to Mr. Beckett in the most sincere way I knew . . . by imitating his work. I wish I had just continued, and whatever would have evolved would have evolved. I would have refound my own voice, really. And it certainly was interesting work. I think *Spared* is wonderful. I love it. Whatever is Beckettian in it just simply *is*. I mean, it's like describing a coat on a man. But it's not the man, is it? It's the coat. That work was in a particular mode . . . it wore a particular coat, that's all. Beckett loved *Spared*. He adored *Spared*. He wrote to me saying he'd stolen from it . . . the play of his with the old man . . . with the hair flowing on to his pillow. I had one note from him saying he was starting this play and that it was a reaction to *Spared* and then, another note, when he'd finished. I was thrilled. It was so flattering, really.

Kane: Did it frighten you that he adored *Spared*?

Horovitz: Frighten me? No. I was ever so happy. At the time, I thought about framing his note. I remember thinking about putting it on the wall for people to see. Of course, I didn't. I haven't even given my notes from him over for publication. I'll leave them to my children. They're mine, and they're private. But in the end, I think that Mr. Beckett and I were sometimes at odds about writing. I felt that his work was elitist, and mine should be populist, working class. It's absurd now to be saying these things out loud, but at the time, I can remember being so incredibly *desperate* to find a point of difference so I wouldn't go through my life imitating Beckett's work. Once you do imitate him—once that amazing voice of his is in your head—it's four walls over backward. I mean it's a crazy way of using language, and once it's in your head it's very hard to stop whistling his particular tune. I was just desperate to get away from that wry son of a bitch . . . because his voice was so *staining*. I can remember convincing myself that his work was really elitist and that it was never going to be for my mother or for working-class Gloucester. Of course, I was dead wrong. When I produced *Happy Days* at the Gloucester Stage Company, the audience loved it. It was a commercial success.

Kane: Beckett is one of the few playwrights that you refer to as "father of choice." Are you referring to him as a literary or intellectual model?

Horovitz: I'm talking about as a man across the table. That's the "father of choice." It's everything that's in the man. It's hardly just the writing, but yet it's the way that man looks at life. It's the way the man talks to me. Anouilh was a kind of friend. His daughter Colombe is one of my best friends, absolutely one of my best friends, and will be 'til we're both dead—her, first, then me. And yet Anouilh would never have been my "father of choice." He wasn't an easy father; he was too much like my own father. He was selfish. Beckett was not selfish, not ever. He was absolutely generous, generous to a fault, with his time, with his money. I can remember him saying, "If you need money, take some. I have more than I need." He was a lovely, lovely person. And yet *Waiting for Godot* isn't my favorite play in the world. It makes me laugh from time to time, but it's not the kind of theater that I love. Loving Beckett was more than than my envying a guy's career. Samuel Beckett was really a friend.

Yes, I miss him. But like Harkavy, I still talk things over with Beckett, nearly every day of my life. And his advice is almost always, as we Gloucester locals say, excellent.

Kane: Was Beckett influential in facilitating your acceptance and production in the French theater, where you are so well received?

Horovitz: I hope not. I think Ionesco certainly was. Anouilh, too. Claude Roy, a lot. I was very guarded about my relationship with Beckett in the early days. Lately our friendship is pretty well known in France. He'd show up at plays of mine. He'd send people to see something, so, yeah, I'm sure Beckett did help. Why kid myself? I'm sure he did, knowing him.

Kane: When you say you hope not, you mean you hope that the work spoke for itself?

Horovitz: Of course. That, too. It's a funny kind of luck that makes a successful writer successful. It's not just the work. I mean, there are so many people doing good work, and then once you have success, you get a lot of support from people thinking they'll catch on to your star. One success leads to another success. It's awful to see people of talent being turned away. And time passes; failure breeds failure. It's not just their careers that turn sour; their writing often turns sour. Their hopes are dashed It's awful; it's just awful. You see so much of it. There are so few playwrights of my generation still writing plays. I'm so lucky. My kids, Gillian, my wife, my popularity in Europe, my little theatre in Gloucester, the playwrights in the New York Playwrights Lab . . . it's all been so incredibly lucky. More than I deserve.

Kane: Even after twenty-five years, you seem to be able to find new inspiration, either as soon as you finish a play or before you've finished another. Do you work on several plays at the same time?

Horovitz: Less than I used to. Now I'm pretty much working on one play at a time. The movie work is often paying the bills. That's a good thing; I think it's a good thing. When I used to make my entire living solely doing plays, there was almost a frenzy about writing a new play. I needed to have so many plays out there working for me. I think I've brought that back into a reasonable proportion. But I am, by nature, frenzied. I think I'll be frenzied even after I'm dead. My grave will be a mess. It's me. I always feel like I'm living two lives at the same time. When somebody asks me, "What have you been doing?" I always pause, kind of embarrassed to answer because I know I've been doing a lot. I'm always a bit ashamed of my success, I guess. This morning the hygienist at the dentist was massaging my gums, and she was saying the most touching things. She was really, really talking about life. You can really get people to open up if you ask the right questions. My mother taught me this. It's quite amazing; everybody wants to talk about life.

Kane: Does that give you a source of material?

Horovitz: Of course. I mean, that's a skill that I've developed. It's not only a skill, but it's a genuine interest. It's my job to get my hygienist to talk about life.

Kane: I remember reading an anecdote many, many years ago about Arthur Miller, who acquired ideas for his plays by listening in on conversations when traveling the subways from Brooklyn to New York.

Horovitz: He seems to be doing it again. He has such an amazing talent, that guy, really an amazing talent. His new work was awful for a while, but then, suddenly, *The Last Yankee* appeared . . . and, like *A View from the Bridge* and *Death of a Salesman*, it is, I believe, an important play. I'm so glad for Arthur Miller. He's so gorgeously unpopular with the New York critics just now. It may be lucky. He's angry and robust at seventy-seven. Maybe he'll stay alive just to show the filthy bastards.

Kane: In *Today, I Am a Fountain Pen* and *Henry Lumper* you employ a choral figure similar to Alfieri in Miller's *A View from the Bridge*, who serves as both historical and social conscience.

Horovitz: *A View from the Bridge* was definitely an influence on *Henry Lumper.* I mean, it is, first and foremost, boldly, an adaptation of *Henry IV* . . . so I guess I was thinking, as long as it's *Henry IV*, it might as well be Arthur Miller, too.

Kane: I believe that in your notes to *Henry Lumper* you say that "everything is fair game."

Horovitz: Yeah, with that play. I don't tend to do a whole lot of nonoriginal work.

Kane: Although you have acknowledged that Ionesco and Beckett are the major influences on your work, on more than one occasion you have referred to Thornton Wilder as your mentor. How did he function as mentor and at what point in your career?

Horovitz: He read the seven plays of my cycle of home-town plays, *The Wakefield Plays.* He was full of flattery, full of praise, but, in one small sentence, he changed the course of my writing for years and years to come. He looked at me, smiled, and said: "There isn't very much Wakefield in these plays." My Gloucester-based plays could never attract that criticism . . . not from the man who'd created Grovers Corners. Thornton Wilder was an amazingly brilliant, sweet, funny, old guy. At the end of his life, he took to wearing the hat that he wore when he played the Stage Manager in *Our Town.* He was so ill at the end. It seemed to me that people were treating him as if he had died ten years before that. Given who he was and what he had accomplished, there was not a lot of interest in him at all. It's so typically American to forget the great older artists in a great sick search for the young and the new. Not many people were calling him . . . Mia Farrow did; she called him a lot. Mostly, Mr. Wilder was alone, up in Connecticut, with his lovely, dotty, old sister, Isabel. I forget how the hell I first met him. How on earth did I meet Thornton Wilder? Not a clue. He just appeared in my breakfast cereal. God! I can't remember! Anyway, for the last year or so of his life, I used to try to meet with him once a week, sometimes for dinner.

Kane: How did Wilder's comment about there "not being very much Wakefield" in *The Wakefield Plays* have an impact on your Gloucester cycle?

Horovitz: Well, he created Grover's Corners, didn't he, and it was so detailed, daily life was so detailed, so absolutely *real*. And here *I* was working from a real place, and there was such an *absence* of detail. In writing *The Wakefield Plays*, I'd succumbed to a deep fear of not really having a proper, distinguished education—really spotty high school, leaving college, getting married way too young, going to drama school in England, not a serious Harvard education like my cousins and uncles or the Kennedys. My time at the Royal Academy of Dramatic Art sounded impressive, but I had this huge amount of reading that I knew I hadn't done. Big black literary holes. I was a bit hysterical about it, really. I mean, I was like a starving man. I got myself accepted to the Ph.D. program at the City University of New York. I had made a few hundred thousand dollars the year before from writing a couple of Hollywood movies. I bought a house in the Village [Greenwich], for cash, and I thought, well, what else do I want? What do I need? I wanted and needed an education. I read everything in sight but after two years of a Ph.D. program in English Lit., I wrote three three-act plays teeming with literary allusion, not life. I became frightened, when I looked at my *Wakefield Plays*, that I had screwed something up, badly . . . that I would, forever more, write that kind of appalling play that is appealing to academics but not at all moving to people, not touching. Irresponsible academic tripe.

I remember when I decided to be a playwright that what led me to it was the emotional power of certain plays that I had seen: *Our Town*, for one, and *Raisin in the Sun*, for another. I mean, they were really anti-intellectual plays, plays for people . . . not unintelligent plays but the antithesis, of say, *Four Baboons Adoring the Sun*, or that other play of Guare's, *Six Degrees of Separation*. I found that one to be not so much a play as a *New York Times* event ... you loved the article, now see the play. Middle-class drivel. I predict that in ten years that play will not be done by anybody at any time. It's only of remote interest for the trendiest of Uptown East Side reasons. There's nothing moving about that play at all. It's not real. It's New York chic. Am I jealous of its success? Maybe just a tad.

Kane: In 1972, you were hired by City College to teach playwriting on the basis of your professional accomplishments and qualifications, yet you falsely indicated that you had earned a B.A. at Harvard University. There was really no need at this point of your career to acknowledge or deny that that you had even attended Harvard or graduated from Harvard. You were accepted, I trust, on the basis of your accomplishments. Yet when *Cappella* was published, the Harvard story emerged. Although you've acknowledged this deception as regrettable, isn't it more than possible that this very bright, lower-middle-class Jewish boy from Wakefield always wanted to go to Harvard so badly that he almost convinced himself that he had? In fact, deception of one kind or another recurs in many of your plays.

Horovitz: To a certain extent it does. To a greater extent, I know that it was the sixties, and it was the kind of thing I had never done, so it seemed so cool to just, you know, say it. It was the spirit of 1968 to just simply reinvent yourself, even with the most outrageous lies. I remember chasing some poor guy with a movie camera, and I wouldn't stop taking his picture, and it was driving him crazy. I thought I was so incredibly cool. Far out, man. There isn't a chance in the world that I would do that now, that I would say I went to Harvard in '61. There was also a hysteria about getting the job, too. In fact, when I first got the job, I wasn't famous at all. I was twenty-eight. I had no money. I had a lot of kids. And to my shock and horror, I reported for a job for which I was obliged to have a university degree, not a drama school certificate. So I took what I needed. I lied. Of course, had I lied and said I had a degree from Salem Teachers College, no one would have known or cared. Because I'm Mr. Success, I took a *Harvard* degree. Why own when you can rent? Like Brackish says, "If the man I *am* met the man I *was* . . ."

Kane: It seems entirely out of character for you to have done this, because you seem so honest and so forthright.

Horovitz: Yuh, well, maybe. . . . Consider this. Maybe I wouldn't seem as honest and forthright as I seem to you today if I hadn't been caught in a big lie in 1968. It's just possible that one can actually learn a lesson in this life and get to say, "Boy, was that ever stupid!" It's so much easier just to tell the truth and get on with it. But the truth is, when I got that job, I was desperate to get the job. Ironically, when I was found out, years later, I *didn't* need the job. I'd had some commercial success.

Kane: When you were fired from the City College for falsifying teaching qualifications, what was the sequence of events that led to your teaching at New York University? Had you already earned your M.A. degree?

Horovitz: No, I was teaching at NYU before I got my Masters degree. I was fired from City College on a Monday, and I started teaching at NYU the next day. The chairman of the Drama Department at NYU, a prince named Carl

Weber, called me up and said, "Come down here and teach; that's ridiculous." And then the next year, I started teaching at Brandeis University. I was a full professor there for two years . . . until my lung collapsed. See? I knew I'd get my collapsed lung in!

Kane: I knew you were at Brandeis, as well. So obviously, you were City College's loss and NYU's gain ?

Horovitz: I was such a good teacher when I was teaching at CCNY. I loved teaching, back then. Many of "my kids" are still writing; Wendy Wasserstein, David Rimmer—they were there with me, my students. That was really the beginning of the New York Playwrights Lab. The Playwrights Lab exists because of City College's firing me. So, thank you, City College. I'd created a graduate seminar in playwriting at CCNY, and I came up with a unique system of teaching playwriting. Everybody I knew was teaching playwriting in the same old manner: a kid would write a play, he or she would bring it in to class, and the whole play would be read to the whole class. Usually student plays don't work. Usually the class would be sound asleep and/or feeling physical pain, and some poor student playwright, who had achieved the miracle of actually finishing a play, would be sitting there, horrified to see sleeping peers. Really, the last thing a student wants to hear is criticism of his or her hundred-page, four-months-in-the-writing play, to hear it's no good . . . or, worse, it's confusing—especially after suffering through two hours of their classmates' hostile fatigue.

Anyway, playwriting was not often taught in a realistic or supportive way. I came up with this idea that everybody had to write five pages a week—no more no less—and then stop. Students would bring in their five pages, and we'd read them and all they were being asked to change was five pages. No more, no less. And, yes, Virginia, grain by grain, the desert is solidly built. After five weeks, the students would each have twenty-five pages that everybody understood . . . and approved of. What that meant is they'd have twenty-five coherent pages and actually know what the play was about themselves. They could answer the big questions: Why do you want to write this play? Why do you think people should give up a night of something else to see this play? What are you trying to do to the world with this play? What's the story? And, ultimately, the biggest question of them all: From this we learn? These are all essential questions that you have to ask yourself when you're in the throes of writing a play . . . questions you don't normally ask yourself when you're a kid, starting out. Instead, as a beginner, you chide yourself, over and over, again, with, "I want to be a playwright. I want to be a playwright. I want to be a playwright." So, anyway, I think, for one reason or another, I hit upon a realistic, constructive, low-risk, low-pain system.

In a word, it worked. Wendy Wasserstein, for example, whom I remember to be absolutely incoherent in her twenty-first year of life . . . but, delicious . . .

Wendy is a charmer . . . but, I mean when I first met Wendy she was writing about showgirls tap dancing on the tops of Buicks in Miami! She was loony, absolutely loony. She *is* those plays of hers; that's exactly the life she came from. She was rebelling against that. It was interesting stuff . . . for about ten minutes, but, then, so incoherent. Five pages a week really worked. And now, look, Wendy is soaring. I'm kidding, of course. I don't mean to take credit for any of Wendy's great success. She's done every bit of it herself. But unlike most teachers of playwriting with most students of playwriting, I didn't stop her, I didn't block her path. I loved her and her wonderful imagination then, and I still do.

I want to say one final thing about my being fired from CCNY, because I think we've taken something that doesn't really mean a great deal to me, and we've talked it to death. The only truly startling thing about that entire incident was the identity of the young man who caught me in the lie and exposed that lie to the world. I was out of the country, in France, codirecting the Paris premiere of *Line*, which won the Critics' Prize, there. My point is, I was doing well by then—very well. *Alfred the Great* and *Cappella* were published by Harper & Row, in hard-cover editions, on the same day. My editor, Frances Lindley needed a bio from me for the two book jackets, and I wasn't around. So she got her own. By fate's most rotten twist, her research assistant got ahold of, yes, a catalog from CCNY, and Harper & Row printed the lie in both editions: Harvard, B.A., 1961. A lowly reporter for the *Harvard Crimson* was reviewing the books, and noticed the Harvard connection. He looked me up in the Big Book of Harvard Graduates and could only find cousins and uncles, not me. He rang me up and asked me why he was having difficulty finding me listed in the Big Book. I answered, "Because I never went to Harvard." And the rock of scandal began to roll out of control. I begged the kid not to print the story. In the end, he sold a short piece on me and my phony bachelor's degree to AP [Associated Press] for something like fifty bucks. A week later, it hit the papers, big time. Huge *New York Times* story.

Two days later, Lenny Baker rang me up, screaming, somewhat hysterically, "Israel! Quick! Turn on your TV! You're on every channel!" And I was. The lying playwright says he's sorry. And, as I mentioned, Carl Weber was among the early callers, and I started teaching at NYU before sundown. So here's the truly astonishing fact: the student reporter for the *Crimson* was none other than young Frank Rich, who is, of course, now the first-string drama critic of the *New York Times.* Between Rich's guilt and my anger, we have not been able to make peace with each other. Frank Rich has hardly reviewed my work at all over the years . . . twice, I believe, in fifteen years . . . and we're talking about maybe fifteen new plays . . . and both times he reviewed me, he wrote savagely negative reports. This has not been a good thing for me, or, I suspect, for Rich, or for the many people who go to my plays in New York City.

As neither Rich nor Horovitz appears to be going away, I hope we can strike a truce one day, soon. Let's start a new subject, Leslie, please?

Kane: As a founding member of the National Playwrights Conference of the Eugene O'Neill Memorial Theatre, you profited from its workshop performances of your completed plays. But you modeled the Playwrights Lab on an entirely different premise?

Horovitz: Yes. The O'Neill Conference was more of a career move than a working place. It was great. I adored every moment I ever spent there, but, simply said, working at the O'Neill was, and probably still is, a high-profile experience. The Lab is the opposite. Here's the secret of the Playwrights Lab: Everybody starts a play at the same time; nobody's allowed to bring anything they've written before; there are no strangers allowed in the room—just us, working, criticizing each other's work; supporting each other. There are few defenses seen at all. Everybody's got no more than five pages invested at any one time. Before each of us writes his or her first five pages, we all talk about the plays we're going to be writing. So we all actually have to think about the big questions early on. Then the first five pages come in, and everybody's asked the same question: Is this a good way to start a play? Is this a good opening gambit? In the Lab, the creative process is really open and shared, and this can be frightening, really frightening. But once you actually start writing your play, you're on a track you wouldn't have been on without your fellow Labbers, your peers. You've got this wonderful support system because you're surrounded by a group of full-time, professional, hard-working, serious writers who are actually paying attention. We're in the right place at the right time. Ours a room brimming with respect and caring.

Kane: Do you always write a play at the same time as the other writers in the Lab?

Horovitz: Absolutely. Always.

Kane: So you are artistic director of this group, but you're writing your new play at the same time?

Horovitz: Yeah, that's the beauty part for me. I remember that when I was fired from City College, the guy who was the head of the department, back then, assumed that after I was out of there, somebody would take over my playwriting class. Not true. When I left, it was like some kind of odd, deep relationship between my students and me that didn't exist in some normal class . . . in, say, Middle English . . . because, I suppose, they were in the midst of this odd process with me, midway through the creation of their plays. So we decided to continue to meet, away from the City College campus—without pay and without tuition. Circle Rep [Circle Repertory Theatre] was then uptown in the West 90s, on Broadway, before they got the Sheridan Square Playhouse, downtown. I called Lanford [Wilson] and Marshall [Mason], and they set it up for me to be able to continue meeting with my students, two or three times a week at Circle. This is way back to *When Are You Coming Home, Red Rider?* days at Circle Rep.   My students included David Rimmer and Wendy Wasserstein and Ronda Peck, and a bunch of other people who are still writing. Obviously, something that was going on between us had some positive effect on them as well.   And then the dust sort of settled, and I taught at NYU and then Brandeis.

Kane: Now we're in mid-seventies?

Horovitz: Yuh. It was probably '73. I taught at Brandeis '74 and '75 using exactly that five-page method, or system. I handpicked the graduate students at Brandeis. Fred Zollo, Janet Neipris, and Liz Coe were among them. The New York Playwrights Lab had really jump-started with that little group of displaced CCNY writers. But then the Lab stalled for the couple of years I was at Brandeis. I suppose I'd put all my energy there, at Brandeis. And I'd treated the graduate students like Labbers, like pro's. I wrote my play *The Primary English Class* along with the Brandeis lab playwrights. I was paid quite a lot of money by Brandeis. I was the Fannie Hurst Professor of Playwriting. It makes no sense, but, never mind. I flew there up to Boston, from New York, one day a week, and I got paid thirty thousand a year for nine months, one day a week. Pas mal. Then when I was in the hospital in Chicago, when my lung collapsed—during the second year I was teaching at Brandeis—the greedy guy who was head of the department sent me a letter in the hospital saying, "So sorry you're ill. I'm going to take over your playwriting classes." So I was out of my job at Brandeis. I was very angry. I'm not quite sure how it came to pass. But while I was in the hospital, after reading his note, I thought, I don't really want to teach.   I don't *need* to teach. I don't ever want to sit in a department meeting again. I hate schools. I don't really want to work with students. I'd like to work with full-time playwrights. So I gathered together a group of writers in New York, and I sold the Actors Studio on the idea of our being guests in their house. God bless Lee Strasberg and Carl Shaeffer for saying yes. That first Lab group included Richard Vetere, Peter Parnell, Bruce Serlin, Mario Fratti, Jeff Sweet, Nancy Fales, Linda Segal . . . a lot of good writers who all still write.

Kane: And that was 1975?

Horovitz: That must have been 1976, because I'd finished a draft of *The Lounge Player,* and then I'd started the first draft *The Widow's Blind Date* . . . both during the first year of the Lab. That same year, Peter Parnell wrote *The Sorrows of Steven,* and Richard Vetere wrote *Rockaway Boulevard.* We were *cookin'*! We did a festival of our new plays in the spring, full productions at the Actors Studio. About four of the plays moved commercially.   Peter's play moved to the Public [Anspacher Theater], intact.   Then, it was just obvious I should go get my money someplace else and just do the Lab that way. It was just such a good thing. It went along for a number of years, and then you burn out. I mean it's like the [Gloucester] Stage Company. There are times when it's very vital, it's very much in the center of my life, and other times I just wish somebody would take over and give me a holiday. The Lab was even more intense because I was writing along with them. In the eighties I let it go for a couple of years. Then, ironically, Joanne Akalitis got after me and said, "Whatever happened to the New York Playwrights Lab? That was great." Rosemarie Tichler helped me reorganize the Lab, this time at the Public Theatre. So I started the New York Playwrights Lab up again a couple years ago. And I can report that it's really working . . . better than ever. What a fantastic group of writers we have!

Kane: Who is in it now?

Horovitz: Erin Cressida Wilson, Marlena Meyer, and Frank Pugliesi, who wrote *Aven'u Boys;* and Jonathan Marc Sherman, who wrote *Women and Wallace;* Richard Vetere, Kenny Lonergan, Nicole Burdette, and Seth Svi Rosenfeld, who wrote *Servy and Bernice 4-Ever;* Dan Reitz, Matt Weiss . . . really serious, hard-working, talented playwrights. I would say that the most interesting writers in New York City are in the Lab right now. Period. No question about it. It's a secret society. There's no kind of commercial pressure on it at all. It's a totally artful experience. Everybody finds the time to take it seriously, to do their work. Some of the pages will be faxed from London. It's quite interesting how everybody gets there.

Kane: In a recent essay you acknowledge O'Neill as a standard, colleague and competitor. Scholars have noted numerous analogues to O'Neill, such as your use of myth and memory, trilogies, and structure. What do you see as O'Neill's greatest legacy to you?

Horovitz: New England. I mean, I think it's a way of taking New England life, clearly. Whenever I see O'Neill, I'm always reminded of that. It's that line more than anything. I mean, I think if you can boil all the plays in the world that are serious plays—and you just sort of boil them all down—they'll have those elements. I think what's special is his use of place. You don't get hit over the head with it, but it's there. I mean, he's really a New England playwright. If you're a New Englander, it just rings so true. And he's very funny. You don't think of O'Neill as being funny, but when you go to any of the plays, its always a great relief that he's so funny. If Beckett's not funny, it's a disaster; it's really a disaster. Smoke would come from his grave, he'd be so upset. Or if I wrote a play and it weren't funny, it would be a disaster. It would be the most pretentious crap imaginable. *North Shore Fish* could be played as a melodrama, and it would be just awful.

Kane: Well, as long as we're talking about New England, you have referred to yourself as a "Yankee Jew." You were brought up in the Catholic community of Wakefield, Massachusetts. How did your family maintain or inspire your cultural connections in a community where there were so few Jews?

Horovitz: When I was a little kid, I always thought there were more than enough Jews in the community, because my two closest friends, Buzzy and Richie, were both Jewish. It was only later that I realized they were the other two Jewish families in the town. My sister married Buzzy's brother, Arnold. My mother plays mah-jongg on Wednesdays with Richie's mother. Of course, I'm exaggerating. There must have been at least twenty other Jewish families in Wakefield, back then . . . but, you get the picture. Not a hotbed of Hebraic thought. I don't know about your family, but I can assume if they were anything like my family, they weren't particularly religious Jews. Did you grow up in Massachusetts?

Kane: No. I grew up in Brooklyn and Long Island. My grandparents were Orthodox Jews.

Horovitz: Oh. It's a completely different experience. The New England experience is this—especially with Jews my age. You grew up Jewish and you were told constantly that you were Jewish, but you celebrated Christmas . . . without a Christmas tree, because then there would be a scandal if the other six Jews saw a Christmas tree in your house. You ate in Chinese restaurants, and you really were very pressured to assimilate into a Christian community. At the same time, you were constantly bombarded with this odd, modern, Jewish identity that did not relate to Orthodoxy—not much religious education and a very strong movement away from Hebrew in the synagogue. We weren't Yankees. We were *Yenkees.*

Kane: If it's impossible, indeed unwise, to attempt to separate O'Neill's life from his work, couldn't one argue the same thing about your work, in which one finds numerous allusions to your life, such as the fleet-footed Archie in *Widow's Blind Date,* the ethnic playwright in *Author! Author!* the returning hero in *The Alfred Trilogy,* the young Jewish boys in your *Saulte Ste. Marie Trilogy? A Rosen by Any Other Name,* in particular, confronts the issues of Jewish identity and of name.

Horovitz: There's a lot going on in *Rosen. A Rosen by Any Other Name* is definitely one of my good ones. I like the way that play works on people; it's very moving. The play is based on a speech that I made as a thirteen-year-old kid during a national oratory contest. The name of the speech, or the topic, was "From Kalitsky to Kaye," and it was about name changing. But I must tell you, as life would have it, that the subject was handed to me on a piece of paper by the organizers of the contest. Everybody had to make an extemporaneous speech, and everybody got a different subject. Everybody's prepared speech was: "We have nothing to fear but fear itself," which was, of course, a line spoken and made famous by none other than that Jew-hater Franklin Delano Roosevelt.

Anyway, I was handed that line and I wrote my prize-winning speech. I was a short kid, too short to stand behind the podium. I was also much much younger than the other competitors. I had to stand in front of the podium to be seen. I won the contest, and I had my life's first great, great victory. In *Rosen*, I found myself, at age fortysomething writing a play that still celebrated that victory. It may be as simple as that. You know, it might be that the essential reason I wrote that play was to get back to it. I mean we do that a lot. We do repeat our successes, over and over again . . . unconsciously, but we do do this. Childhood successes are enormously important, aren't they? By the by, I used the "We have nothing to fear but fear . . . " public-speaking motif again in *Unexpected Tenderness*. Only with this play, I'm not hiding behind anything. I'm out there, exposed. *Unexpected Tenderness* is a play that will be quite startling to people . . . certainly to my sister, Shirley.

Kane: I thought there might have been, without stretching it, some connection between the writing of *Rosen* and the impending birth of your twins.

Horovitz: It would have been deeply unconscious, as I had first written the plays for Canadian television, years before I ever met Gillian. So there was little thought of having children with her. In fact, I was just barely coping with raising the three children I had already. Those three original Saulte Ste. Marie-based TV plays were successful on Canadian television. Unfortunately, it was like talking about a big fish I'd caught somewhere in the Great Lakes. I would have to stop people and tell them about this great success I had in Canada. The original plays were based, in part, on a collection of stories by a Toronto lawyer named Morley Torgov. The book had been given to me. I had been called in for a business meeting with John Hirsh, who was running CBC's Televison Drama department back then. Poor dear guy, gone from AIDS. John—do you know who John Hirsh was?—he was a director at the Stratford Festival. He was born in a Nazi concentration camp during the Second World War. Can you imagine how essentially gloomy John was? Anyway, he wanted me to write a sitcom, and the basic idea of the show was completely stupid. It was called "Rimshot." Anyway, I said "No, thank you." He gave me the books with Morley's stories and said, "We're also interested in this." When I got out to the airport to fly home to New York, Toronto and I were snowed in. I sat waiting for a plane for hours and hours, and I read the whole book of stories. They reminded me so much of my childhood in Wakefield, Massachusetts. I went back into Toronto, to John's office, and I said, "I'll do these; these are good." They paid about ten thousand bucks for a ninety-minute TV play in those days, and I had a lot of kids (three kids, then), and I knew I'd need to earn about thirty thousand, so I said to Hirsch, "I'll be doing three plays; I see this as a trilogy."

Kane: So, identity issues aside, the inspiration for the *Saulte Ste. Marie Trilogy* was monetary? What you're saying is, "I've got these three kids; I need to make a quick thirty thousand."

Horovitz: Sort of. Remember, however, that I could have made a lot more if I'd done the sitcom John had suggested, "Rimshot." There was something in Morley's stories that grabbed hold of me. I got really caught up in writing the second play, *Rosen*. Nothing in that play exists in Morley Torgov's book at all. As for the money motive, there's an old joke, a funny kind of truth-nontruth story, about a critic interviewing Tolstoy, asking, "Why do you write so much Mr. Tolstoy?" Supposedly Tolstoy answered, "I have a lot of kids." I mean, "Why do you write so much?" is such a totally asinine question, and "I have a lot of kids" is a perfectly reasonable answer. As I get older, the why-write-so-much question amuses me more and more. My pal Peter Carey, who won the Booker Prize a few years back for *Oscar and Lucina*—Pete's a great writer—is feverishly working, endlessly too. And I asked him, one day, "Why are you working so hard, Pete?" and he said, "I've got these kids." Everybody I care about comes up with "these kids" for an answer, whether they have kids or not.

Kane: But you started to say *Rosen* was different.

Horovitz: Rosen somehow caught my attention, all by itself. It was just one of those plays that wrote itself. I came back to my little oratory contest victory, and then I came back to that moment when I was a kid. I was born right after my grandfather, who was named Israel, died. My grandmother and cousin and aunt went on a plane to collect his body. Their plane crashed, and they were killed. I was born a couple of weeks later into what had not been a totally joyous period in Horovitz family history. Against my mother's will and better judgment, I was named Israel instead of Arthur—her first choice. My full name is Israel Arthur Horovitz. Irrespective of my legal name, my folks always called me Arthur. When I was bar mitzvahed, to my shock and amazement, my photograph was published on the front page of the *Wakefield Daily Item* with a yarmulke and a tallis. The headline read: "Israel Arthur Horovitz is confirmed." The kids at school were just beside themselves with joy that they had this major Jew-boy name to kid me about.

When I was seventeen, I wrote my first play, *The Comeback*, and I signed it Israel Horovitz. It was the first time in my life that I had acknowledged my legal name. I was just sick of Jewish jokes and the anti-Semitic shit that I had taken in my sweet little town. I didn't reclaim the name *Israel* out of any deep religious fervor. It wasn't out of any kind of deep Jewish experience, either, other than good old Yankee persecution. I was a kid during the Second World War. After hearing about what went on in the concentration camps, I found it easy to say, "Fuck you all! I've got Jewish blood in my veins, and I'm proud of it." And I grabbed the name *Israel*. I'm not altogether glad about that, because it's such a strong Jewish identity . . . one that's betrayed by the reality of my life. I don't have a strong Jewish identity other than my name. And as I get older, I have less and less interest in organized religion, anybody's religion. But I wouldn't want to be mistaken for Protestant, or Catholic to be sure. I'm a Jew. That's my team.

Kane: Your *Saulte Ste. Marie Trilogy*, particularly *Rosen*, delicately balances the larger issues of Jewish life with the more intimate themes of family relationships, heritage, and heroism. *Rosen* appears to be the most personal of all your plays. Was it also consciously autobiographical?

Horovitz: Yes and no. Those two things. Morley [Torgov] grew up in a little town in Canada. His people were mercantile Jews. What I see that's autobiographical is the father-son relationship and my fantasy of teaching my father, the way the kid in *Rosen* teaches his father. Ultimately Barney Rosen says to Stanley, his son, "I'm so sorry, Stanley. Can you forgive me?" There used to be a Stanley line in the play, "Of course, I forgive you; you're my father." Sol Frieder, an actor who's become Hannah and Oliver's (my twins') surrogate grandfather, was sitting in the back of the theater, and I heard him whisper, "Why should a son have to forgive a father? And why should a father have to be forgiven?" . . . So I brought in a rewrite, and now, when the father says, "Oh, Stanley can you forgive me?" Stanley looks at his father and replies, simply, with, "You're my father." And then they embrace. I never had such a moment like that with my own father, ever—not ever. Even when my father was crippled with Parkinson's disease and dying, he had a tremendous anger and power, and not the vaguest intention of ever saying "thank you" to anyone, for anything. He was mostly an angry guy—without the benefit of nine years of psychoanalysis with Dr. Harkavy. So what? Is *Rosen* autobiographical? What *isn't* autobiographical in the end, if the writer is writing from the heart, writing to touch people? . . . unless you're simply imitating other plays? So you try to pull all the pieces together—you say to yourself, "That moment's Morley, and that moment's me"—but, in the end, there are three plays that I have written about fathers and sons, with three distinct lives . . . of their own.

Kane: Previously you described yourself as a very arrogant, stubborn, angry man, and sometimes violent man whose work often depicted that violence. Yet now you appear to be much more mellow. Has living in Gloucester mellowed the man and the artist?

Horovitz: People keep telling me how relaxed I am. Some people say, "You are the most relaxed person I know." And I'll say back to them, "God, there's so much turmoil inside!" and they'll say, "Really? I think of you as the most relaxed person I know." And I'm stunned. I'm just stunned . . . because, many a morning, I'm awake at four o'clock, pacing the floor in a complete frenzy. But I do know who I am. I know who I am; I know what I do. I know what my place is, and, in the end, I'm grateful for my losses and my victories. I mean, that's the truth of it. As much as I enjoy anything at all, I enjoy my life and who I am and the people around me. I have all of the anxieties that anybody with my shaped head could have. And why not? These days, I'm less likely to turn around and punch somebody in the nose than I used to be. I'm perfectly capable of doing it; it's always my *impulse* to do it. The big thing psychoanalysis does for you is get you that little extra beat of time in which you say, "Well, I wanna punch him in the mouth, but I probably shouldn't do that."

Kane: Or, I don't have to?

Horovitz: I don't even know if you ever get to that. I think honestly you say to yourself, "If I do that, I'll regret it." I think that's the second step. Maybe down the road you say, "I don't have to do that." But I'm still at a point in my life when I'm under pressure in a relationship that I want to hit somebody or I'll still say some dumb things. But I think I'm more capable now of diffusing people's anger. I really used to feed it.

Kane: Earlier, you mentioned responding to Sol Frieder's observation that a line did not ring true in *Rosen*. You seem exceptionally responsive to the rewrite process, as evidenced by the fact that many of your plays have gone through successive rewrites and revisions after they have been completed. I am thinking of *Widow's Blind Date*, for example.

Horovitz: I rewrite endlessly—sometimes inappropriately. *The Primary English Class* springs to mind as a nut case in point. I made what I thought was a huge discovery, ten years after the Diane Keaton production of *The Primary English Class* had closed in New York. I discovered that Mrs. Pong, the old Chinese lady, never came back from the ladies' room, and wouldn't it be better if she came back? I thought the play shouldn't end on the teacher's being defeated, as it had, but, instead, it should end on the old Chinese lady's coming back and insisting that the teacher teach her. Now the old Chinese lady returns to the classroom and says to the teacher, "Okay, let's go."

I tried out the rewrite during a revival at The Gloucester Stage, and the audience just *loved* the new ending. It was so *uplifting*. I had to pay to have the publisher of the acting edition reprint and make the change. Nuts! But I'd thought about the play and asked myself, Why am I trying to bum the audience out with a comedy yet? Nice thing about plays versus life: you just simply rewrite them. I think having the Gloucester Stage Company has had a strongly positive effect on me and my work. I mean, I'm deeply aware of what I call dicking around with people's nights out. I see the same Gloucester people in our audience over and over again, and I love them. They arrive at a play, as people are wont to do, with questions of life's meaning . . . questions of existence, really. People want to be taken very seriously . . . even by a comedy.

Kane: As founder, artistic director, and resident playwright of the Gloucester Stage Company, you have weathered many threats to its financial stability and viability, as recently as last summer [1993]. Why do you struggle to maintain the theatre? You don't have to.

Horovitz: I don't know why. I can say this: My parents used to entertain something like thirty people on the weekends, every weekend. I remember, while growing up, there'd be a houseful of people. My mother loved cooking for them, entertaining them. By contrast, my father would be in the corner. He couldn't really get involved. He wanted to, but he couldn't really figure out how to get in. Part of my father is me, not really figuring out how to have friendships the way I'd like to have them. The other part of me runs Gloucester Stage. It is my mother, able to have large groups of people liking her and depending on her. I don't have a lot of friends. I used to but, with five kids to occupy my spare time, I just don't, not for years now. Instead, I have the theatre and I have the Playwrights Lab, and it's another kind of friendship I have with people, a working friendship. I'm not sure that I have time for the other kind. When I get back to New York after being away, I always think, "Well, who are my friends? Who do I call now?" It's very worrisome. I travel all the time. When you live like you do, you have a couple of friends in the neighborhood; that's what you buy into but when you constantly travel from city to city, the way I do, it's so . . . *different.* I have a lot of friends in Paris. I don't quite understand why I do, but I do. Maybe because I'm more popular there. Maybe that's a factor. You know, actually, that I'm more welcome because my work is more popular there, or something.

Kane: You had a very long friendship with Joe Papp, didn't you?

Horovitz: Yeah, I did.

Kane: Joe Papp profoundly influenced the careers of many playwrights from the 1960s to the 1990s. What was the nature of your relationship with Joe Papp, whose Public Theatre staged or workshopped several of your plays?

Horovitz: He used to tell me I was his favorite Jewish playwright. He always said that over and over again. I don't know why. Everybody knows that Spinoza was Joe's favorite Jewish playwright.

Kane: Was that intended as a compliment?

Horovitz: God only knows. Joe had a lot of stormy relationships. My relationship with him had really changed years and years ago. We had a really bad time together in the early to mid 1980s. After the reviews came out—all positive—I thought Joe was going to move my play *Sunday Runners in the Rain* to Broadway. He had no intention of doing that. I was furious. I felt betrayed. We had a confrontation . . . almost a fist fight. Certainly we had a different kind of friendship after that set back. I loved Joe, but I think he always promised more than he could deliver. That was Joe: he wanted to be everybody's perfect papa. I'm told he used to really have quite a violent relationship with [David] Rabe. Some people say that they used to close the door and go at it. Fistfights. Who knows, really? I loved Joe, and I miss him, and, as a producer at Gloucester Stage, I imitate him whenever I can. Joe was a really large personality . . . a very passionate guy . . . egomaniacal off the charts. I mean, off the charts. His sense of himself was enormous. Joe Papp is for me, and will always be, Mr. New York. A few years ago, I started to write a movie called *Mr. New York*, with a guy like Joe. I abandoned it after fifty pages or so. I preferred my memories to my invention. You can't be born in Wakefield, Massachusetts, like I was, and ever be what Joe was. New York City was really his town . . . to a certain extent Paul Simon has that too. Like Joe, Paul's got an ease in New York City; it's all just kind of like his high school reunion.

Kane: Previously you were talking before about friendships. The impression that I have is that you have a warm relationship with Paul Simon.

Horovitz: Yeah, but we're not as current in each other's lives as I wish we could be, as we were when we were both single . . . which is to say between marriages. I think we still love each other . . . still think of each other as friends. But so much time has passed so quickly.

I think the turning point for me with all conventional friendships came when Gill and I got married. I wanted so much for our marriage to work. I kept thinking this is not gonna be a marriage that's gonna end a couple years after it starts. I gave it my all. And then, our having kids, twins yet. There was so little time for other people. And what a great marriage Gill and I have. Now I have a tendency to huddle together with my little family whenever I can. And I mean my whole family, all five of my kids.

When you look back over life, you realize that every year was entirely different and that you can never be what you just were. For me, this is both the most exciting thing about life and the most frightening thing about life: it just keeps changing and changing and changing. I mean, just in a year, the number of people who've come and gone in my life is unthinkable. Some are dead; some are simply busy elsewhere. I try to maintain this odd belief that things will always be the way they are. I'm constantly saying to myself, This is the standard. And then the little rabbi in my ear whispers, "There is no standard; nothing alive ever stays as it was." It's true: nothing sticks . . . so, then, after you come to grips with how quickly life changes, you have a constant hysteria about letting go of anyone you love. When I take a trip to Boston for a couple of days for a board meeting, to see a play, whatever, I say good-bye to my wife and kids, and I wonder if I'll see them again. It's not a passing thought; it's a waking nightmare. It consumes me. Don't you think it's the randomness with which tragedy strikes that drives people the craziest? It's the one thing in life we can't accept: the randomness of tragedy. We're always manufacturing some kind of insane logic, you know, some kind of logic that just isn't there, to try to take control over the things that are totally uncontrollable.

Kane: In *North Shore Fish*, for example, a sensitive group portrait of people allied by geography, their Catholic upbringing, and their impending obsolescence, you make a provocative statement about the quantum relationship between the loss of work and loss of hope. To what do you attribute your keen sensitivity to an individual's rational—or irrational—fears?

Horovitz: See, the thing that I find so heartbreaking is—well, let me try to say it this way: I was thinking that to ever really speak French beautifully, I'd have to say the same word over and over a hundred times. It's the repetition that creates character. If your life takes a bad turn, and you repeat your bad luck, say, a hundred times, well, you own *that*.

I think about my friend Mick, in Gloucester, a lot. Mick works on the fish pier; sometimes he drives a truck. Mick's as intelligent as I am. There's no question about it; he has the same basic, God-given intelligence. But every day he repeats his daily life experience [of driving a truck], he becomes more and more *that*. Every day I repeat my experience—go to France, direct my plays, do interviews like this. It makes me *this*. I'm having more fun than Mick, making more money, getting better strokes. It's not fair. It's just not fair. Something's gone wrong. It's not that Mick's life is bad. It's not . . . not bad. It's just that it's not big. It's just that Mick's life is smaller than it should be for a man of Mick's intelligence. I look at Mick, and I don't know what to do for him. I mean, I feel responsible somehow, because I'm a thinking person and something's *wrong*. It's a pity. It's just a pity. To say I feel guilty, well, sure, what else is new? I'm a *Jewish* thinking person.

Kane: We were talking before about your friends in Gloucester and competition they might feel. Uniting metaphor with meaning—and the physical and psychic violence that it generates—competition has characterized your work for nearly twenty-five years. Is competition the price of proving one's worth?

Horovitz: I just see competitiveness as basic human nature, really. I think that I just got on to it as a subject for my plays, early on. Competitiveness was so strong in my life that it was something I could both recognize and feel trapped by at the same time.

Kane: Competition with your father or just competition in general?

Horovitz: Competition in general. I'm sure at the same time I was trying to prove something to my father as well. That's human nature. I was certainly a competitive fellow. I was a serious athlete when I was a kid, too. I suppose that contributed to my competitiveness later on, in the New York theatre scene. I remember having a short play on in an omnibus evening off-Broadway in the late 1960s with fifteen other playwrights. I had this all-consuming need to have the best play, get the best reviews, to win the prize.

Kane: How has your competitive marathon running influenced your writing?

Horovitz: Kind of hard to tell which influences which. I mean, there are two things I do, without fail, every day of my life: I run and I write. As I age, I get better at my writing game. Running's another story. At this point in my life, I can't win races anymore, unless I'm racing against people with serious physical defects. I used to enter races to try to win, or at least to try to come home with a trophy of some kind, even if only an age group trophy. Now I don't think about winning. I'm older and slower. I'm still competitive . . . I still want to win, but I work against the impulse to kill myself trying. It's too frustrating. I love being around Gill when she wins. When Gill won the English National Marathon Championship last year, I was so proud . . . so thrilled. Competitiveness does energize me—even somebody else's. I mean, I still recognize what's good about competition. It helps, of course, to be very, very well adjusted to life and its frailties. I'm not.

Kane: Do you know anyone who is?

Horovitz: Well, I suppose we don't know many people who are, because beautifully adjusted people don't often become *known* people, famous people. You need a competitive edge, or you just never break through. I can imagine someone being so well adjusted, they constantly say, "Why bother? It's not worth it." I think everybody gets to a point in their life—not everybody—but a *lot* of us get to a point in life when we ask ourselves, "What was that all about?" Does the world really need ten more plays? Does the world really need another movie, need another poem?" I don't know the answer. My honest answer would change from day to day. Some days, I'll have an idea for a play that is so vivid I can see and hear the audience reacting to it. I'm moved by those musings. Of course, even I realize the limitation of writing plays to reach people. The theatre has a very direct relationship to people at large but in a tight little context. Another day, I'll discover something about life that will shake me. Four o'clock this morning, I was up, awake, writing. I'd been awakened by an idea. Do you know that little play of mine called *The 75th*?

Kane: I love that little play.

Horovitz: I do too. I've always wanted to write a second act for that play. For years now I've wanted to either write a second act or write a companion play called *75A* . . . one that has *The 75th* as its curtain-raiser, and then their later, at-the-end-of-life relationship. I had this thought last night, and it was totally original for me. I mean, I'm sure it's been thought about and written about by a hundred other people. Anyway, the two old people from *The 75th* . . . they're discussing their shared past. He was discussing who he was in relation to her, and she says something like, "We've lived so long and we've seen so much; you know that we really are *history*. If only we'd written it down at the time. Kind of like a living history, we are." He says, "No, I don't agree. When you write it down at the time, it's not history; it's common knowledge. History requires that you wait until you can't quite remember what happened, and *then* you write it down." It's a lovely thought, isn't it? History is so creative, really. This interview is, for me, creative. What you ask, what I answer, how we reinvent ourselves. So, anyway, that small thought about history somehow energized me. I do want to get at that second act for *The 75th*. It's not an idea that will cure cancer or replace night baseball. It's just a thought, a new piece for an old play.

Kane: In *Strong-Man's Weak Child*, a trinity of dreams, desire, and deception is colored by the metaphysical reality of a child's death. I believe it is the only play of yours that dramatizes the death of a child. Does this focus on darker themes signify a new direction for your work?

Horovitz: I don't know about that, Leslie. I don't know. I mean that's why I was surprised by *Fighting over Beverley*, because it doesn't bear a strong resemblance to *Strong-Man's Weak Child*—not at all. I think that maybe spending a lot of time in France, where there's so little interest in naturalistic plays, has influenced me. If you were going to put across a naturalistic play in France, it has to be astonishingly brilliant because there's just no interest in the genre. They've done all that, and they're on to something else. *Strong-Man's Weak Child* was so successful for me. I mean, I liked it so much. So, no, I didn't just set out to do something more in that vein. Instead, I said to myself, "Oh, you can't do that again. You've just done that. Do something totally different."

Kane: You have said that *Fighting over Beverley*, the ninth play in the Gloucester cycle, was initially a valentine to your wife, Gillian. How did it evolve into a serious letter to your mother?

Horovitz: I started out to write a kind of love letter to Gillian, who was born in England, in South London, saying to her, "You've given up your country and your family and your friends, and you've taken on this new place, where you can never quite belong, and your children won't ever really have English accents like yours, and it's all in the name of love and marriage. And I can see that it's too much to give, that it's not quite fair, not quite right. So, I want to give you something that shows you at least that I notice this terrible sacrifice that you've made." I started out to write the play that could say that, but I hated it, and I dropped it. Simply put, the idea was great, but play didn't work.

Kane: It appears from the manuscript date that you have been working on *Beverley* for the last two years.

Horovitz: It's a completely different play than the one I started out writing . . . about four years ago, in fact. I started writing a play that was more like *Today, I Am a Fountain Pen*. It was light, and it was sexy and romantic and sweet. Beguiling. But it did absolutely nothing for me, and so I just stopped. Then I started over last year, essentially using the central idea of the old version's third act. The first time around with *Beverley*, the same actors played themselves at twenty, forty, and sixty—a three-act play. In the third act, a Brit who was jilted at twenty by Beverley reappears in her life at age sixty-five, and he says to her, "He's had you for forty-five years. Enough's enough. I'm taking you back to England with me."

Kane: That's a great line.

Horovitz: That's virtually all I kept of the first attempt. So I started out writing a love letter to Gillian, and I ended up, I think, writing a very serious letter to my mother and to my daughters. I mean, I think it's definitely a response to my mother and her marriage to my father, who was a very cruel, tough guy, a very complicated guy. Not that she's uncomplicated, me old mum. She was clearly my father's wife. But looking back over my life, I can only imagine what sense of responsibility people who are eighty today felt when they were kids.

Kane: Do you mean the commitment to stay married regardless of personal unhappiness? Haven't you previously argued that divorce is the worst thing that parents can do to their children?

Horovitz: There was really a sense of staying married back then. You got into a bad marriage and it was tough luck, kiddo. You stayed in it. So having said, "Divorce is about the worst thing you can do to kids," I now look at my mother and say, "Staying in a loveless marriage is about the worst thing you can do to yourself." That's all I've exposed here—a terrible dilemma.

Divorce is a dreadful thing to do to kids. It brands them, confuses them for life, and there's nothing they can do about it. It's completely forced upon them. You tell yourself, "But I've done it, already; I can't change the past." True. What's gone is gone. But you can treat your children to increased attention, given the fact that you've hurt them. I decided that it's a hell of a lot better to recognize that I've done something wrong than pretend I've done nothing wrong.

Kane: Can you say that *Fighting over Beverley* seems to complete the Gloucester cycle?

Horovitz: Let's hope. I'm desperately trying to end the thing, yes.

Kane: For the past fourteen years, you have fashioned yourself as the voice, heart, and conscience of Gloucester, Massachusetts, codifying a regional dialect, calling attention to a dying fish business, the price of gentrification, and the growing drug trade. Is there more to say, or have you exhausted the subject?

Horovitz: I can't still feel that my spiritual center is in Gloucester, Massachusetts, at this particular time in my life. But I'm sure if I spent more time there again, as I did ten years ago, that sense would come back to me. In truth, I feel like I've come to the end of something with my writing about life in Gloucester, and *The Gloucester Plays.* I feel like I can relax a bit. I want to publish all of the Gloucester-based plays, soon. I'll need to do some clean-up work. I need to polish *Strong-Man's Weak Child.* I got sidetracked by writing the movie script [*Strong-Men*], and now I have to bring the play up to snuff again. And I've got to pull *Sunday Runners in the Rain* together as well. It's a big mess. I want to revise it and publish an acting edition. I've never published it, anywhere. Then I want to get the entire cycle of Gloucester-based plays collected. It's time to step back and see what I've got there.

Kane: Nominated for a New York Drama Desk Award and a Pulitzer Prize, *North Shore Fish* might have been the play that enabled you to achieve commercial success and major critical acceptance. Do you regret that it has not?

Horovitz: Of course, it bothers me. It's pity it didn't go to Broadway, like *Park Your Car in Harvard Yard* did. It's a drag. For about ten minutes, it looked as though Cher was going to play Florence, in a Broadway production that never materialized. I don't know what went wrong, but something went wrong. Then a few years later, I'd hoped that *The Widow's Blind Date* would to be a commercial success in New York, the way it was in Gloucester, and Paris, and Los Angeles. The New York production was a tragic turn in the play's life. The *New York Times* sent a newly hired third-stringer [drama critic], named Laurie Winer, who wrote a nasty little review, saying *Widow* was essentially awful . . . like a Clint Eastwood movie. Lucky for Clint, Laurie's clout didn't extend beyond Bleecker Street, and Clint Eastwood has been able to have some success since then. Anyway, the rat wrote a mean-spirited and totally inaccurate pan . . . even getting the names of the three actors in my play bollixed up. *The Times* dumped her two weeks later and even printed an odd retraction correcting her mistakes. But, of course, *Widow* never recovered from the negative review and closed a few months after it opened. *Widow* still doesn't get done as much as it should in this country. It's a shame. I think it'll find it's own strong life, here in America, eventually, because actors will like to do it, and they'll rediscover it. A bad review in the *Times* is like a drive-by shooting.

Of course, I've had more than my share of raves in the *Times,* and I've rarely been heard complaining about any of those, no matter how many inaccuracies they contained.

Kane: Samuel Beckett has said that if one could leave a couple of gems, that would be a success. Do you believe that *The Wakefield Plays* and *The Gloucester Plays* are your major accomplishments?

Horovitz: Major accomplishments? Gosh and golly. I think *Stage Directions* is a kind of gem, maybe. I haven't seen *The Wakefield Plays* on stage in such a long time. *The Wakefield Plays* don't get done as often as many of my other plays. I shouldn't say that; the short plays get done a lot—*Hopscotch, The 75th, Stage Directions, and Spared.* In fact, they are done all the time. But, the longer plays—*The Alfred Trilogy*—never really caught on after their initial productions. I don't really know why. Maybe they're too heady. I mean, I can look at *The Gloucester Plays* and think to myself, "Okay, time to get on to the next thing." You know, you just put your work out there and let the world pick and choose . . . determine the winners. Beckett would be hard pressed to have figured out which his gems were.

You know, you have certain favorites at certain times. I love *Stage Directions* at the moment, because I really had fun directing it in France . . . and it was a certified success. It's like no other play I've ever written or seen. In my Paris production, I had a live cellist on stage, scoring the show as it went. I used a huge piece of white satin, an old backdrop, folded on the lip of the stage—there's a sofa and two armchairs on stage, that's all. As the cello played—in quite nice lighting—the stagehands came out and ran with this cloth flowing over their heads, and they covered the furniture, in the way that furniture's covered in the home of people recently dead. And the play began. It was really quite beautiful. We staged the play in a converted dance studio. Instead of using a small mirror on stage, as I'd initially indicated in the text, one entire wall was mirrored, covered at first by a huge black curtain. The audience didn't suspect there was a mirror behind it. Midway through the play, when the older daughter defies Jewish law and uncovers the mirror [in the home of her recently deceased parents] by pulling back the curtain, the audience was suddenly seeing the play directly, head on, and seeing it a second time in the mirror's reflection. They were both seeing the play and seeing themselves seeing the play. The emotional stakes went up and up and up. Listen to me going on this way.

Stage Directions—we called it *Didascalies* in France—was, for me, really quite an exciting play to direct . . . as were both *Strong-Man's Weak Child* and *The Widow's Blind Date.* And I remember, vividly, standing at the back of the Music Box Theatre, night after night, with my twins, Hannah and Ollie, watching Jason Robards and Judith Ivey perform *Park Your Car in Harvard Yard.* The play worked so well; the audience was so moved. It was so gratifying, so lucky, to see that I was reaching people, touching people, bringing them some comfort. I mean, I can't watch *The Indian Wants the Bronx* easily now. It feels mean-spirited, terrified, and terrifying. When I watch *Line* these days, I find much of it embarrassing. But, you know, *Line* is about to start its nineteenth year of consecutive performance off-Broadway, at the 13th Street Repertory Theatre, so who am I to complain? All I can say, really, is it's not for me, at this time in my particular life, but it seems to be perfect for lots and lots of other people. So how can a writer chose a favorite play? Do you know *Mrs. Klein*, Nicky Wright's play about the psychoanalyst? Mrs. Klein was a disciple of Freud. She psychoanalyzed her own children and found them to be quite ordinary. She published her findings, and her children were undone. One child ended up committing suicide. The pronouncement of their being ordinary was devastating to them. I think to really look over your plays and say, "I prefer *Rats*," is like looking over your children and saying, "I prefer the middle girl." It's a silly game. People and preferences are constantly changing. Everyone I have ever met—child or otherwise—has a totally unique and different quality, and every play I've ever written represents a totally different time of my life, in an ever-changing life. You hope that, in the end, the whole thing spells Mother. That's all I hope for, really, you know, at the end—that the whole catastrophe makes some sense, that there's a truth to be found in my work, and that there's a sense of what life was like on our little dot on the planet Earth in our time . . . that I've left this stuff behind me and that people will get a sense of our particular catastrophe, our particular turmoil, and, also, I suppose, a sense of how life could have been better, a sense that we've perhaps looked at our past life, together and, well, *learned* something. Otherwise, I ask you, what's the point?

My job is to think and to look at life and to look at people and to respond to all that. So it's of no concern to me, really, if the damn thing is successful, or if it's my favorite play at the moment, or even if it's a couple of gems. I mean, what I like or dislike so much depends on what I just ate or how, at the moment, I feel about life around me, about myself. At the end of my life, all this writing will have had to have served some purpose; people will have had to have *used* it—taken comfort in it, somehow balanced the lives they had with the lives they might have had. And I, the writer, have to balance the plays I've written with the plays I could write.

Primary Bibliography

PUBLISHED PLAYS

Acrobats and *Line*. New York: Dramatists Play Service, 1971. *Line* reprinted as *Le ler*. Paris: Avant-scène, 1973.

Alfred the Great. New York: Dramatists Play Service, 1974; New York: Harper & Row, 1974.

The Chopin Playoffs. New York: Dramatists Play Service, 1987.

A Christmas Carol: Scrooge and Marley. Adapted from Charles Dickens, *A Christmas Carol*. New York: Dramatists Play Service, 1980.

Dr. Hero. New York: Dramatists Play Service, 1973.

Faith. New York: Dramatists Play Service, 1989.

First Season: The Indian Wants the Bronx, Line, It's Called the Sugar Plum, Rats. New York: Random House, 1968.

The Former One-on-One Basketball Champion and *The Great Labor Day Classic*. New York: Dramatists Play Service, 1982.

The Good Parts. New York: Dramatists Play Service, 1983.

The Great Labor Day Classic. New York: Dramatists Play Service, 1982.

Henry Lumper. New York: Dramatists Play Service, 1990.

The Honest-to-God Schnozzola. New York: Breakthrough Press, 1971.

Hopscotch and *The 75th* (Parts One and Two, *The Quannapowitt Quartet*). New York: Dramatists Play Service, 1977.

The Indian Wants the Bronx. New York: Dramatists Play Service, 1968; In *Off-Broadway Plays*. Harmondsworth, U.K.: Penguin, 1970.

Israel Horovitz: 16 Short Plays: Line, It's Called the Sugar Plum, The Indian Wants the Bronx, Rats, Morning, The Honest-to-God-Schnozzola, Play for Germs, Shooting Gallery, Acrobats, The Great Labor Day Classic, The Former One-on-One Basketball Champion, Hopscotch, The 75th, Stage Directions, Spared, Faith. Newbury, V.T.: Smith and Kraus, 1994.

An Israel Horovitz Trilogy: Today I Am a Fountain Pen, A Rosen by Any Other Name, The Chopin Playoffs. Garden City, N.Y.: Fireside Theatre, 1987.

It's Called the Sugar Plum. New York: Dramatists Play Service, 1968.

Leader and *Play for Trees*. New York: Dramatists Play Service, 1971.

Mackerel. Vancouver, Canada: Talonbooks, 1979.

Man with Bags. Adapted from Eugene Ionesco's *L'Homme aux valises*. Translated by
   Marie-France Ionesco. New York: Grove, 1977.
Morning. New York: Samuel French, 1969. Reprinted as *Clair-Obscur*. Paris:
   Gallimard, 1972. In *Morning, Noon and Night*. With Terrence McNally and
   Leonard Melfi. New York: Random, 1969.
North Shore Fish. New York: Dramatists Play Service, 1989.
The Primary English Class. Dramatists Play Service, 1976.
Rats. New York: Dramatists Play Service, 1968.
A Rosen by Any Other Name. New York: Dramatists Play Service, 1987.
Shooting Gallery and Play for Germs. New York: Dramatists Play Service, 1973.
Stage Directions and *Spared* (Parts Three and Four, The Quannapowitt Quartet). New
   York: Dramatists Play Service, 1977. *Stage Directions* and *Hopscotch* reprinted
   as *La Marelle et Didascalies*. Paris: L'Avant-scène, 1993.
*Three Gloucester Plays: Park Your Car in Harvard Yard, Henry Lumper, North Shore
   Fish*. Garden City, N.Y.: Fireside Theatre, 1992.
Today I Am a Fountain Pen. New York: Dramatists Play Service, 1987.
Uncle Snake: An Independence Day Pageant. New York: Dramatists Play Service,
   1976.
*The Wakefield Plays: Alfred the Great, Our Father's Failing, Alfred Dies, Hopscotch,
   The 75th, Stage Directions, Spared*. New York: Bard/Avon, 1979.
The Widow's Blind Date. New York: Theatre Communications Group, 1981.
   Reprinted as *Le Baiser de la veuve*. Paris: Edilig, 1984. Revised and reprinted.
   New York: Dramatists Play Service; Garden City, N.Y.: Fireside, 1989.
Year of the Duck. New York: Dramatists Play Service, 1988.

OTHER PLAYS

Capella (with David Boorstin). Adapted from Horovitz's novel, 1978.
The Comeback, 1958.
The Death of Bernard the Believer, 1960.
Fighting over Beverley, 1992.
Firebird at Dogtown, 1986.
The First, the Last, the Middle: A Comedy Triptych (with Terrence McNally and
   Leonard Melfi), 1974.
The Hanging of Emmanuel, 1961.
Hop, Skip, and Jump, 1963.
The Killer Dove, 1963.
The Lounge Player, 1977.
This Play Is about Me, 1961.
Le Première, 1972.
The Reason We Eat, 1976.
The Simon Street Harvest, 1964.
Sunday Runners in the Rain, 1980.
Turnstile, 1974.

BOOKS

Capella. New York: Harper & Row, 1973.
Nobody Loves Me. Paris: Editions de Minuit; New York: Braziller, 1976.
Spider Poems and Other Writing. New York: Harper & Row, 1973.

TELEPLAYS

Bartleby the Scrivener, adapted from Herman Melville's short story. Baltimore:
    Maryland Public TV, 1977.
A Day with Conrad Green, adapted from Ring Lardner story, 1978.
The Deer Park. Adapted from a novel by Norman Mailer. Lorimar Productions, 1979.
Growing Up Jewish in Sault Ste. Marie. Adapted from Morley Torgov's novel, *A Nice
    Place to Come From*. Canadian Broadcasting, 1978.
The Making and Breaking of Splinters Braun, 1976.
Play for Germs. Segment of *V. D. Blues*. New York: WNET-TV, 1972.
Start to Finish, 1975.

SCREENPLAYS

Acrobats. Adapted from his play of same name. Walker Stuart Productions, 1972.
Alfredo. Metro-Goldwyn-Mayer, 1970.
Author! Author! Twentieth Century Fox, 1982. Starring Al Pacino.
Believe in Me (Originally titled *Speed is of the Essence*). Directed by Stuart Hagmann
    with Israel Horovitz. Starring Jacqueline Bisset and David Sarrazin. Metro-
    Goldwyn-Mayer, 1970.
Berta, 1982.
Camerian Climbing, 1971.
The Deuce. Tri-Star, 1991.
Fast Eddie, 1980.
Fell, 1982.
Letters to Iris. 1988–89.
Light Years. Based on the novel by James Salter. 1985.
Line. Adapted from his play of same name. Kaleidoscope Films, 1970.
Machine Gun McCain. English adaptation by Horovitz of a story by Roli from the novel
    Candyleg by Ovid Demaris. Directed by Giuliano Montaldo. With John
    Cassavettes, Peter Falk and Gena Rowlands. Euroatlantica/Columbia, 1970.
A Man in Love. Written with Diane Kurys. Directed by Diane Kurys. With Peter
    Coyote, Peter Riegert, and Jamie Lee Curtis. Cinecom, 1987.
The Pan, 1989.
Payofski's Discovery, 1988.
The Quiet Room.
The Sad-Eyed Girls in the Park, 1971.
The Strawberry Statement. Based on the novel by James Simon Kunen. Directed by

Stuart Hagmann and Israel Horovitz. With Bruce Davison and Kim Darby. Produced by Irwin Winkler and Robert Chartoff. Metro-Goldwyn-Mayer, 1970.

Strong-Men. Adapted from his *Strong-Man's Weak Child.* Producer, Ned Tannen. Tri-Star, 1991.

SELECTED OTHER WORKS

"Author's Notes." *Henry Lumper.* New York: Dramatists Play Service, 1990, 90–95.

"Introduction." *Three Gloucester Plays.* Garden City, N.Y.: Fireside Theatre, 1992, v–vii.

"The Legacy of O'Neill." *Eugene O'Neill Newsletter* 11, no. 1 (Spring 1987): 3–10.

"Naked Feet." *Boston Running News* 5, no. 2 (September–October 1980): 60–69.

"Naked Feet: 'The Changing of the God.'" *Boston Running News* (November–December 1983): 36–40.

"On Words and Silence." *Dramatist Guild Quarterly* 11 (1974): 19–22.

"Tragedy." *Dramatist Guild Quarterly* 9 (1973): 5–13.

Selected Secondary Bibliography

Barnes, Clive. Review of *Alfred the Great. New York Times*, 14 August 1974, 28.
————. Review of *The Honest-to-God Schnozzola. New York Times*, 22 April 1969, 40.
————. Review of *Line* and *Shooting Gallery. New York Times*, 22 March 1976, 20.
————. Review of *Morning, Noon and Night. New York Times*, 29 November 1968, 52.
Beaufort, John. "The American Tourist Is Still Good for Laughs." *Christian Science Monitor*, 21 January 1982, 18.
————. Review of *The Primary English Class. New York Times*, 17 February 1976, 38.
Berkrot, Peter. "Israel Horovitz." *American Theatre* (October 1992): 39–40; 98–99.
Bigsby, C.W.E. *A Critical Introduction to Twentieth Century Drama*. Vol. 3. New York: Cambridge University Press, 1985.
Blank, Edward L. "Playhouse Has World Premiere." *Pittsburgh Press*, 18 March 1973, 4.
Clurman, Harold. "Theatre." *Nation,* 12 February 1986, 221.
Cohn, Ruby. *New American Dramatist 1960–1990*. 2d ed. New York: St. Martin's Press, 1991.
Denby, David. Review of *Author! Author! New York*, 19 July 1982, 52.
DiGaetani, John L., ed. "Interview." *Search for Post-Modern Theatre*. Westport, Conn.: Greenwood Press, 1991.
Disch, Thomas M. Review of *Park Your Car in Harvard Yard. Nation*, 20 January 1992, 66.
————. Review of *The Widow's Blind Date*. Circle in the Square, New York. *Nation*, 18 December 1989, 766.
Evory, Ann, ed. *Contemporary Authors: A Bio-Bibliographical Guide to Current Authors and Their Works*. Detroit: Gale Research Co., 1978.
Feingold, Michael. "Two Playwrights Clowning Around." *New York Times*, 29 February 1976, 5.
Forsberg, Myra. "A Playwright Seeks the Truths of His Childhood." *New York Times*, 2 March 1986, H4, H26.

Gaddini, Salli. "Horovitz Plays Enhance Symposium." *UWM Post*, 18 November 1976, 7.

Gerard, Jeremy. Review of *Park Your Car in Harvard Yard*. Music Box Theater, New York. *Variety*, 11 November 1991, 58.

————. Review of *Park Your Car in Harvard Yard*. Morris A. Mechanic Theater, New York. *Variety*, 7 October 1991, 203.

Giantvalley, Scott. "Israel Horovitz." In *Critical Survey of Drama: English Language Series*, 3. Ed. Frank Magill. Englewood Cliffs, N.J.: Salem Press, 1985.

Gill, Brendan. "Triumph and Disaster." *New Yorker* 7 December 1968, 139–40.

Gold, Sylviane. "Life at the Fish Factory." *Wall Street Journal*, 19 January 1987, 16.

Gottfried, Martin. *Opening Nights: Theater Criticism of the Sixties*. New York: G. P. Putnam's Sons, 1969.

————. Review of *Acrobats* and *Line*. *Women's Wear Daily*, 17 February 1971. Rpt. *New York Theatre Critics' Reviews* (1972): 350.

————. Review of *The Indian Wants the Bronx*. *Women's Wear Daily*, 18 January 1968. Rpt. *New York Theatre Critics' Reviews* (1968): 268.

————. Review of *The Primary English Class*. *New York Post*, 17 February 1976. Rpt. *New York Theatre Critics' Reviews* (1976): 336.

Gussow, Mel. Review of *Chopin Playoffs*. *New York Times*, 16 May 1986, C3.

————. Review of *Dr. Hero*. *New York Times*, 22 March 1973, 55.

————. Review of *North Shore Fish*. *New York Times*, 12 January 1987, C20.

————. Review of *A Rosen by Any Other Name*. *New York Times*, 5 March 1986, C19.

————. Review of *Today I Am a Fountain Pen*. *New York Times*, 3 January 1986, C3.

————. Review of *Year of the Duck*. *New York Times*, 20 October 1987, C18.

————. "When the Group Becomes the Star." *New York Times*, 25 January 1987, 4.

Harris, Leonard. Review of *Line* and *Acrobats*. WCBS-TV. 15 February 1971. Rpt. *New York Theatre Critics' Reviews* (1972): 350.

Hartigan, Patti. "Horovitz's Life as a Town Bard." *American Theatre* (December 1989): 58–59.

Haun, Harry. "Mixed Joys of Jewish Life." *Playbill* (September 1986): 4–10.

Jacobi, Martin J. "Israel Horovitz." In *American Playwrights since 1945*, ed. Philip C. Kolin. Westport, Conn.: Greenwood Press, 1989.

Johnson, Malcolm L. Review of *Reason We Eat*. *Hartford Courant*, 14 November 1976, F9.

Kael, Pauline. Review of *Author! Author!* *New Yorker*, 26 July 1982, 66.

Kalem, T. E. "Cosmic Jokers." *Time*, 1 March 1971, 67.

Katzman, Don. Review of *Hopscotch* and *The 75th*. *Straight Creek Journal*, 3 February 1977, 9.

Kelly, Kevin. Review of *Park Your Car in Harvard Yard*. *Boston Globe*, 19 November 1991, C8.

————. Review of *Strong-Man's Weak Child*. *Boston Globe*, 24 August 1990, 31, 38.

Kennedy, Louise. Review of *Fighting over Beverley*. *Boston Globe*, 7 September 1993, 53.

Kerr, Walter. " 'Futz'—And Eugene O'Neill." *New York Times*, 30 June 1968, B1.

————. Review of *Dr. Hero*. *New York Times*, 22 April 1973, 1.

Kovac, Kim Peter. "Israel Horovitz." In *Dictionary of Literary Biography: Twentieth*

Century American Dramatists, 7: 301–308. Ed. John MacNicholas. Detroit: Gale Research Co.

Kroll, Jack. Review of *Author! Author! Newsweek*, 5 July 1982, 72.

———. "Theater of Crisis." *Newsweek* 5 May 1969, 118.

Lawson, Carol. "Four Horovitz Plays Going into Rehearsal." *New York Times*, 7 March 1979, C2.

Little, Stuart W., and Cantor, Arthur. *The Playmakers*. New York: Dutton, 1970.

Mackay, Barbara. Review of *The Quannapowitt Quartet. Denver Post*, 2 February 1977, D29.

Norton, Elliot. Review of *Alfred the Great. Boston Herald American*, 4 December 1973, 28.

Oliver, Edith. Review of *Acrobats* and *Line. New Yorker* 27 February 1971, 82–84.

———. Review of *Park Your Car in Harvard Yard*. Music Box Theater, New York. *New Yorker*, 18 November 1991, 126.

———. Review of *A Rosen by Any Other Name*. American Jewish Theater, New York. *New Yorker*, 24 March 1986, 111.

———. Review of *The Widow's Blind Date*. Circle in the Square Downtown, New York. *New Yorker*, 20 November 1989, 110.

———. "The Soft-Edged Pirandello." *New Yorker* 3 May 1969, 107–9.

Pasolli, Robert. Review of *Line. Village Voice*, 7 December 1967, 36.

Rich, Frank. Review of *The Good Parts. New York Times*, 7 January 1982, C3.

———. Review of *Park Your Car in Harvard Yard. New York Times*, 8 November 1991, C1.

Sagal, Peter. "The Mellowing of Israel Horovitz." *Boston Magazine* 86 (October 1986): 239–48.

Schickel, Richard. Review of *The Primary English Class. Time*, 1 March 1976. Rpt. *New York Theatre Critics' Reviews* (1976): 337.

Shepard, Richard. "Three Playwrights Talk Shop." *New York Times*, 10 December 1968, 54.

Simon, John. Review of *Faith, Hope and Charity*. South Street Theater, New York. *New York*, 16 January 1989, 80.

———. Review of The Good Parts. Astor Place Theater, New York. *New York*, 18 January 1982, 70.

———. Review of *Park Your Car in Harvard Yard. New York*, 18 November 1991, 95.

———. Review of *The Widow's Blind Date*. Circle in the Square Downtown, New York. *New York*, 20 November 1989, 129.

Sogliuzzo, A. Richard. "Israel Horovitz." *Contemporary Dramatists*. 4th ed. Ed. D. L. Kirkpatrick. Chicago: St. James Press, 1988, 264–67.

Sterritt, David. "I Feel a Violent Revolution Coming." *Christian Science Monitor*, 22 July 1970, 11.

Sullivan, Dan. Review of *The Indian Wants the Bronx* and *It's Called the Sugar Plum. New York Times*, 18 January 1968, 47.

Tallmer, Jerry. Review of *Today I Am a Fountain Pen. New York Post*, 21 August 1986, 29.

Watts, Richard, Jr. Review of *The Indian Wants the Bronx* and *It's Called the Sugar Plum. New York Post*, 18 January 1968. Rpt. *New York Theatre Critics' Reviews* (1968): 268.

Weiner, Bernard. "A Prolific Playwright Who 'Sort of Got Out of Control.'" *San Francisco Chronicle*, 17 March 1977, 46.

Westerbeck, Colin L., Jr. Review of *Author! Author! Commonweal*, 10 September 1982, 468.

Wetzsteon, Ross. "*Author! Author!*—It's Horovitz." *New York*, 2 August 1982, 28–35.

Williams, Barry B. "Images of America." *Theatre Journal*, 34 (May 1982): 223–32.

About the Editor and Contributors

ROBERT COMBS is Associate Professor of English at George Washington University, Washington, D.C. Author of *Vision of the Voyage: Hart Crane and the Psychology of Romanticism,* he teaches modern American poetry, drama, and short fiction. Recently, he has been active in curriculum revision at George Washington University, making the American literature program more culturally inclusive.

THOMAS F. CONNOLLY teaches in the English Department at Suffolk University, Boston, and has contributed articles to the *Cambridge Guide to American Theatre, The St. James International Dictionary of the Theatre,* and *The Blackwell Companion to Twentieth Century Theatre.* He regularly writes theatre and book reviews for the *Eugene O'Neill Review.*

WILLIAM DEMASTES is Associate Professor of English at Louisiana State University. He is the author of *Beyond Naturalism: A New Realism in American Theatre* (1988), *Clifford Odets: A Research and Production Sourcebook* (1991), and numerous articles on modern drama in a variety of journals.

ANDREW ELFENBEIN is an Assistant Professor of English at the University of Minnesota–Twin Cities. His book *Byron and the Victorians* will be published shortly. His current research involves the interrelations between gay and lesbian representatives during the Romantic era.

STEVEN H. GALE is the University Endowed Professor of Humanities at Kentucky State University. Previous teaching experience includes at the University of Southern California, the University of California at Los Angeles, the University of Puerto Rico, and the University of Liberia (Fulbright Professor of British and American Literature). He has published one hundred articles on a wide range of subjects and written and edited fourteen books among them four on Harold Pinter (including *Butter's Going Up* and the standard annotated bibliography). He is the editor of *Encyclopedia of American Humorists* and *Encyclopedia of British Humorists*. He is now working on a volume on Pinter's screenplays, and he has a novel and filmscript under consideration. Gale is president of the Harold Pinter Society and coeditor of the *Pinter Review: Annual Essays*.

SUSAN C. HAEDICKE is Visiting Assistant Professor in Theater at the University of Massachusetts, Amherst. She also works as a professional dramaturg for Horizons Theatre in Washington, D.C. Her publications include articles in *Essays in Theatre, Theatre Topics*, and *Journal of Dramatic Theory and Criticism* and the forthcoming *Approaches to Teaching Arthur Miller's* Death of a Salesman.

ANN C. HALL taught drama at Marquette University and is currently serving as the Dramaturg and Education Director for the Contemporary American Theatre Company, Columbus, Ohio. In addition to publishing numerous articles in modern drama, she has recently published, *A Kind of Alaska: Women in the Plays of Eugene O'Neill, Harold Pinter, and Sam Shepard*.

MARTIN J. JACOBI is Associate Professor of English at Clemson University. Included among his publications are works on Arthur Miller, Lanford Wilson, and Luigi Pirandello. He also publishes on rhetorical theory and composition. He is the coauthor, with Bernard Duffy, of *The Politics of Rhetoric: Richard Weaver and the Conservative Tradition* (Greenwood Press, 1993).

LESLIE KANE is Professor of English at Westfield State College. She is the author of *The Language of Silence: On the Unspoken and the Unspeakable in Modern Drama* and the editor of *David Mamet: A Casebook*. Her critical essays and reviews on Harold Pinter, David Mamet, Samuel Beckett, Marsha Norman, Sam Shepard, Arthur Miller, Lanford Wilson, and Luigi Pirandello have appeared in numerous journals and critical collections, including the *Pinter Review, World Literature Today, American Drama, Theatre Journal, Yearbook of English Studies, American Theatre*, and *Feminine Focus: The New Playwrights and Public Issues/Private Tensions*. Vice-President of the Harold Pinter Society, President of the David Mamet Society, and Fulbright Scholar, Kane is writing *Weasels and Wisemen*, a study of Jewish identity in the work of Harold Pinter and David Mamet.

LILIANE KERJAN is Professor of Theatre and American Studies at the University of Rennes. She is the author of *The Theater of Edward Albee*, and translator of Peter Swet's *The Interview*, and she has contributed to collections of essays and published numerous articles on American theatre in journals and press, including *La Quinzaine Litteraire.* She has been a Fulbright Scholar, a Salzburg Fellow, and a critic at the O'Neill Theater Center.

DENNIS A. KLEIN is professor of Spanish at the University of South Dakota, Vermillion. He has published and lectured widely on the fields of Hispanic literature and world drama. His most recent books are *Peter Shaffer,* revised edition, and *Garcia Lorca's Tragic Trilogy: Blood Wedding, Yerma and the House of Bernarda Alba.* Additionally, he serves as head bibliographer for the Spanish section of the Modern Language Association's *International Bibliography.*

ROBERT SCANLAN is the Literary Director of the American Repertory Theatre, Cambridge, Massachusetts. A lecturer on dramatic arts at Harvard University, he also directs the Dramaturgy Program at the ART Institute for Advanced Theatre Training. He has specialized throughout his career in the works of Samuel Beckett and was recently elected president of the Samuel Beckett Society, his two-year term to begin in 1995.

ROBERT SKLOOT is a teacher, play director, and former chair of the Department of Theatre and Drama, University of Wisconsin–Madison. His writing on modern drama includes two books on the theatre and drama of the Holocaust. He has served as Fulbright Professor of Drama in Israel and Austria.

JOHN WATKINS is an Associate Professor of English at Marquette University. His essays on Chaucer, Spenser, and Byron have appeared in literary journals, and his book, *The Specter of Dido: Spenser and the Virgilian Tradition,* is forthcoming.